Commentary

on

Plato's *Symposium*

on

Love

Marsilio Ficino

an English translation by
Sears Jayne

Spring Publications
Woodstock, Connecticut

Published by Spring Publications;
299 East Quassett Road;
Woodstock, Connecticut 06281

Third printing of the Second Revised Edition 1999.
This book printed on acid-free paper by McNaughton & Gunn.
Cover design by Patricia Mora and Maribeth Lipscomb.

Another translation of this work—entitled *Marsilio Ficino's Commentary on Plato's Symposium* and published by the University of Missouri at Columbia—was previously copyrighted by Sears Jayne in 1944. The present translation is completely new, with an entirely new introduction, notes, and bibliography. It does not correspond to the 1944 version in any way.

Library of Congress Cataloging-in-Publication Data

Ficino, Marsilio, 1433-1499.
Commentary on Plato's Symposium on love.

Translation of: De amore.
Bibliography: p.
1. Love—Early works to 1800. 2. Aesthetics,
Medieval. 3. Plato. I. Title.
B785.F43D3913   1985   177'.7   84-20255
ISBN 0-88214-601-7

for Mae

Acknowledgments

It has been over forty years since the first edition of this work was published. During that period I have received help and encouragement toward a second edition from several people. Among them I must mention with special gratitude Paul Kristeller and the late D. P. Walker. In the early stages of preparing the new edition, I had extensive help from Eve Adler, and at later stages from Penny Pickett and Andrea Sununu. Both the Guggenheim Foundation and Brown University have at various times thrown coins into this sluggish fountain, hoping to bring it back to life. My wife has endured with angelic patience the writing of both editions and the long interval between. Finally, I want to thank James Hillman, Thomas Moore, Randolph Severson, and Mary Helen Sullivan for their generous help in seeing the work through the press.

Sears Jayne
Brown University

Contents

Introduction

Commentary on Plato's *Symposium* on Love

Introduction

I. Some Problems of Interpretation

As Professor Kristeller has often pointed out, the interpretation of the works of Ficino ought to be left to historians of philosophy, but for various reasons the *De amore* has been neglected by the philosophers and taken over by people in other disciplines. Perhaps the most striking fact about the neglect of the *De amore* among historians of philosophy is that they do not treat it seriously as a commentary on Plato's *Symposium*[1] possibly because the *De amore* discusses only six short passages of the *Symposium*,[2] or possibly because Ficino himself gave them little encouragement to do so. The full title of the work in Ficino's autograph manuscript is *Commentary on Plato's Symposium on Love*,[3] but when Ficino translated the work into Italian in 1474, several years before he permitted it to be published, he called it simply *Sopra lo amore (On Love)*, and he gave it the title *De amore* in two of the three lists of his own works which he left.[4] In the last and fullest of these, he lists in one group all of his formal commentaries on the dialogues of Plato: the *Argumenta*, the *Commentarium in partem Philebi*, and the *Commentarium in Timaeum*, but the *De amore* he lists by that name and among his early treatises, with the following added note:

> The author was persuaded to compose this book by his dear friend Giovanni Cavalcanti, a great and good man, who argued that it would summon the lost lovers of earthly beauty to return to the love of immortal beauty.

In his letters, too,[5] he habitually refers to the work as his *De amore*. He uses the same title in referring to the work in his *Life of Plato*,[6] and in the prefatory letter to the Latin version of the work itself he refers to it, not as a commentary on the *Symposium*, but as a treatise on love.[7]

Modern readers of the *De amore* have given it a variety of interpretations.[8] For Paul Kristeller, Ficino is primarily a philosopher, and the *De amore* is important as an exposition of a central concept in Ficino's philosophy, the concept of appetite.[9] For D. P. Walker, on the other hand, Ficino is a reviver of the ancient theology and a student of magic; for Walker the *De amore* is much less important among Ficino's own writings than the *De vita* or the *Epistolae*.[10] Catholic scholars such as Giuseppe Anichini and Father James Devereux[11] interpret the *De amore* as an effort to delineate the relation between the love of God and the love of self, following a dichotomy set up by Thomas Aquinas. Marian Heitzman sees the crucial influence as coming not from St. Thomas but from Augustine and Avicenna.[12] The Protestant theologian Anders Nygren[13] uses Ficino's *De amore* to support a thesis that the Christian concept of *agape* was corrupted during the renaissance by the Greek concept of *eros*. The psychologist James Hillman regards Ficino as one of the revolutionary founders of modern thought and sees the *De amore* as a document in the history of archetypal psychology.[14]

By far the most widespread interpretation of the *De amore*, however, is the view that the book belongs to the genre of the literary *trattato d'amore*.[15] The history of this genre was first outlined in 1525, in Mario Equicola's survey of treatises on love up to his own time.[16] In that survey Ficino's *De amore* appears in the following ambience:

Guittone d'Arezzo (c. 1230–1294)
Guido Cavalcanti (c. 1250–1300)
Dante Alighieri (1265–1321)
Francesco Barberino (1294–1348)
Francesco Petrarca (1304–1374)
Giovanni Boccaccio (1313–1375)
Marsilio Ficino (1433–1499)
Francesco Diacceto (1446–1522)
Giovanni Pico della Mirandola (1462–1494)
Gianfrancesco Pico della Mirandola (1469–1533)

Working from Equicola's base, scholars have extended the list of *trattatisti d'amore* in both directions: backward to show the antecedents of Ficino in prose discussions of the *dubbi* of love, such as the *De amore* of Andreas Capellanus,[17] and forward to show the progeny of Ficino through Castiglione, Hebreo, and Bembo, to Bruno.[18] The main point made by most literary scholars is that Ficino was responsible for shifting the emphasis in treatises on love from an Aristotelean (and medieval) emphasis on the physiology and psychology of love to a Platonic (and renaissance) emphasis on love as desire for ideal beauty.

II. The Circumstances of Composition

Marsilio Ficino (1433–1499)[1] was the son of the personal physician of Cosimo de' Medici. During the years 1462 to 1473,[2] Marsilio was employed by the Medici family as a translator, and most of the first six of those years he devoted to translating the works of Plato from Greek into Latin.[3] It was immediately after the completion of this Plato translation that he wrote the *De amore*. His autograph manuscript of the work (Vatican lat. 7705) is dated July 1469.[4]

Almost at once, on 6 August 1469, as if to test the religious orthodoxy of his work, he sent copies of it to two members of the clergy: a Hungarian Bishop named Joannes Pannonius (1434–1473) and Cardinal Francesco Piccolomini of Siena (1439–1503).[5] One month later (September 1469), Ficino received from Cardinal Giovanni Bessarion in Rome a copy of Bessarion's *In calumniatorem Platonis*.[6] Ficino did not return to the *De amore* for five years, during which he took holy orders[7] and published an Italian treatise called *The Christian Religion*.[8]

The occasion of his returning to the *De amore* was apparently a request from Lorenzo de' Medici that Ficino make an Italian translation of the work for two of Lorenzo's friends, the same friends for whom Lorenzo had ordered Italian translations of the Hermetic *Pimander* and Dante's *De monarchia* several years before.[9] Before making his translation of the *De amore*, Ficino took the occasion to add a number of passages to the Latin text. These revisions consisted chiefly of headings for the seven "Speeches" and titles for the chapters, but he also added several new passages, of which seven had to do with astrology.[10]

Neither this new Italian version nor the Latin original was published for some time. Ficino borrowed some passages from the Latin version for his *Platonic Theology*,[11] which was published in 1482, but it was not until two years later (1484) that the *De amore* as a whole was finally published for the first time, appearing under the title *Commentary on Plato's Symposium on Love* in Ficino's Latin translation of the *Works* of Plato.[12] The Italian version was not published until 1544, forty-five years after the death of its author.

III. The Argument

One of the most accurate assessments of Ficino's *De amore* ever written is a statement by one of Ficino's contemporaries, a professor of Aristotelean philosophy named Agostino Nifo (c. 1473–1546), who says of it: "Amplifying Plato's views on love partly by allegorizing Plato and partly by adding to him, Ficino made a not unskillful compilation of many different ideas about love."[1] The best way to go about a first reading of the *De amore* is to think of it exactly as Nifo suggests, not as a commentary on the *Symposium*, but as a compilation of ideas about love.

We should ask of each section of the work in turn, "What does this section say?" By "section" I do not mean either Speech (*Oratio*) or Chapter. The present divisions into Speech and Chapter are late additions to the text and may be ignored. What matters is the individual section or block of material on a single subject. If we read the work block by block, we see that it has the structure outlined in the following table. For convenience and clarity I have noted in this table the present Speech and Chapter divisions on the left, and on the right I have noted the primary source on which each section seems to me to be based.

Ficino's De amore

Speech I	Possible Source
CHAPTER	
1 Cavalcanti frame	
2 Cavalcanti frame	
3 Causes of love	
Hypostases	Plotinus 3.5

4 Nature of love
   Effects of love   *Sympos.* 178c–180d

Speech II
CHAPTER
1 Hypostases   Dionys. *DN* 4.7–16
2 Hypostases   ibid.
   Hypostases   ibid.
3 Hypostases   Plotinus 5.5.4
   Beauty   Plotinus 5.8
4 Hypostases   Plotinus 5.1.8
5 Hypostases   Plotinus 5.3.12
6 Effects of love
7 Hypostases   Plotinus 3.5.2
8 Effects of love   Aquinas *ST* 1–2.Q.28
   Causes of love   Aquinas *ST* 1–2.Q.27
   Causes of love   (added 1475)
9 Nature of love; cf. VII.10   Aquinas *ST* 1–2.Q.27

Speech III
CHAPTER
1 Cosmic love   Dionys. *DN* 4.10–16
2 Cosmic love   ibid.
3 Cosmic love   *Sympos.* 186b–187d
4 Cosmic love   Dionys. *DN* 4.10–16
5 Cosmic love

Speech IV
CHAPTER
1 Fable of Aristophanes   *Sympos.* 189c–193d
2 Nature of man   Aquinas *ST* 1–2.Q.63
3 Nature of man; cf. VI.12–13   Proclus *El.* 80, 184–88
4 Nature of man   *Phaedrus* 248c
5 Nature of man   Aquinas *ST* 1–2.Q.57–63
6 Nature of man   Aquinas *ST* 1–2.Q.61.5

Speech V
CHAPTER
1 Beauty (e)   Aquinas *ST* 1–2.Q.27.1
2 Beauty (h)   Plotinus 1.6
3 Beauty (h)   ibid.
4 Beauty (h)   Plotinus 5.8
   Beauty (h)   Plotinus 1.6
5 Beauty (h)   ibid.
6 Beauty (e)   Aquinas *ST* 1–2.Q.62
7 Agathon's description of Eros   *Sympos.* 195b–196b
8 Agathon's description of Eros   *Sympos.* 196b–196e

4 Causes of simple love: blood, spirits   Medical authorities
5 Causes of simple love: blood, spirits   Dino del Garbo
6 Effects of simple love: homosexuality   Lucretius
7 Causes of simple love: blood, spirits   Medical treatises
8 Causes of simple love: blood, spirits   ibid.
9 Causes of simple love: blood, spirits   ibid.
10 Nature of reciprocal love: eyes;   Literary tradition
    cf. II.9 above
11 Cures of love   Medical treatises
12 Effects of simple love: madness   ibid.
13 History of soul: descent, four steps   Proclus *Alcibiades*
14 History of soul: ascent, four madnesses   *Phaedrus*
15 History of soul: four madnesses, cont.   *Phaedrus*
16 Praise of Socratic love
    Socrates: as a teacher   Proclus *Alcibiades*
17 Praise of God   Hermes *Pim.* 13

The sources noted here reflect all three of the main layers of Ficino's studies up to 1469:

1. 1452–56   Platonists available in Latin, including *Liber de causis*, Pseudo-Dionysius, and Proclus
2. 1456–62   Scholastic studies and medical studies
3. 1462–69   Greek Platonists, especially Plato and Plotinus

The main argument of the *De amore* as a treatise on love may be paraphrased as follows: the cosmos consists of a hierarchy of being extending from God (unity) to the physical world (multiplicity). In this hierarchy every level evolves from the level above it in a descending emanation from God and desires to rise to the level above it in an ascending return to God. This desire to return to one's source is called love, and the quality in the source which attracts this desire is called beauty. The human soul, as a part of the hierarchy of being, is involved in this same process of descent from God and return to God; in human beings the desire to procreate inferior beings is called earthly love, and the desire to rise to higher levels of being is called heavenly love. Human love is therefore a good thing because in both of its phases, descending and ascending, it is part of a natural cosmic process in which all creatures share.

IV.   The Method

For most modern readers, the chief difficulty experienced in reading the *De amore* is not the unfamiliarity of its ideas but the unfamiliarity of its method. Most modern works of prose are either works of fiction or of non-fiction; the *De amore* is a little of both. I shall try first to explain Ficino's use of fictions in the work. I shall then discuss his use of multiple opinions.

The Fictions

The *De amore* purports to be an account of a historical event, a banquet attended by nine actual Florentines. The report is written in the first person by Ficino, who records not only what happened but everything that was said. In the order of their ages, the nine people who attended the banquet were as follows:[1]

Bishop Agli, age 70 (Bishop of Fiesole)	Marsilio Ficino, age 36 (translator of Plato)
Dr. Dietifeci, age 68 (Ficino's father)	Carlo Marsuppini, age c. 25 (Ficino's student)
Bernardo Nuzzi, age c. 45 (Ficino's teacher)	Cristoforo Marsuppini, age c. 23 (Ficino's student)
Cristoforo Landino, age 45 (Ficino's teacher)	Giovanni Cavalcanti, age 21 (Ficino's friend)
Tommaso Benci, age 42 (Ficino's admirer)	

According to Ficino, as soon as dinner was over two of the senior members of the group, the Bishop and the physician, were called away. The remaining seven people then elected Giovanni Cavalcanti the guest of honor and settled down for a round of seven speeches. What happened after the last speech Ficino does not say; the work ends with the closing remarks of the seventh speech. Because the narrative involves actual people, the reader at first supposes that the banquet actually occurred. But one soon recognizes that it did not and that Ficino's real point in telling about it was not to record the event for posterity but only to use the fiction as a way of saying certain things about love.

Just as the banquet is a fiction, so is the idea that the point of the occasion was to discuss the *Symposium*. Like the banquet fiction, this fiction begins ambitiously and then fades. The evening begins with a reading aloud of the entire *Symposium* by Bernardo Nuzzi, presumably in Ficino's Latin translation. Then, since there are seven guests and seven sections of the *Symposium*, each guest is supposed to comment on one section of the dialogue. What actually happens, however, is that only five of the guests give speeches, the second and seventh speeches do not mention the *Symposium* at all, and in only one, the sixth, is there a sentence-by-sentence commentary on any part of Plato's dialogue. The actual relation of the evening's discussion to the *Symposium* is shown in the accompanying table (p. 10) of the speakers and their subjects.

There are two minor points of interest about Ficino's treatment of the *Symposium*. One is that the main reason he gives Porus and Penia a detailed commentary is that he found that commentary ready-made in Plotinus and simply borrowed it.

The other point concerns the last section of the *Symposium* (215b–223d), the speech of Alcibiades, one of the admirers of Socrates. In part of that speech, Alcibiades describes his efforts to seduce Socrates by lying naked beside him in bed. This section of the dialogue (216d–219e) had been notorious (as one of the bawdy passages of Greek literature) throughout the Middle Ages, even when the text of the dialogue itself was not known.[2] When the dialogue was first recovered, in Italy early in the fifteenth century, this was the first passage to be translated into Latin.[3] Evidently Leonardo Bruni, who translated it, thought the dialogue as a whole did not live up to its bawdy reputation since he did not bother to translate the rest of the dialogue. But the reputation of this passage made a special difficulty for Ficino.

Ficino's solution to this problem is ingenious. He simply ignores Alcibiades' comment on Socrates as a bedfellow and instead adds to Speech VII a section praising Socrates as a teacher. His material for this section he takes partly from Diogenes Laertius and partly from Plato's *Apology*, but primarily from another work which does essentially what he himself was doing in the *De amore*, namely Proclus's *Commentary on I Alcibiades*.[4] In this work Proclus celebrates Socrates as a teacher of the doctrine of Socratic love to Alcibiades, and in the course of the work he outlines the whole of the Platonic theology of love.

Although the *Symposium* does not contribute very much to the doctrinal content of the *De amore*, employing the form of a commentary on

Ficino's speaker	Plato's speaker and topics	Sections of Plato and topics actually discussed by Ficino's speaker
I. Giovanni Cavalcanti	Phaedrus: antiquity and nobility of Cupid	definition of terms; *Sympos.* 178c–180d
II. Giovanni Cavalcanti	Pausanias: two kinds of love (heavenly and earthly)	cosmic hypostases
III. Giovanni Cavalcanti	Erixymachus: human love part of a universal natural force	cosmic love; *Sympos.* 186b–187d
IV. Cristoforo Landino	Aristophanes: fable of split creatures	fable of Aristophanes, *Sympos.* 189c–193d; nature of man; love as moral force
V. Carlo Marsuppini	Agathon: whether love is beautiful or not	theory of beauty; *Sympos.* 195b–e, 197a–b
VI. Tommaso Benci	Socrates: Porus and Penia, ladder of love, immortality, love as daemon	Porus and Penia; *Sympos.* 203d–e; ladder of love; immortality; daemons; *Sympos.* 207d–208b
VII. Cristoforo Marsuppini	Alcibiades: praise of Socrates	Cavalcanti poem; physiology of love; four madnesses; *Phaedrus*; praise of love, of God, and of Socrates; *Apology, I Alcibiades*

the *Symposium* was important to Ficino. The point was that it was conventional before Ficino's time to write one's own treatise in the form of a commentary on some other work. The history of this convention is outlined in Professor Nelson's book,[5] and I need not repeat it. The chief models for Ficino were Dante and Guido Cavalcanti. The logical analogue for Ficino would have been to write his treatise on Platonic love as a commentary on a Platonic poem, just as Cavalcanti had written his treatise on Aristotelean love as a commentary on an Aristotelean poem.

But Ficino decided to use the *Symposium* of Plato as his vehicle. It was an appropriate vehicle because it was on his subject and because it was new; his was the first complete translation of the dialogue ever written. It was because of the convention of the commentary as a substitute for the discursive treatise that Ficino wrote his treatise on love in the form of a commentary, and it was because of the relevance of the *Symposium* to his own subject, Socratic love, that he chose to attach his commentary to the *Symposium*. But, as in the case of the banquet fiction, Ficino does not carry out the commentary fiction systematically because both fictions are there only for the sake of the argument which he wanted to advance, his defense of human love.

The Multiple Opinions

Cosmic Love

By cosmic love Ficino means the cycle of emanation and reversion in the cosmos as described by Proclus, the Pseudo-Dionysius, and the author of the *Liber de causis*. This cosmos is a series of concentric circles, with the highest form of being, the abstract One, at the center, and successively lower forms emanating outward to the physical world which forms the outermost circle. Though Ficino had doubtless read and probably used all three of these authors, I think it very likely that his immediate model was the *Convivio* (or *Symposium*) of Dante.[6] Ficino had begun his Platonic studies in 1456 at the behest of a leading Dantist, Cristoforo Landino,[7] and it is likely that Landino suggested the *Convivio* to him as a model. Dante's *Convivio*, like Ficino's *De amore*, is a banquet, a philosophical feast in which Dante celebrates as his key idea the cosmic nature of love. He describes the universe as a hierarchy in which every level of being is united in a desire to ascend to God.

> The highest desire of everything, given to it by nature in the beginning, is to return to its own source. Since God is the source of our souls and made them in his image, our souls desire above all to return to God. (4.12.14–19)

The universe is made coherent by the cosmic love for God which pervades all creation:

> Love is the heartbeat of the whole universe. Everything participates in it according to its own special love, from simple bodies, to composite bodies, to plants, to animals, to man. (3.3.2–11)

Dante's immediate source for this vision may have been the Pseudo-Dionysius's *Divine Names*, but the same conception also appears in the *Liber de causis*, which Dante cites by name:

> Every substantial form proceeds from its own first cause, which is God, as the *Liber de causis* says. Therefore its being derives from God, it is preserved by God, and it naturally desires to be united to God, to strengthen its own being. (3.2.4–7)

Dante's stress on the personality of God as the source of the outpouring of being and the object of every creature's search for being is certainly Christian rather than Proclean. Ficino, too, can sound very Christian (e.g., the chapter heading of VII.17), but in places he sounds neither Christian nor Proclean, but Plotinian, as where he stresses the point that the One is above being (e.g., I.3). In VI.16 we are told that the stages of love are: World Body, World Soul, Angelic Mind, and God; but in VII.13 that the levels are Nature, Opinion, Reason, and Intellect.[8] In still other places (e.g., IV.3–4), Ficino speaks as if man were not a participant in the ebb and flow of cosmic love at all, but only a spectator who stands apart and tries to make up his mind whether to love God or himself. In still other places, we hear that not all creatures are involved in the process of cosmic love after all: the artist, for example, loves not God but the idea of order (III.3); the wolf loves not God but himself; and on that account hates lambs (III.4), which are presumably beneath him in the hierarchy of being and thus constitute an exception to the Proclean rule that higher orders desire to create lower orders, not to destroy them. In short, the concept of cosmic love in the *De amore* is not based on any single authority and indeed is not any one concept. What Ficino is trying to do in the *De amore* is to defend the propriety of personal love by showing that it is merely a natural part of a perfectly respectable cosmic process; he is simply trying to persuade the reader, by celebrating the universality of love in the world, that love is a good thing: "So my friends, I urge and beg you to give yourselves to love without reservation, for it is not base but divine" (II.8).

The Human Soul

As we have seen, Ficino had at his disposal in writing the *De amore* three principal groups of authorities, the "Latin" Platonists, the Scholastic theologians, and the "Greek" Platonists whom he had just translated.[9] In writing about the human soul, Ficino skips eclectically from one to another among these three sources.

On the history of the soul, for example, he states both the heretical Platonic view that the soul descends from a previous existence (IV.4) and the orthodox Christian view that the soul is created by God directly on earth and rises toward bliss in heaven (IV.5). In several places he reviews the whole history of the soul in Platonic terms, covering its descent and its ascent (e.g., VII.13-14), but he also gives a Thomistic account of the soul's pursuit of divine virtues (IV.5-6) which is no less vivid than his Plotinian account of the soul's "upward way" through the hypostases (VI.18-19). On the question of the soul's faculties, he is usually Aristotelean: thus in VI.6 he discusses the process of perception in terms of the Aristotelean outer and inner senses, and his conception of the imagination[10] accords loosely with those of Avicenna and Albert. Elsewhere (e.g., VI.15) he says that "Intellect is not a natural and inherent faculty of the soul." Still elsewhere (VII.13) he distinguishes Intellect from Reason as parts of the soul, in the usual Platonic way. At the critical point in the description of the soul's functions, where he must say whether the soul constructs its universals by abstraction, or rather merely compares particulars with universals which are innate, he says, "there immediately appears in the Intellect another species of this image" (VII.1).

Beauty

In Ficino's earlier defenses of love (the *De divino furore* and *De voluptate*), he had not found it necessary to discuss beauty at all, because his major sources there, Proclus and his heirs, had defined love as a desire to return to the cause, to recover the more perfect being from which all creatures have degenerated in the process of being created. But both of the Greek authors whom Ficino had been reading more recently, Plato and Plotinus, define lòve as the desire for beauty.[11] Thus in the *De amore*, beauty becomes an important subject. Unfortunately, as soon as Ficino tried to define beauty, he found himself once more confronting a disagreement between the Platonists and the Aristoteleans. The Platonists defined beauty as an abstract universal existing separately in the mind of God, whereas the Aristoteleans defined beauty as an abstraction generated by the individual human mind from many particular sense experiences. Moreover, most medieval and renaissance theorists,[12] from Bonaventure to Alberti, believed that beauty was a form which was given to matter, an order or arrangement imposed upon objects of experience, whereas the Platonists held that beauty was an abstract quality in which physical objects participated in various degrees.

Ficino's solution to these differences of opinion is, as usual, to present them all and let the reader take his choice. Thus in the opening section of the *De amore* (I.3–4), he gives as the basic working definition of beauty simply the commonsense definition which he knew that his artist friends would approve, the pragmatic Aristotelean definition employed by Alberti, that beauty is a way of ordering experience. Elsewhere, however (V.5), he also gives the Platonic definition of beauty as participation in an undefinable Ideal. In still another place (V.6), he tries to combine the two concepts by drawing an analogy with the concept of infused virtue in Aquinas: it is true, he says, that beauty is a quality or grace infused into a thing by God, by an act of grace, but a thing can be prepared to receive this grace by arranging its parts, by imposing arrangement, order, or harmony upon it; though the virtue of beauty is actually an infused virtue, it will be given only to objects which have acquired the natural virtue of order and harmony. Just as the idea of qualities infused by grace is not original with Ficino, so his application of the idea to the particular problem of the nature of beauty is not his own either. It may be found in the same work which we have already cited as one of his sources for the concept of cosmic love, the *Convivio* of Dante.[13]

Human Love

In the Platonic theology of the school of Proclus, love is conceived of as a cosmic force in which individual human beings participate willy-nilly, along with all other creatures, falling and rising, emanating from and reverting to the One, just as all the rest of the universe does. The Proclus school sees man as merely one of the participants in the universal two-stage cosmic process, following first the urge to be a cause oneself and then the urge to return to one's own cause. Human love is in effect indistinguishable from its cosmic matrix, and the individual will is not really free. The human soul is merely a spark of light emanating from the divine sun. In some places the *De amore* appears to endorse this view:

> . . . the ray of beauty which is both Plenty and the father of love, has the power to be reflected back to what it came from, and it draws the lover with it. But it descends first from God, and passes through the Angel and the Soul, as if they were made of glass; and from the Soul it easily emanates into the body prepared to receive it. Then from that body of a younger man it shines out, especially through the eyes, the transparent windows of the soul. It flies onward through the air, and penetrating the eyes of an older man, pierces his soul, kindles his appetite, then leads the wounded soul and the kindled appetite to their healing and cooling, respectively, while it carries them with it to the same place from which it had itself descended, step-by-step, indeed, first to the body of the beloved, second to the Soul, third, to the Angel, and finally to God, the first origin of this splendor. (VI.10)

In other places, however, Ficino appears to endorse a view more like that of Plato and Plotinus: the soul begins in heaven, falls into the body, and then reascends to heaven, but the individual soul is free to eschew the desire for the body which causes it to fall and free also to decide when, or if, it will turn to the desire for ideal beauty, which causes it to rise. That is, once born into the flesh, man is free to choose between earthly love and heavenly love:

> He who uses love properly certainly praises the beauty of the body, but through that contemplates the higher beauty of the soul, the Mind, and God, and admires and loves that more strongly. (II.7)

In still other places Ficino appears to be thinking in terms of Aquinas's view of love as a matter of choosing between love of self and love of God:

> so that we shall seem to have first worshipped God in things, in order later to worship things in God, and to worship things in God for this reason, in order to recover ourselves in Him above all, and in loving God we shall seem to have loved ourselves. (VI.19)

Thus the section on human love in the *De amore* follows the same method as the other four sections: it presents different views of human love without trying to argue out their relative merits or to resolve the obvious contradictions among them. Here, as elsewhere, Ficino prefers to say, "We think that both of these opinions are true, but each for a different reason" (VI.1).

Of the three main kinds of love, the last kind, "simple" (i.e., physical) love, is given the most emphatic position, and it is also described in the least ambiguous way, giving a mainly traditional physiological account of the causes and cures of love considered as a disease of the spirits and blood.[14] But even here Ficino introduces one new authority, namely Lucretius. Able at last to make some public use of the Lucretian studies of his youth,[15] he cites Lucretius[16] six times in support of the argument that physical love must be a good thing because it is physiologically natural.

The Rationale

Most historians have explained Ficino's method on the ground that he is a syncretist: that he believed that Platonism was compatible not only with Christianity but also with all three of the other classical philosophies, and with the theologies of ancient Greece, Babylonia, and Egypt as well.

Another possible rationale which has been given for Ficino's method is that it stems from his anti-rationalism, that the reason he does not conduct a clear, logical argument is that he does not believe that reason leads to truth. There are two main versions of this defense of Ficino. One is the defense of Eugenio Garin,[17] who says that Ficino's method is poetic rather than philosophical, that while the rest of us are listening to the voice of reason Ficino is listening to the imagination, and this is why he prefers fictional to discursive form in the *De amore*. Another version of this defense is that of James Hillman[18] who believes that Ficino is the first modern thinker to attend properly to the voice of the unconscious. According to Hillman, the reason Ficino says whatever pops into his head to say is that he believes the conscious mind has no monopoly on truth: like modern psychologists, Ficino believes that we should not block out or suppress ideas just because they are unfamiliar or irrational.

There is a good deal to be said for the argument that Ficino is an anti-rationalist. What we call the unconscious Ficino called divine inspiration,[19] and he firmly believed that there was no need for him to understand any sentence which came into his mind to say, since all sentences were put there by God;[20] St. Thomas himself had pointed out that God does not think discursively.[21]

But I think that there may be a slightly different explanation for the method of the *De amore*. It was intended to say one thing to the initiate and something else to the rest of the world; it was meant to have two meanings, one esoteric and the other exoteric.

The renaissance conception of esotericism[22] is only a particular version of the ancient principle that writers who wish to conceal their meaning from some readers while making it available to others have always used one of two techniques for doing so. One is the technique of saying something which is perfectly clear but which will mean one thing to an uninstructed reader and another to an instructed reader. Myth is an example of this technique: to the child the myth is only a story; to an instructed reader the myth may be an allegory of some deeper meaning. The other technique is to use language which does not mean anything to anyone who does not know the code. This is the technique of encipherment, such as the system of using numbers in place of letters, or letters in place of other letters, or code names instead of ordinary names. In the renaissance each of these two techniques was associated with an ancient philosopher, the first with Plato and the second with Aristotle. It was no accident, from the point of view of Ficino's age, that the standard Aristotelean account of the nature of love should have been embodied in a poem which makes no sense to the uninstructed reader, Cavalcanti's *"Donna me prega"*; or, on the other hand, that the standard account of Plato's view of love was embodied in a myth, the story of Porus and Penia, which makes one kind of sense as a narrative on its own terms but which also makes a different kind of sense when interpreted allegorically by Plotinus.

A related distinction between the Platonic and Aristotelean methods of writing was that Plato wrote non-discursively, casting his ideas in the form of imaginary dialogues and myths, whereas Aristotle wrote discursively, casting his ideas in the form of systematic treatises on physics, metaphysics, ethics, politics, etc. "The Platonic style is more poetic than philosophical," says Ficino.[23] The result of this renaissance presumption about the Platonic and Aristotelean methods was that any renaissance reader would have expected a work which pretended to be Platonic as opposed to Aristotelean to be non-discursive as opposed to systematic and to contain an esoteric as well as an exoteric meaning.

The distinction between esoteric and exoteric meaning was particularly important to the Florentine Platonists for a social reason as well.[24] Florence was a far more democratic society than most societies in northern Europe, and there was a tendency in Florence for the elite class to try to shore up the merely financial basis of its superiority by artificial intellectual devices; lacking the argument of birth which sufficed in other societies to sustain the dichotomy between the upper and lower classes, they tried to reinforce the distinction between the haves and the have-nots by generating an intellectual dichotomy between those who understood and those who did not. Though Ficino himself was a have-not, he was employed by the social elite of the Medici circle, and almost everything he wrote up to the death of Piero was designed to serve the ends of developing an intellectual elitism to reinforce the Medici's financial elitism.

Because the *De amore* was written as a Platonic work and because it was written for the Medici, any renaissance reader would have expected it to follow the Platonic mode of non-discursive form but also to conceal some more esoteric meaning than was apparent on the surface. This is, in fact, the way in which Giovanni Pico della Mirandola read the *De amore*. He ignored the external paraphernalia of the banquet discussion of the *Symposium* and discussed the work as if it were a treatise on love. This is the way Ficino intended the *De amore* to be read. He intended that any ordinary person outside his own group be preoccupied by the fictions (the banquet and the commentary) which constitute the exoteric fable. What he intended for his friends to see in it was its esoteric meaning, the reasoned defense of 'Socratic' love. The fictions and the multiple authorities, the confusing aspects of the method of the work, are deliberate strategies of the technique of esotericism, the desire to write a work which says different things to different groups of people. Because the work was written for an esoteric elite, it had throughout the renaissance special appeal to such elites, not only in Italy, but also in France, Spain, and England. That influence is the most striking feature of its subsequent history.

V. Subsequent History

The *De amore* did not depend for its survival upon the Plato volume of 1484 in which it was first published.[1] The work had already been circulating for fifteen years in manuscript copies and had established a flourishing life of its own as a pet book of court aristocrats. The book had been written in the first place as an esoteric work for aristocrats, and it served the same purposes in other courts as it had served in the court of the Medici. The popularity of the book among the nobility then was analogous to the popularity among leisured Americans today of "privileged secret" books such as books on special diets or techniques of meditation. For almost two hundred years, the *De amore* was an 'in' book in courts all over Europe. Since the people who read the *De amore* and talked about it were the same people whose patronage supported the artists of the period, the beneficiaries of that patronage were not slow to incorporate the secrets of Ficino into their works of art. For example, the allegorization of mythology in the *De amore* was borrowed by Bandinelli and Dürer for engravings and by Botticelli for paintings.[2] Similarly, the section of the *De amore* on the theory of beauty (V.1-6) was used by Lomazzo for his treatise *Idea del tempio della pittura* and by Tasso for his dialogue on art called *Il Ficino*.[3]

The main appeal, however, of the *De amore* to the court audience was of course the fact that it dealt with the subject of love. Discussions of the nature of love had long figured in the social life of the Italian ducal courts,[4] and the *De amore* gave these courts something new to discuss, the topic of idealized love. Though the work had been written for and about men, its doctrine that the love of the body is a step toward a higher kind of love was especially welcomed by women. With their help, the popularity of the *De amore* lasted almost two hundred years, from 1469 to about 1660, and especially in four countries: Italy, France, Spain, and England. In Italy this influence took the form mainly of prose treatises on love, which were based on the *De amore*. In France there were also such treatises, but there were also many poems, romances, and plays which used Ficino's ideas. In Spain and England the influence of the *De amore* fell mainly on poetry and drama. We shall now look at each of these four countries in more detail.

The scale of the influence of the *De amore* in Italy is suggested by Marcel's list of thirty-three Italian works influenced by it during the first century of its existence.[5] The most important of the Italian prose treatises in this list appeared in the following order.

1469 Latin *De amore* written and distributed in manuscript
1474 Italian *De amore* written and distributed in manuscript
1484 Latin *De amore* published in *Opera Platonis*
1486 Giovanni Pico della Mirandola, *Commento*
1495 Mario Equicola, *Il libro de natura d'amore* (5 editions)
1501 Leo Hebreo, *Dialoghi d'amore* (11 editions)
1505 Pietro Bembo, *Gli Asolani* (7 editions)
1508 Francesco Diacceto, *De amore*
1518 Baldessare Castiglione, *Il Cortegiano* (16 editions)
1542 Sperone Speroni, *Dialogo d'amore*
1544 Italian versions of *De amore* (two) published
1544 Giuseppe Betussi, *Il Raverta*
1545 Francesco Sansovino, *Ragionamento*
1547 Bartolomeo Gottifredi, *Specchio d'amore*
1547 Tullia d'Aragona, *Dell' infinita d'Amore*
1553 Benedetto Varchi, *Le lezzioni*
1554 Pompeo della Barba, *Expositione*
1567 Flaminio Nobili, *Trattato dell'amore*
1581 Francisco de' Vieri, *Lezzioni*
1581 Niccolo Vito de Gozze de Raguse, *Dialoghi della bellezza*
1585 Giordano Bruno, *Degli Eroici furori*

In the immediate circle of Ficino's friends, the *De amore* was received mainly with enthusiasm. Lorenzo de' Medici, for example, used it almost at once for his own commentary on his own love poems and explains in a letter of 1474 that his love for Ficino is the love described in the *De amore*.[6] A little later (1477), one of Ficino's readers in Pistoia, Antonio Ivani, praises the *De amore* by saying that his own experience bears out Ficino's view that spiritual love is superior to "natural love," for his wife and children are a terrible burden to him.[7] In 1495, as we have seen, Mario Equicola accorded Ficino a place of honor in his history of treatises on love, and in 1508 one of Ficino's students, Francesco Diacceto, paraphrased the *De amore* in a treatise of his own with the same title.[8] Among Ficino's immediate contemporaries, his own student Giovanni Pico della Mirandola was the most hostile critic of the *De amore*, so hostile that his sharpest barbs, in the *Commento* (1486), were suppressed until modern times.[9] As if to provide a *tertium quid* to the disagreement between Ficino and Pico, Pico's nephew, Gianfrancesco Pico della Mirandola, published in 1516 a treatise showing that both Ficino and Pico were wrong[10] and that the only proper way to deal with the subject of love is in Christian terms.

Among the many Italian treatises on love which owed something to Ficino, by far the most influential, both inside and outside Italy, were the *Dialoghi d'amore* of Leo Hebreo and the *Il Cortegiano* of Baldassare Castiglione.[11] Both of these works were edited, translated, and borrowed from widely, far exceeding in their influence the other three major Italian authorities on Platonic love: Pico, Bembo, and Bruno.

The direct impact of Ficino's *De amore* in France[12] began with paraphrases in French of short passages from the work, first by Champier (1503),[13] then by Heroet (1536), and then by Corrozet (1541).[14] The entire *De amore* was first translated into French in 1542 (by de la Haye); there was a second French translation in 1578 (by Boderie). Meanwhile the *De amore* was being used as a source for other works in France, both in prose and in poetry. The chief borrowings in prose were by Taillemont (1551), Le Caron (1556), and LeRoy (1558).[15] In poetry[16] the *De amore* influenced works by Heroet, Corrozet, Tyard, Des Autelz, Peletier, Scève, DuBellay, Ronsard, de Baif, Habert, and Boderie, among others. With the exception of a period between 1559 and 1576, the *De amore* was popular among the French aristocracy through the whole of the sixteenth century. This vogue continued through the first half of the seventeenth century as well, affecting not only prose and poetry but also romances, fetes, and plays, before it finally faded about 1660.[17]

In Spain,[18] as in France, the chief audience for the love-theory of Ficino's *De amore* was the aristocracy, but during the sixteenth and seventeenth centuries the theory was known in Spain mainly through the works of Léon Hebreo[19] and Castiglione,[20] both of whom were much more popular in Spain than Ficino himself. Among the Spanish writers who did use the *De amore* directly, the most important were the playwright Lope de Vega and the poets Fray Luis de Léon, Garcilaso de la Vega, and Fray Pedro Malón de Chaide.[21]

In England[22] Ficino's *De amore* was known as early as 1500, when a copy of Ficino's Latin *Opera Platonis* of 1484 is found at Cambridge.[23] But the status of Plato in England was entirely different from the prestige which he enjoyed in France. Between 1485 and 1578 there were more than a hundred different editions of various works of Plato in France; in England during the same period, not one. Between 1485 and

1578 the most influential statement of the theory of Platonic love, so far as England was concerned, was that in Castiglione's *Courtier*,[24] which arrived in England in 1531 and was translated into English in 1561. The watershed year for Plato (and Ficino) in England was 1578. In that year the French Calvinist Jean de Serres (c. 1540–1598) dedicated the first volume of a new Latin translation of Plato to Queen Elizabeth I,[25] and in the same year, as we have seen, Guy Le Fevre de la Boderie published his new French translation of Ficino's *De amore*. It was Boderie's French *De amore* which was mainly responsible for the influence of the *De amore* in England. This influence begins in 1581 with an allegorical court entertainment called *The Fortress of Perfect Beauty*,[26] which was probably written in part at least by Sir Philip Sidney. Between 1581 and 1589 the *De amore* was largely ignored in England. Then, between 1590 and 1596 it was used by both Chapman[27] and Spenser[28] for exercises in the classical hymn. The years 1596 to 1600 are again mainly blank for Ficino. There was a brief flurry of interest in Platonic themes between 1601 and 1602, but these derive from sources other than the *De amore*.

During the reign of James I, Ficino was studied at Oxford by the theologian Thomas Jackson,[29] but the love-theory of the *De amore* appears mainly in the poets, including John Donne, Thomas and Henry Vaughan, William Habington, William Drummond, Thomas Howell, Thomas Traherne, and Francis Kynaston.[30]

In the Caroline period there was a great burst of interest in all of Ficino's works, both at court (where Henrietta Maria encouraged the writing of plays[31] on Platonic love, by Daniel, Carew, Montague, Suckling, Jonson, and Heywood), and at Cambridge,[32] where Henry More, John Smith, and Peter Sterry, followed at Oxford by John Norris, studied and imitated Ficino's writings. Still, in 1655, when Thomas Stanley wrote the first English history of philosophy (London, 1655–62), in the section on Platonism, the work which he quotes in order to explain the theory of Platonic love is not Ficino's *De amore* but Pico's *Commento*.

By comparison with the influence of Ficino in France, his influence in England was relatively limited. But even on the continent, as economic and social change gradually destroyed the social elites which saw themselves reflected in the *De amore*, the special attraction of Ficino's treatise, and of the dialogue to which it pointed, lost its appeal. So, in the whole of the seventeenth century there was only one separate edition of the *Symposium*, and that was an Italian translation by Dardi Bembo left over from the previous century (Venice, 1601). In England the Enlightenment administered the *coup de grace* to renaissance Platonism.[33] The typical enlightenment attitude toward Plato and Ficino may be seen in Samuel Parker's ironic *A Free and Impartial Censure of the Platonick Philosophy*:

> That Platonisme is almost nothing but an allegorie is too notorious to want a proof. Plato's two famous dialogues, viz his *Symposium* and his *Phaedrus*, ranked by Ficinus among his metaphysical and theological treatises, treat of nothing but love and beauty, and of them, too, in poetick schemes and fables.[34]

and in Bolingbroke's *Epistles* to Pope:

> The lofty madness of Plato and the pompous jargon of Aristotle . . .
> Plato, their great master in metaphysical pneumatics, gave them in his vague and figurative manner of writing sufficient foundation for either of these opinions. . . .
> Plato, who disgraced philosophy as much as Homer elevated poetry by the use of allegory. . . .
> I remember to have read somewhere in Plotinus, or in some other madman of that stamp. . . .[35]

The resurgence of Hellenic studies in Germany in the late eighteenth century stirred a brief Platonic revival in England about 1804, when Thomas Taylor translated a number of Platonists into English, but no one revived Ficino's *De amore*, and the *Symposium* itself was still read with so much suspicion that in 1831 a character named Dr. Folliott in Thomas Love Peacock's novel *Crotchet Castle* says,

> I am aware, Sir, that Plato, in his *Symposium*, discourseth very eloquently touching the Uranian and Pandemian Venus, but you must remember that in our Universities Plato is held to be little better than a misleader of youth.

There was a brisk revival of interest in Plato's *Symposium* in the later nineteenth century in parts of Western Europe, but none of the scores of commentators on the *Symposium* during that period paid much attention to Ficino. The twentieth-century revival of Ficino's *De amore* derives almost entirely from the efforts of modern scholars to understand the philosophy, literature, and visual arts of the Renaissance.

VI. The Translation

The translation given here replaces a translation which I published in 1944 under the title *Marsilio Ficino's Commentary on Plato's Symposium.*[1] That work, which was written as a M.A. thesis at the University of Missouri during World War II, has since been superseded in all three of its parts: the Introduction has been rendered useless by subsequent biographical and philosophical scholarship on Ficino, and the Latin text and the English translation have been rendered obsolete by Raymond Marcel's 1956 edition of Ficino's autograph manuscript of the *De amore.*[2] I have accordingly made an entirely new translation and have written an entirely new introduction. I have not reprinted the Latin text, since that is easily available in Marcel's edition. That edition is a transcription of Ficino's autograph in Vatican manuscript lat. 7705, collated with most of the other extant manuscripts. My translation is based primarily on Marcel's edition; that is, the reader may presume that he can find the Latin original of any sentence in my translation by consulting the corresponding section of Marcel's edition, except where my notes specifically direct him to some other text. Such notes occur only infrequently and only where I have preferred a reading from one of the following sources:

1. Vatican manuscript lat. 7705 itself, which I have collated throughout in microfilm. I have not translated the marginal postillae in this manuscript; they may be consulted in Marcel's edition.

2. Oxford manuscript Canonicianus latinus 156, which contains Ficino's autograph marginal corrections; this, too, I have collated.

3. Additions or corrections from other manuscripts as reported by Father Devereux in his collation of all extant manuscripts in *RQ* 28 (1975): 173–82.

4. My own collation of all the printed editions, published with my 1944 translation.

My translation takes into account other translations[3] as follows:

M. Ficino (Italian, 1474)

K. P. Hasse (German, 1914)

R. Marcel (French, 1956)

A. R. Diaz (Spanish, 1968)

J. J. S. Peake (English, 1968) [V.3–6 only]

G. Neal (English, 1979) [VI.11–19 only]

M. Allen (English, 1981) [VII.14 only]

Notes

I.

1. See, for example, works 1950–57 surveyed by Harold Cherniss in *Lustrum* 4 (1959) : 189–97, and more recent works discussed in the latest edition of Plato's *Symposium*, by Sir Kenneth Dover (London, 1980).

2. See analytical table, p. 10 above. The passages are:

   1. 178c–180d

   2. 186b–187d

   3. 189c–193d

   4. 195b–197b

   5. 203b–e

   6. 207d–208b

3. Marcel inserts a comma into this title and translates the title as if "On Love" were the subtitle of the work: "Commentary on Plato's *Symposium*, or On Love." But the phrase "On Love" is a subtitle of the *Symposium* itself, not of Ficino's own work, as Ficino's translation of the dialogue shows. See Raymond Marcel edition (Paris, 1956), p. 136.

4. See Paul O. Kristeller, *Supplementum Ficinianum* (Florence, 1937), 1 : 3; cited as *Suppl.*

5. Marsilio Ficino, *Opera* (Basle, 1576), pp. 621, 629, 631, 656, 657.

6. Ibid., p. 765.

7. See Marcel, *Life*, p. 341, translation on p. 179 below.

8. For recent interpretations of Ficino's philosophy in general, see Paul O. Kristeller, "L'état présent des études sur Marsile Ficin," in *Platon et Aristote à la Renaissance*, Colloque international de Tours (Paris, 1976), pp. 59–77.

9. Paul O. Kristeller in *The Philosophy of Ficino* (New York, 1943).

10. D. P. Walker, *Spiritual and Demonic Magic from Ficino to Campanella* (London, 1958).

11. For Anichini and Devereux, see Section II of the Bibliography below. The view of the Thomistic background which I have mentioned is that of Pierre Rousselot, *Pour l'histoire du problème de l'amour au moyen age*, Beiträge zur Geschichte der Philosophie des Mittelalters 6 (Münster, 1908). The self-love concept derives from Aristotle's *philautia* in *Nic. Ethics* 9.8. Another renaissance treatise on love which deals with this problem more directly is that of Francesco Patrizi. See edition by John C. Nelson (Florence, 1963). For a different view of St. Thomas's theory of love see H. D. Simonin, "Autour de la solution thomiste du problème de l'amour," *AHDLM* 6 (1931) : 174–272.

12. Marian Heitzman, "L'agostinismo avicennizzante e il punto di partenza della filosofia di Marsilio Ficino," *GCFI* 16 (1935) : 295–322, 460–80; 17 (1936) : 1–11.

13. Anders Nygren, *Agape and Eros* (London, 1932); among Nygren's critics see especially Jean Danielou, *Platonisme et théologie mystique* (Paris, 1944), pp. 199–208.

14. James Hillman, *Re-Visioning Psychology* (New York, 1975), pp. 197–202.

15. The two major works are: John C. Nelson, *The Renaissance Theory of Love* (New York, 1958); and Jean Festugière, *La philosophie de l'amour de Marsile Ficin*, 2d ed. (Paris, 1941). But see also Raymond Marcel, "Le platonisme de Pétrarque à Léon Hébreu," *Association Guillaume Budé, Congrès de Tours et Poitiers* (Paris, 1954), pp. 293–319; Nesca Robb, *Neoplatonism of the Italian Renaissance* (London, 1968); and Edouard F. Meylan, "L'Evolution de la notion d'amour Platonique," *Humanisme et Renaissance* 5 (1938) : 418–42.

16. *Libro di natura d'amore* (Venice, 1525). Equicola's list includes one French work also, the *Roman de la Rose*, which he places between Barberino and Boccaccio. Equicola wrote the work in Latin about 1495; it was translated into Italian by his nephew. See Ivonne Rocchi, "Per una nuova cronologia e valutazione del *Libro de natura de amore* di Mario Equicola," *GSLI* 93 (1976) : 566–85.

17. The best general work on the tradition before Ficino is Bruno Nardi, *Dante e la cultura medievale*, 2d ed. (Bari, 1949), but Karl Vossler's older *Die philosophischen Grundlagen zum süssen neuen Stil des Guido Guinicelli, Guido Cavalcanti, und Dante* (Heidelberg, 1904) is still useful.

18. There are at least eight books surveying this group of treatises. The best of them is Paolo Lorenzetti's *La bellezza e l'amore nei trattati del cinquecento*, Annali della scuola normale superiore di Pisa, Filos. et filol., vol. 28 (Pisa, 1922). But see also John Nelson, *The Renaissance Theory of Love* cited above, and Luigi Tonelli, *L'amore nella poesia e nel pensiero del rinascimento* (Florence, 1933). Other works covering the same field are listed in the Bibliography under the names of Lorenzo Savino, Giuseppe Zonta (ed.), Michele Rosi, and Giuseppe Saitta (*La Teoria dell' amore . . .*).

II.

1. The standard biography of Ficino is that by Raymond Marcel (Paris, 1958).

2. These dates are conjectural. The first is suggested by Paul O. Kristeller, *Studies in Renaissance Thought and Letters* (Rome, 1956), pp. 196–98. The second is the year of Ficino's taking of holy orders (Kristeller, *Suppl.*, 1 : lxxvii).

3. April 1463 to Autumn 1468. See Ficino, *Opera*, pp. 657, 782, and 1537, and Paul Kristeller, "Marsilio Ficino as a Beginning Student of Plato," *Scriptorium* 20 (1966) : 41–54.

4. See Raymond Marcel, introduction to his edition of the *De amore* (Paris, 1956), p. 41 and facsimile opposite p. 33. See also Sebastiano Gentile, "Per la storia del testo del 'Commentarium in Convivium' di Marsilio Ficino," *Rinascimento* 21 (1981) : 3–27.

5. Kristeller, *Suppl.*, 1 : 87–89.

6. Ficino, *Opera*, p. 616.

7. Kristeller, *Suppl.*, 1 : lxxvii.

8. Ibid., pp. lxiii–lxix and lxxviii–lxxix. The Latin version, written first, is in *Opera*, pp. 1–77.

9. Bernardo del Nero and Antonio Manetti. See dedication in Kristeller, *Suppl.*, 1 : 89–91. Marcel (*Life*, pp. 46–47) dates the additions before 1475. There is a modern edition of Ficino's *De monarchia* by Alessandro Torri (Livorno, 1844). The Italian *De amore* was published by Cosimo Bartoli in 1544; it incorporates the chapter divisions and additions made in 1474.

10. The passages are listed by James Devereux, "The Textual Tradition of Ficino's *De amore*," *RQ* 28 (1975) : 173–82. See Marcel (ed., p. 47) and Kristeller, *Suppl.*, 1 : cxxiii–xxv. Marcel suggests the possibility that the astrological additions were prompted by Ficino's reading of the *De principiis astrologiae* of Alcabitius or the commentary thereon by Cecco d' Ascoli.

11. E.g., pp. 108, 163, 175–81, 248 in Marcel's edition of *Platonic Theology*, vol. 2.

12. See Paul O. Kristeller, "The First Printed Edition of Plato's Works and the Date of its Publication (1484)," in *Science and History: Studies in Honor of Edward Rosen* (Wroclaw, 1978), pp. 25–35.

III.

1. *De pulchro* (Leyden, 1641), p. 2. The work was first published in 1529.

IV.

1. For the two sons of Carlo Marsuppini (1398–1453) I have not been able to find dates. For the others the following references may be consulted:

> Landino (1424–1498): Manfred Lentzen, *Studien zur Dante-Exegese*
> *Cristoforo Landinos* (Cologne, 1971).
> Nuzzi (fl. 1486): Kristeller, *Suppl.*, 2 : 348.
> Cavalcanti (1448–1509): Kristeller, *Suppl.*, 1 : 118.
> Agli (1399–1477): Kristeller, *Suppl.*, 2 : 335.
> Benci (1427–1470): Kristeller, *Suppl.*, 1 : 135.
> Dietifeci (1401–1479): Marcel, *Life*, p. 123.

There is no good life of Cavalcanti. Marcel says that Cavalcanti was born in 1444, citing a letter—written in 1474 (*Opera*, p. 724)—in which Ficino says he thinks Cavalcanti is thirty years old. Della Torre (p. 647) says that Cavalcanti was born in 1448, citing a biography by Scipione Ammirato, *Della famiglia de' Cavalcanti* (Busta Passerine II, in the Biblioteca Nazionale, Florence, fol. 15ʳ). Cf. *Archivio Med. a il Princip.* 10 : 638, 29 : 585, 69 : 17. Kristeller (*Suppl.*, 1 : 118) accepts Della Torre's date, and so do I. Ficino claims (*Opera*, p. 741) to have met Cavalcanti first when Giovanni was four years old (5 lustra before 30 January 1477). The authority for regarding 1467 as the year of their first close association is Ficino's dedication of the *De amore*, where he says that he was thirty-four when he first felt Cavalcanti's love (Marcel, *Life*, p. 341). Although Ficino's banquet is fictional, there undoubtedly was an actual banquet rather like it on 7 November 1468; see Ficino, *Opera*, p. 782. Kristeller suggests that the actual banquet was prompted by Francesco Bandini; see "An Unpublished Description of Naples by Francesco Bandini," in Kristeller's *Studies*, p. 396.

2.   For example, Aulus Gellius (*Noctes Atticae* 1.99) reports the case of a student who was eager to read Plato's *Symposium* because he had heard that it contained an account of the sexual exploits of Alcibiades.

3.   By Leonardo Bruni, about 1436. See Eugenio Garin, "Ricerche sulle traduzioni di Platone nella prima metà del secolo XVI," *Medioevo e Rinascimento: Studi in onore di Bruno Nardi* (Florence, 1955), 1 : 367.

4.   See Ficino, *Opera*, pp. 1908–928 and Kristeller, *Suppl.*, 1 : cxxxiv–xxxv.

5.   John C. Nelson, *Renaissance Theory of Love*, chap. 1 and 2.

6.   The standard account of Ficino's debt to Dante is the short essay by Jean Festugière, "Dante et Marsile Ficin," *Comité français catholique pour la célébration du sixième centenaire de la mort de Dante Alighieri*, Bulletin du Jubilé (Paris, 1922), pp. 535–43. See also Kristeller's "Scholastic Backgrounds . . . ," *Studies*, p. 262, where he lists Ficino's references to Dante. André Chastel's chapter in *L'Art et humanisme* (Paris, 1959), "Dante, l'académie platonique et les artistes," pp. 106–24, is more general. Festugière's account, which stresses the fact that at least five of Ficino's associates in the "Academy" where active Dantists (Manetti, Benivieni, Attavanti, Verino, and Landino), could well be amplified by evidence from texts. For example, in the *De amore* there are several similarities to the *Convivio*: Ficino, like Dante, uses the technique of giving first a literal and then an allegorical reading of a text. Ficino, like Dante, in the course of distinguishing between the intellectual and the moral virtues, asserts that the intellectual virtues are superior, though the moral virtues are better known. Ficino uses the term *splendor* as a technical term for beauty, as Dante does (*Conv.* 3.15. 5.16–17). And most interesting of all, Ficino explains human individuation very much as Dante does.

7.   "In 1456, when I was in my twenty-third year, and you [i.e., Philippo Valori] were just being born, I began my first serious study by writing a four-book introduction to Platonism [the *Institutiones*]. This book was suggested to me by a good friend of mine who is also a very learned man, Cristoforo Landino. But when he and Cosimo de' Medici read what I had written, though they complimented me on it, they advised me not to publish it until I had learned a little Greek and absorbed more Platonism from primary sources. For what I had written in that work came partly from my own invention and partly from such reading as I had done up to that time in the Latin Platonists. So I started to read the Platonists and Plato in Greek, and I gradually used the material from the original essays in later writings" (*Opera*, p. 929).

8.   On the problem of Ficino's various lists of the cosmic hypostases, see Michael Allen, "Ficino's Theory of the Five Substances . . . ," *JMRS* 12 (1982) : 19–44.

9.   For Ficino's debt to Aquinas see Paul Kristeller, *Le Thomisme et la Pensée Italienne de la Renaissance* (Montreal, 1967); see also his *Studies*, pp. 35–55.

10.   See Robert Klein, "L'imagination comme vêtement de l'âme chez Marsile Ficin et chez Giordano Bruno," *Revue de métaphysique et de morale* 61 (1956) : 18–39.

11.   On the conflict between Proclus and Plotinus in Ficino's thinking about the theory of beauty, see the article by Oskar Walzel, "Von Plotin, Proklos und Ficinus . . . ," *DVLG* 19 (1941) : 407–29.

12.   See especially Edgar de Bruyne, *Etudes d'esthétique médiévale* (Bruges, 1946); Henri Pouillon, "La beauté, propriété transcendentale, chez les scolastiques (1220–1270),"

AHDLM 15 (1946) : 263–329; and Anthony Blunt, *Artistic Theory in Italy 1450–1600* (Oxford, 1940).

13. *Convivio* 4.21.4–10. See also 3.2.1–42. In the *De monarchia* of Dante, which Ficino translated into Italian in 1467, Dante endorses Boethius's view that true nobility is a special worth which God gives to souls which have been prepared to receive it. This concept of the relative preparation of the soul to receive a divine gift is analogous to Ficino's explanation (*De amore*, V.6) of how it happens that individual people are not all equally beautiful: though all participate in the same single, perfect beauty, some souls are better prepared to receive beauty than others. I think it likely that the *De amore* passage may have been influenced by the *Convivio*. But similar ideas may also be seen in the *Liber de causis*, in Aristotle (*Phys.* 1.187.a.28) and in Plotinus (*Enn.* 2.31.11). Ficino's awareness of these earlier sources may be reflected in his describing the passive or possible intellect of Aristotle as the "receiving" intellect (*Opera*, p. 240).

14. See John L. Lowes, "The Loveres Maladye of Hereos," *MP* 11 (1913–14) : 491–546. Most general medical treatises included a section, variously entitled *De amore*, *De ereos*, or *De iliacu*, on the disease of love. Ficino apparently used the treatises of Avicenna, Arnold of Villanova, and especially of Rhazes, whom he mentions by name.

15. Garin (in "Recenti interpretazione," p. 304) derides the notion that Ficino went through a "Lucretian period" in 1457–58, citing letters from this period in which Ficino mentions Platonism. But the evidence of a dominating interest in Epicureanism during those years is undeniable. It began when he read Lucretius during a summer which he spent at Campoli, as the guest of the Canigiani family. He wrote a commentary on Lucretius that September and later burned it. (See his admission in *Opera*, p. 933: "I suppressed a commentary on Lucretius which I wrote as a boy; I burned it, just as Plato did his tragedies and elegies.") His letters throughout the fall of 1457 show him preoccupied with Lucretius. For example, the letter to Mercati of 15 Oct. 1457, the letter to Morali of 29 Nov. 1457, and the letter to one or the other (probably) of 4 January 1458. The first and probably most important motive for his interest in Lucretius was simply that his program for the study of philosophy had been laid out on the basis of covering the four classical schools in this order: Peripatetics, Stoics, Platonists, and Epicureans. (See *Opera*, pp. 986 and 1801.) The fourth and remaining school, which he had not previously studied, was Epicureanism. But there was also another reason for his studying Lucretius. He regarded himself as a committed Platonist, and he had been told (by George of Trebizond in the attack on the Platonists which he published in 1455) that Epicurus was a disciple of Plato.

16. See *De amore*, VII, pp. 162, 163–64, and 168; in addition, Lucretius is alluded to on pp. 121 and 166.

17. See his important essay, "Immagini e simboli in Marsilio Ficino," *Medioevo e Rinascimento: Studi e ricerche* (Bari, 1954) : 288–310.

18. See *Re-Visioning Psychology*, pp. 197–202.

19. See *Opera*, pp. 612–15, 927.

20. See *Opera*, p. 986.

21. *Summa contra Gentiles* 1.57.

22. For the background of this discussion of the techniques of esotericism, see D. P.

Walker, "Esoteric Symbolism," in *Poetry and Poetics from Ancient Greece to the Renaissance*, ed. G. M. Kirkwood (Ithaca, 1975), pp. 218–32. For the special importance of the distinction between esoteric and exoteric in Florentine Platonism, see Bohdan Kieszkowski, *Studi sul platonismo del rinascimento* (Florence, 1936), p. 42. It could be argued that Ficino's use of indirection is merely an example of the rhetorical device of dissimulation recommended by Quintilian (Book 9), but Ficino's techniques go far beyond the bounds of what renaissance rhetoricians understood as the figure of dissimulation.

23. *Opera*, p. 1129.

24. See Klibansky, Saxl, and Panofsky, *Saturn and Melancholy* (London, 1964), pp. 75–97.

V.

1. See Professor Kristeller's important essay "The European Significance of Florentine Platonism" in *Medieval and Renaissance Studies* 8 (1968) : 206–29.

2. For Bandinelli see Panofsky's *Studies in Iconology* (New York, 1962); for Dürer see Klibansky, Saxl and Panofsky, *Saturn and Melancholy*. For Botticelli, see Ferruolo, Gombrich, Wadsworth, and Wind. The full references for these works and many others dealing with the influence of Ficino on the visual arts are given in Section VIII of the Bibliography. Notice especially the article of Parronchi suggesting the influence of Ficino on Michelangelo's Sistine ceiling.

3. See Giovanni Paolo Lomazzo, *Idea del tempio della pittura* (Milan, 1590), chap. 26, "La bellezza," pp. 83–96, especially pp. 83–84, the discussion of *ordo, modus*, and *species*. For Nifo see his *De pulchro* (Leyden, 1641), chap. 14, 15. For Tasso see especially his *Il Ficino* and discussion in Annabel M. Patterson, "Tasso and Neoplatonism . . . ," *SRen* 18 (1971) : 105–33. For the renaissance theory of beauty in general, see especially Anthony Blunt, *Artistic Theory in Italy 1450–1600*, and André Chastel, *Marsile Ficin et l'Art* (Geneva, 1954). For Ficino's debt in aesthetics to Plotinus and Proclus, see Oskar Walzel, "Von Plotin, Proklos und Ficinus," *DVLG* 19 (1941) : 407–29. Also useful are N. Ivanoff, "La beauté dans la philosophie de Marsile Ficin et de Léon Hébreu," *Humanisme et Renaissance* 3 (1936) : 12–21 and Erwin Panofsky, *Idea* (Columbia, S.C., 1968).

4. See T. F. Crane, *Italian Social Customs of the Sixteenth Century* (New Haven, 1920).

5. See Marcel edition, pp. 121–22. The best work on this Italian influence is Paolo Lorenzetti, *La bellezza e l'amore nei trattati del cinquecento*.

6. See Ficino, *Opera*, p. 621; Ficino's reply is on p. 622. See also James B. Wadsworth, "Lorenzo de' Medici and Marsilio Ficino: an Experiment in Platonic Friendship," *Romanic Review* 46 (1955) : 90–100.

7. See Kristeller, *Suppl.*, 2 : 246–47. Ivani had written earlier, calling the *De amore* a "divine" work, and Ficino had acknowledged this praise (*Opera*, p. 772). On Ivani, see Kristeller, *Suppl.*, 2 : 324.

8. On Diacceto see Kristeller, *Studies*, pp. 287–336; Kristeller gives a short analysis of Diacceto's *De amore* (1508) on pp. 308–10. An Italian translation by Diacceto, *I tre libri d' amore* (1511), was published in Venice in 1561.

9. An expurgated version was published in Florence in 1519, but the full text was

not published until 1942, by Eugenio Garin.

10. *De amore divino* (Rome, 1516).

11. See Pugliese's article in Section II of the Bibliography. The neat biological evolution among these treatises described by Edouard Meylan in "L' Evolution de la notion d'amour platonique," *Humanisme et Renaissance* 5 (1938) : 418–22 seems to me too good to be true. Similarly, I doubt that it is useful to divide them all into Ficino-line (i.e., spiritual love) treatises versus Hebreo-line (i.e., physical love) treatises, as some critics have tried to do. If anyone, Pico, not Hebreo, was regarded as the antithesis to Ficino by renaissance readers.

12. For France the best survey of the early influence is Jean Festugière, *La philosophie de l'amour de Marsile Ficin.* But see also Marcel's section on French works influenced by the *De amore*, in his edition, pp. 114–29, and the works of Lajarte, Lefranc, Levi, Mönch, Perry, Renaudet, Walker, and Weber listed in the France section of the Bibliography.

13. See Book 4, "Le livre de vraye amour" of Champier's *La nef des dames vertueuses*, ed. James Wadsworth (Hague, 1962). The fullest study of Platonism in the Lyons circle is Wadsworth's book *Lyons 1473–1503* (Cambridge, Mass., 1962).

14. See the book by Tiemann.

15. See Gundersheimer and Margolin.

16. On Platonism in the poets, see especially Merrill and Schmidt. The essays by Gadoffre and Hornik are also useful.

17. For discussion see the works by Adam, Brody, Huit, Johnson, Leclerc, and Mathieu-Castellani.

18. The best single introduction to Platonism in Spain is the long essay by Menendez y Pelayo listed in the Spain section of the Bibliography.

19. On Hebreo see especially, in the Spain section of the Bibliography, the works by Damiens, Fontanesi, Guy, Ivanoff, Perry, and Pflaum.

20. See especially works under Krebs and Morreale.

21. See the works by Arciniegas, Darst, Hathaway, Jones, Trueblood, and Vinci.

22. The standard works on Platonism in England are the books by Cassirer and Harrison listed in the Britain section of the Bibliography.

23. Grace Book B. Part 1.13.

24. See the books by Dannenberg and Schrinner.

25. S. K. Heninger, "Sidney and Serranus' *Plato*," *ELR* 13 (1983) : 146–61.

26. See article by Norman Council.

27. On Chapman see especially the works listed under Battenhouse, Schoell, and Waddington.

28. On Spenser see especially the works listed under Dees, Ellrodt, Fowler, Quitslund, and Welsford.

29. On Jackson see the article by Sarah Hutton.

30. On the Platonizing poets of the reign of James, see especially the works listed under Cinquemani, Doggett, Durr, Guffey, and Sicherman.

31. On Platonism in the Caroline drama, see especially the works by Gordon, Reyher, and Sensabaugh.

32. On the Cambridge Platonists see, in addition to Cassirer, the works by Lichten-

stein, Pinto, and Staudenbauer. On Norris see Mackinnon.

33. See Frank B. Evans, "Platonic Scholarship in Eighteenth Century England," *MP* 41 (1943) : 103–10.

34. Samuel Parker, *A Free and Impartial Censure of the Platonick Philosophy* (Oxford, 1666), p. 74.

35. Henry St. John, Viscount Bolingsbroke, *Works*, ed. D. Mallet (London, 1777), 2 : 443, 535 and 4 : 52, 95.

VI.

1. *Marsilio Ficino's Commentary on Plato's Symposium* (Columbia, Missouri, 1944).

2. *Marsile Ficin: Commentaire sur le Banquet de Platon* (Paris, 1956).

3. I have ignored the two complete French translations made during the Renaissance (by Jean de la Haye and Guy le Fevre de la Boderie) and also various other incomplete French translations of the work. These are described (pp. 123–29) by Raymond Marcel, whose own French translation, published in the same volume with his edition of the Latin text, is the only authoritative version in that language. I have also ignored the Roumanian translation by Sorin Ionescu (Bucharest, 1942). For fuller references see Bibliography, Section I.

Commentary of Marsilio Ficino
of Florence
on the
Symposium of Plato
On Love

Speech I

Chapter 1

[No title]

PLATO, THE FATHER of philosophers, died at the age of eighty-one, on November 7, which was his birthday, reclining at a banquet, after the feast had been cleared away.[1] This banquet, in which both the birthday and the anniversary of Plato are equally contained, all of the ancient Platonists down to the times of Plotinus and Porphyry[2] used to celebrate every year. But after Porphyry these solemn feasts were neglected for twelve hundred years. At last, in our own times, the famous Lorenzo de' Medici, wishing to renew the Platonic banquet, appointed Francesco Bandini master of the feast.[3] Therefore, since Bandini had arranged to celebrate the seventh day of November, he received with regal pomp at Careggi, in the country, nine Platonic guests: Antonio degli Agli, Bishop of Fiesole; Ficino, a physician; Cristoforo Landino, a poet; Bernardo Nuzzi, a rhetorician; Tommaso Benci; Giovanni Cavalcanti (our friend, whom the guests named Hero[4] because of his virtue of soul and handsome appearance);[5] and the two Marsuppini brothers, Cristoforo and Carlo, sons of the poet Carlo Marsuppini. Lastly, Bandini wanted me to be the ninth, in order that, with Marsilio Ficino added to those already mentioned, the number of the Muses might be achieved.

When the feast had been cleared away, Bernardo Nuzzi took the book of Plato which is entitled *Symposium on Love* and read all the speeches of this Symposium. When he had finished reading, he asked the rest of the guests each to expound on one of the speeches. They all consented. When the lots had been drawn, that first speech of Phaedrus fell to Giovanni Cavalcanti to explain. The speech of Pausanias fell to Antonio the theologian; of Eryximachus, the physician, to Ficino the physician; of the poet Aristophanes to Cristoforo the poet; of young Agathon to Carlo Marsuppini. To Tommaso Benci was given the disputation of Socrates; and that of Alcibiades to Cristoforo Marsuppini. This kind of lot they all approved. But the bishop and the physician found it necessary to leave, the one for the care of souls, the other for the care of bodies; they left their parts in the speaking to Giovanni Cavalcanti. The rest turned toward him and, ready to listen, fell silent. Then that hero exhorted them as follows.

Chapter 2

By what rule love should be praised
What is its dignity and greatness

Distinguished guests, a most agreeable lot has fallen to me today, by which it has turned out that I am to take the part of Phaedrus the Myrrhinusian. Of that Phaedrus, I say, whose friendship Lysias[6] of Thebes, the great orator, valued so highly that he tried to win him over by means of a speech composed with much lucubration; Phaedrus, whose appearance Socrates admired so much that one day, on the banks of the Ilissus River, Socrates was so excited by the beauty of Phaedrus that he became carried away, and recited the divine mysteries, though he had previously claimed that he was ignorant of all things, not only heavenly but also earthly. Phaedrus, by whose talents Plato was so much impressed that he dedicated to Phaedrus the first fruits of his studies. To him the epigrams, to him the elegies of Plato, to him his first book on beauty, which is entitled *Phaedrus*. Since, therefore, it has been judged that I am like this Phaedrus (not by me certainly, for I do not claim so much for myself), but first by the falling of the lot, and then by your applause, with these favorable auspices, I shall gladly comment on his speech first. Then I shall take the parts of Antonio and Ficino, to the best of my ability.

In dealing with any subject, gentlemen, any philosopher who is a follower of Plato examines three points:[7] what precedes it, what accompanies it, and what follows it. If these are good, he praises the thing itself; but if bad, he criticizes it. The perfect praise, therefore, is one which reviews a thing's past origin, tells its present form, and shows its future consequences. On the basis of its antecedents a thing is praised as noble, on the basis of its present nature, as great, and on the basis of its effect, as useful. Therefore, on the basis of those three points these three qualities are included in praises: nobility, greatness, and utility. Therefore, our Phaedrus, having considered first the present excellence of Love, called him *a great god.* He added *worthy to be admired by gods and men.*[8] And properly so. For we rightly admire things which are great. Certainly he is great to whose domination men and gods, as they say, are all subject. For, according to the ancients, the gods as well as men fall in love. This is what Orpheus[9] and Hesiod[10] mean when they say that the minds of mortals and immortals are conquered by Love. In addition, Love is said to be *worthy to be admired,* since every man loves that whose beauty he admires. Certainly the gods, or as our theologians[11] say, the angels, admire and love divine beauty, and men admire and love the beauty of the body. And this certainly is the praise of Love based on the present excellence which attends it.

Phaedrus next praises him on the basis of antecedents, when he says that he is the *oldest of all the gods.*[12] In this, when his ancient origin is told, Love's nobility shines. Thirdly, he will praise him on the basis of effects, where his wonderful usefulness will be apparent from his consequences. But we shall talk about his ancient and noble origin first, and about his future usefulness afterward.

Chapter 3

On the origin of love

In the *Argonautica*,[13] when Orpheus, in the presence of Chiron and the heroes, sang about the beginnings of things, following the theology of Hermes Trismegistus,[14] he placed Chaos before the World, and located

Love in the bosom of that Chaos, before Saturn, Jove, and the other gods; and he praised Love[15] in these words: *Love is the oldest, perfect in himself, and best counseled.* Hesiod,[16] in his *Theology,* Parmenides[17] the Pythagorean, in his book *On Nature,* and Acusilaus[18] the poet agreed with Orpheus and Hermes. Plato, in the *Timaeus,*[19] describes Chaos in a similar way, and places Love in it. And in the *Symposium*[20] Phaedrus recounted the same thing.

The Platonists define *chaos* as an unformed world, and *world* as a formed chaos. According to them there are three worlds, and likewise there will be three chaoses. The first of all things is God, the author of all things, whom we call "the Good" itself. He creates first the Angelic Mind, then the World Soul, as Plato calls it, and last the World Body. That supreme God we do not call a world, because *world* means *ornament, composed of many,* whereas God must be completely simple. But we do declare Him to be the beginning and end of all the worlds. The first world made by God is the Angelic Mind. The second is the Soul of the universal Body. The third is this whole machine which we see.

In these three worlds three chaoses are also considered. In the beginning God creates the substance of that Mind, which we also call its essence. This essence at that first moment of its creation is formless and dark. But because it is born from God, it turns toward God, its beginning, through a certain innate appetite. Turned toward God, it is illuminated by His ray. By the splendor of that ray, its appetite is increased. The whole of that increased appetite reaches out to God. As it reaches out, it receives form. For God, who is omnipotent, imprints on the Mind, reaching out toward Him, the natures of all things which are to be created. On the Angelic Mind, therefore, are painted, in some spiritual way, so to speak, all the things which we perceive in these bodies. There[21] come into being the spheres of the heavens and of the elements, the stars, the natures of the vapors, and the forms of stones, metals, plants, and animals.

These forms of all things, conceived in that celestial Mind, by a certain fomenting of God, we do not doubt are the Ideas. That Form or Idea of the heavens[22] we often call the god Uranus. The Form of the first planet we call Saturn, of the second, Jove, and so on for the rest of the planets. Also, that Idea of our fire we call the god Vulcan, of air Juno, of water Neptune, and of earth Pluto. Thus all the gods assigned to certain parts of the lower world are the Ideas of those parts collected in that celestial Mind.[23]

But before that perfect conceiving of the Ideas by the forming God came the reaching out of the Mind to God. Before this reaching out came the increasing of the appetite; before this the infusion of the ray; before this that first turning of the appetite; before this the unformed essence of the Mind. Further, that still unformed essence we call Chaos. Its first turning toward God we call the birth of Love. The infusion of the ray, the food of Love. The ensuing increase of appetite, we call the growing of Love. The reaching out to God, the impetus of Love. The forming of the Ideas, the perfecting of Love. The combination of all the Forms and Ideas we call in Latin a *mundus*, in Greek a *cosmos*, that is, an ornament. The grace of this *world* or *ornament* is Beauty, to which that Love, as soon as it was born, attracted the Mind; and it led the Mind, formerly ugly, to the same Mind made beautiful. Therefore the condition of Love is that it carries things off to beauty, and joins the ugly to the beautiful.

Who, therefore, will doubt that Love immediately follows Chaos, and precedes the World and all the gods who are assigned to the parts of the World, since the appetite of the Mind precedes its receiving of the Forms, and it is in the already formed Mind that the gods and the World are born? Therefore Orpheus rightly called Love *the oldest* of the gods. Also *perfect in himself*, as if to say, self-perfecting. Since that original appetite of the Mind seems to act spontaneously in drawing its own perfecting from God and in offering it to the Mind, which is formed by it, and to the gods, who are born from it.

Orpheus also called Love *the best counseled*. And rightly. For all wisdom, to which counsel belongs, was given to the Mind, because it turned toward God through Love and shone with His glory. The mind is turned toward God in the same way that the eye is directed toward the light of the sun; next it sees the light of the sun; third, in the light of the sun it perceives the colors and shapes of things. Therefore the eye, at first dark and, like Chaos, formless, loves the light while it looks toward it; in so looking, it is illuminated; in receiving the ray, it is informed with the colors and shapes of things.

But in the same way that the Mind, just born and formless, is turned by Love toward God and is formed, so also the World Soul turns itself toward the Mind and God, from which it was born. And although it is at first formless and a chaos, when it is directed by Love toward the Mind, having received from it the Forms, it becomes a world. In the same way also, the Matter of this World,[24] although in the beginning it lay a formless chaos, without the ornament of Forms, immediately because of a love innate in itself, it directed itself toward the Soul and offered itself obedient to it, and through this conciliating love, receiving from the Soul the ornament of all the Forms which are seen in this world, from a chaos became a world.

Therefore there are three worlds, and three chaoses. In all of them finally, Love accompanies chaos, precedes the world, wakens the sleeping, lights the dark, gives life to the dead, gives form to the formless, perfects the imperfect. Greater praises than these can hardly be expressed or conceived.

Chapter 4

On the usefulness of love

But thus far we have been talking about its origin and nobility; now I think we should talk about its usefulness. Certainly to list every one of the benefits of love conferred upon the human race is superfluous, especially since they can all be comprehended briefly. For all consist in this: that we avoid evil and pursue the good. For Man the evil and the sinful are the same, and the good and the virtuous are the same. Certainly all laws and doctrines strive for nothing else except to teach men to shun sinful things and to do virtuous things. But this goal, which almost innumerable laws and arts eventually reach only with difficulty after a long time, Love achieves all by itself in a moment. For shame deters men from sin, and the desire for glory incites them to virtue. Nothing occasions these two motives in men more easily and quickly than Love.

When we say "love," understand "the desire for beauty." For this is the definition of love among all philosophers. Beauty is a certain grace which most often originates above all in a harmony of several things.[25] It[26] is three-fold. For from the harmony of several virtues in souls there is a grace; from the harmony of several colors and lines in bodies a grace arises; likewise there is a very great grace in sounds from the harmony of several tones. Beauty, therefore, is three-fold: of souls, of bodies, and of sounds. That of souls is known through the intellect; that of bodies is perceived through the eyes; that of sounds is perceived only through the ears.[27] Since, therefore, it is the intellect, seeing, and hearing by which alone we are able to enjoy beauty, and since love is the desire to enjoy beauty, love is always satisfied through the intellect, the eyes, or the ears. What need is there for smell? What need is there for taste, or touch? These senses perceive odors, flavors, heat, cold, softness and hardness, and similar things. None of these is human beauty since they are simple forms, whereas the beauty of the human body requires a harmony of different parts. Love regards the enjoyment of beauty as its end. That pertains only to the intellect, to seeing and to hearing. Love, therefore, is limited to these three; an appetite which follows the other senses is not called love, but lust or madness.

Moreover, if love of a man desires beauty itself, and if the beauty of the human body consists in a certain harmony, and if harmony is temperance, love demands only those things which are temperate, moderate, and decorous. Thus the pleasures of taste and touch, which are so violent and wild that they remove the intellect from its proper state and perturb the man, love not only does not desire, but hates and shuns as things which because of their intemperance are contrary to beauty. Venereal madness leads to intemperance, and therefore to disharmony. Therefore it likewise seems to lead to ugliness, whereas love leads to beauty. Ugliness and beauty are opposites; therefore any motions which carry us to them seem to be opposite to each other. Therefore the desire for coitus (that is, for copulation) and love are shown to be not only not the same motions but opposite. To this fact attest the ancient theologians who attributed the name of love to God. This later theologians also strongly confirm. No name which is suitable for God is common with sinful things. Therefore anyone who is of sound mind ought to be careful lest he heedlessly apply the term love, a divine name, to foolish perturbations. Let Dicaearchus[28] blush, and anyone else who dares to slander the Platonic majesty,[29] on the ground that he indulged too much in love. For we can never indulge too much, or even enough, in passions which are decorous, virtuous, and divine. Hence it happens that every love is virtuous, and every lover is just. For every love is beautiful and proper and naturally loves the proper. But since the stormy passion by which we are swept into lewdness leads us to ugliness, it is judged to be the opposite of love.

Therefore, to return, at last, to the usefulness of love, the shame which deters us from sin and the desire[30] which makes us zealous for virtue arise from love easily and quickly. First because love, since it seeks the beautiful, always desires decorous and admirable things, and since it hates the ugly, necessarily shuns sinful and indecent things.[31] Second, if two people love each other, they watch over each other and want to please each other. Since each is watched by the other, like those who never lack a witness, they abstain from sin. Since they try to please each other, they are always undertaking praiseworthy things with a burning zeal, so that they may not be held in contempt by the beloved, but may be thought worthy of a reciprocation of love. But Phaedrus explains this principle at length and gives three examples of loves. One of the love of a woman for a man, where he speaks about Alcestis, the wife of Admetus, who was willing to die for her husband.[32] Another of the love of a man for a woman, as of Orpheus for Euridice.[33] Third of the love of a man for a man, as of Patroclus for Achilles.[34] Where he shows that nothing renders men braver than love. But it is not my intention for the present to examine the allegory either of Alcestis or of Orpheus. For these stories illustrate the power and dominion of love more forcefully if they are told as history than if they are thought to have been meant allegorically.[35]

Therefore let us concede without argument that Love is a great and wonderful god, and also noble, and very useful, and let us indulge in love in such a way as to be content with his own end, which is beauty. We enjoy this with the same faculty by which we know it. We know it with the intellect, the sight, and the hearing. Hence with these faculties we enjoy it. With the other senses we enjoy not beauty, which Love desires, but something else, which the body desires. Therefore we shall hunt beauty with these three faculties, and by means of the beauty which appears in sounds and bodies, as if by means of certain footprints, we shall track down the beauty of the soul. We shall praise the former, but be satisfied only with the latter; and we shall always strive to remember that the greater the beauty was, the greater the love is.[36] And where the body is certainly beautiful but the soul is not, let us love the body very little if at all, as a shadowy and fleeting image of beauty.

Where the soul alone is beautiful, let us love this enduring beauty of the soul ardently. But where both beauties occur together, let us admire them vehemently. And in this way we shall show that we are truly from the Platonic family. That certainly knows nothing except the festive, happy, heavenly, and celestial. But let this suffice now about the speech of Phaedrus; let us come to Pausanias.

Notes

1. Plato (c. 428–c.348 B.C.); the actual month and day of his birth are not known.

2. Plotinus (c. 204–270). The Alexandrian philosopher. Ficino later translated his *Enneads* (see Kristeller, *Suppl.*, 1 : cxxvi–xxviii). Porphyry (c. 232–c. 304) was a pupil of Plotinus, and also his biographer, and the editor of the *Enneads*. Ficino borrows the information in this paragraph from Porphyry's *Life of Plotinus*. See also Ficino's "De vita Platonis," *Opera*, pp. 763–70.

3. The banquet described here is fictional, but a similar banquet was actually held. See Introduction, section IV, n.1.

4. An approximate English equivalent of the term "hero" is "King of the Revels," but the term "hero" also involves a technical meaning; it is a category of creatures between daemons and men in the hierarchy of being. The class is discussed by Proclus (in the *Commentary on I Alcibiades* and in the *Platonic Theology* 7.46) and also by Jamblichus, in *De mysteriis* (Ficino, *Opera*, pp. 1874–876). Ficino refers to Cavalcanti as a "hero" elsewhere also (*Opera*, p. 624).

5. Ficino consistently translates *indoles* by *apparenza*.

6. Lysias (c. 459–380 B.C.) was an Athenian, not a Theban. His relation to Phaedrus and the incident on the Ilissus River are described in Plato's *Phaedrus* 229a–234c.

7. The idea that Platonists think in triplets is common in Ficino and in other authors; for example, see the opening sentence of Apuleius's *De deo Socratis* and the opening of Pico's *Commento*.

8. Plato *Symposium* 178a.

9. Orpheus *Hymn* 55 (To Venus) 4–6 (Abel, p. 87).

10. Hesiod *Theogony* 121–22.

11. Supplied on authority of the Italian translation.

12. Plato *Symposium* 178a–b.

13. Orpheus *Argonautica* 419–25 (Abel, p. 18).

14. Hermes Trismegistus *Pimander* 3.1.

15. The printed editions read: "Orpheus . . . amorem in ipsius chaos sinu locavit, laudavitque his verbis." The manuscripts read: ". . . in ipsius chaos sinu locavit, laudabitque his verbis." Marcel omits *laudavitque* altogether in his text and translation (p. 138).

16. Hesiod *Theogony* 116 ff. Cf. Plato *Symposium* 178b.

17. Parmenides *Frag.* 13 (Diels, *Die Fragmente der Vorsokratiker* [Berlin, 1934],

1 : 243). Cf. Plato *Symposium* 178b.

18. Acusilaus *Frag.* 1 (Diels, *Die Fragmente*, 1 : 53). Acusilaus (fl. 550 B.C.) wrote the *Genealogies* and a prose version of Homer. The passage referred to here is from the *Genealogies* but is apparently known only from the allusion to it in Plato's *Symposium* 178b.

19. Plato *Timaeus* 30a.

20. Plato *Symposium* 178b.

21. That is, in the Angelic Mind.

22. That is, the sphere of the fixed stars. The name of the mythological equivalent, which Ficino gives as *Coelum*, I translate *Uranus*.

23. Marcel's *superne* should read *superna*.

24. This phrase, frequently repeated, means "the physical world," or the World Body.

25. See V.1 below.

26. That is, grace.

27. Plotinus 1.6.1. Cf. VI.13 below.

28. Dicaearchus of Messene (c. 347–285 B.C.), a pupil of Aristotle, was a geographer and historian. The extant fragments of his works are edited by Fritz R. Wehrli in *Die Schule des Aristoteles*, 2d ed. (Basel, 1967), vol. 1. The allusion here is probably to a quotation in Cicero's *Tusc.* 4.34.71 (Wehrli, p. 21). The point of mentioning Dicaearchus at all, however, is that George of Trebizond cites him as authority for the sexual impropriety of Plato's life; Ficino's phrase "anyone else" probably refers to George.

29. That is, the character of Plato.

30. That is, the desire for glory; see par. 1 of this chapter and also the Italian translation.

31. The idea that love desires only the good and the beautiful (never the evil or ugly) is advanced here in terms very close to those in Plotinus *Enneads* 3.5.1. Cf. also Aquinas *ST.* 1–2. Q.27.1.

32. Plato *Symposium* 179b.

33. Plato *Symposium* 179d.

34. Plato *Symposium* 179e.

35. In Pico's *Commento*, Stanza 4, Pico accuses Ficino of not understanding Plato's allusions to these myths.

36. The Vatican manuscript reading *id servare* seems to me an error. I follow the other manuscripts, the printed text, and Ficino's Italian translation in reading *observare*.

Speech II

Chapter 1

God is goodness, beauty, and justice; beginning, middle, and end

THE PYTHAGOREAN PHILOSOPHERS believed that the trinity was the measure of all things, for the reason, I think, that God governs things by the ternary number, and also that things themselves are completed by the ternary number.[1] Hence Vergil said, "God rejoices in the odd number."[2] Certainly that supreme author first creates all things, second, attracts them to Himself, and third, perfects them. Likewise, all things first flow from that eternal source when they are born; then they flow back again to it, when they seek their own origin; and finally, they are perfected, after they have returned to their source.[3] Orpheus sang this when he called Jupiter the beginning, middle, and end of the universe.[4] The beginning inasmuch as He produces things, the middle inasmuch as He attracts His products back to Himself, and the end inasmuch as He perfects them when they return to Him. Hence we can call that ruler of the universe good, beautiful, and just, as He is often called in Plato. He is good, I say, when He creates; when He attracts, beautiful; and when He perfects each thing according to its merit, just. Beauty, therefore, whose property is to attract, stands between goodness and justice. From goodness it certainly flows; it flows toward justice.

Chapter 2

How divine beauty gives birth to love

This divine beauty has generated love, that is, a desire for itself, in all things. Since if God attracts the World to Himself, and the World is attracted, there exists a certain continuous attraction (beginning from God, emanating to the World, and returning at last to God) which returns again, as if in a kind of circle, to the same place whence it issued. And so one and the same circle from God to the World and from the World to God is called by three names. Inasmuch as it begins in God and attracts to Him, it is called Beauty; inasmuch as emanating to the World it captivates it, it is called Love; inasmuch as returning to its author it joins His work to Him, it is called Pleasure.[5] Love, therefore, beginning from Beauty, ends in Pleasure. This was expressed in that famous hymn of Hierotheus and Dionysius the Areopagite,[6] where these theologians sang as follows: "Love is a good circle which always revolves from the Good to the Good." For Love is necessarily good since it is born from the Good and returns to the Good.

For it is the same God whose beauty all things desire, and in possessing whom all things rest. From there, therefore, our desire is kindled. There the desire of lovers rests, and is not spent, but satisfied.[7] Not without reason does Dionysius compare God to the sun,[8] for just as the sun gives light and warmth to the body, so God offers the light of truth and the warmth of love to souls. We certainly infer this comparison from the sixth book of Plato's *On the Republic*,[9] in the way which I shall explain. Obviously the sun creates both visible bodies and seeing eyes; into the eyes, in order that they may see, it infuses a shining spirit; and the bodies, in order that they may be seen, it paints with colors. But neither the ray proper to the eyes nor the colors proper to the bodies suffice to bring about vision unless the one light itself above the many, from which the many lights proper to eyes and bodies are distributed, arrives, illuminates, arouses, and strengthens.

In the same way, that first act of all, which is called God, bestowed upon each thing, in creating it, species and act.[10] Obviously this act, because it was received in a created thing and in a passive subject, is weak and incapable of performing work, and the perpetual and invisible single light of the divine sun is always shining over all things; it warms, brings to life, stimulates, perfects, and strengthens. Orpheus divinely says about this: "Warming all things, and himself spreading over all things."[11] Insofar as He is the act of all things and strengthens them, He is called good. Insofar as He stimulates and calms, soothes and arouses, He is called beautiful. Insofar as, in objects which are to be known, He attracts to them those three powers of the knowing soul: intellect, sight, and hearing, He is called beauty. Insofar as, in the cognitive power He connects it to the known object, He is called truth. Finally, insofar as He is good, He creates, rules, and perfects; insofar as He is beautiful, He illuminates and infuses with grace.

Chapter 3

Beauty is the splendor of the divine goodness,
and God is the center of four circles

And not without point, the ancient theologians located goodness in the center and beauty in the circle. Or rather goodness in a single center, but beauty in four circles.[12] The single center of all is God. The four circles around God are the Mind, the Soul, Nature, and Matter. The Mind is a motionless circle. The Soul is self-moving. Nature is movable in another but not by another. Matter is movable by another and in another. On the other hand, the reason why we call God the "center" and the other four, "circles," we explain briefly thus:

The center of a circle is a point, single, indivisible, motionless. From it many lines, which are divisible and mobile, are drawn out to the circumference, which is like them.[13] This divisible circumference revolves around the center as its axis. And the nature of the center is such that, although it is single, indivisible, and motionless, it is nevertheless found in many, or rather in all, of the divisible and movable lines everywhere.[14] For everywhere, it is a point in a line.[15] But since nothing can be touched by what is dissimilar to it, every line drawn from the circumference to the center must touch a mid-point of this kind, each in some point of its own which is single, simple, and motionless. Who will deny that God is rightly called the center of all things since He is present in all things, completely single, simple, and motionless? But all things produced from Him are many, composite, and in some way movable, and as they flow from Him so they flow back to Him, in the manner of lines and[16] a circumference.

In this way, Mind, Soul, Nature, and Matter, proceeding from God, strive to return to the same, and from every direction they revolve in toward Him as best they can. And just as the center point is found everywhere in the lines and in the whole circle,[17] and through its own point each of the lines touches the mid-point of the circle, so God, the center of all things, who is the simplest unity and the purest act, puts Himself into all things, not only because He is present to all things, but also because to everything created by Him He gave a certain inmost potency, most simple and most distinctive, which is called the unity of that thing,[18] from which and to which, as from and to their own center the rest of the parts and potencies of the thing hang. Clearly it is proper that created things collect themselves to this their own center, to this their own proper unity, before they cling to their creator, in order, as we have now often repeated, to be able, by clinging to their own center, to cling to the center of all things. The Angelic Mind rises to its own apex or head before it ascends to God. The Soul also, and the rest in the same way. And of those invisible circles, that is, the Mind, the Soul, and Nature, the circle of the visible world is an image. For bodies are the shadows and signs of souls and minds. But a shadow and sign corresponds to the shape of that whose shadow and sign it is. Therefore those four are not wrongly called four circles.

But the Mind is a motionless circle because its operation as well as its substance always remains the same, and it functions in the same way: it always understands in the same way and wills in the same way.[19] On the other hand, the Mind can sometimes be called movable, merely from the fact that, like all other things, it proceeds from God and turns itself toward Him.

The World Soul, and any other soul, is a movable circle. For the Soul by its own nature learns through discourse and functions through periods of time, but discourse from one to another and temporal functioning are undoubtedly called motion. But if there is any stability in the cognition of the Soul, it is stable thanks to the Mind rather than to the Soul.

Nature also is a movable circuit. When we say Soul, we mean, following the custom of the ancient theologians, the power placed in the

Soul's reason and sensation; when we say Nature, we mean the power placed in the Soul's faculty of procreation.[20] The former power in us they called properly Man; the latter, an idol or image of Man. The faculty of procreation is clearly called movable for this reason: because it carries out its work through periods of time. But it differs from that property[21] of the Soul in this: that the Soul is moved *through* and *in* itself. *Through* itself, I say, because it is the beginning of motion. *In* itself also because the operation of reason and sensation resides in the very substance of the Soul. From these[22] no effect necessarily results in the body. Now the power of procreating, which we call Nature, is certainly moved *through* itself, since it is a certain power of the self-moved soul. But the procreative power is said to be moved *in* another, because its entire function is confined *in* the mass of the body. For it nourishes, increases, and propagates the body. Matter, however, or the mass of the body, is a circle movable both *by* another and *in* another. *By* another certainly, since it is necessarily activated by the soul. *In* another, however, because the motion of the body occurs in the space of place.

Now, therefore, we can clearly understand for what reason the theologians place goodness in the center and beauty in the circumference.[23] If the goodness of all things is the one God Himself, through whom all things are good, then beauty is the ray of God, infused in those four circles revolved around God in a certain way. This ray forms in those four circles all the species of all things. Those species we are accustomed to call in the Mind, Ideas; in the Soul, Reasons; in Nature, Seeds; and in Matter, Forms. Therefore in the four circles there seem to be four splendors. The splendor of Ideas in the first, of Reasons in the second, in the third of Seeds, of Forms in the last.

Chapter 4

How Plato's passage on the divine things is explained

This mystery is what Plato meant in the letter to King Dionysius, when he asserted that God is the cause of all beautiful things, that is, the beginning and origin of all Beauty:

> *Around the King of all,* he says, *are all things. All things because of Him. He is the cause of all beautiful things. The second around the Second. The third around*

the Third. The human soul wishes to understand what those things are by looking at those things which are related to itself; but none of these proves adequate. For around the King Himself and the things which I have mentioned, nothing is of that kind; and what is after this the soul says.[24]

Around the King means not inside but outside the King. For in God there is no compositeness. What that word *Around* means, Plato explains when he adds *All things because of Him. He is the cause of all beautiful things,* as if to say that all things are *around* the King for this reason: because to Him as their end, all things of their own nature return, just as from Him as their beginning they are all produced. *Of all beautiful things,* that is, of all the beauty which shines in the above-mentioned circles. For the Forms of bodies are returned to God through the Seeds, these through the Reasons, and these through the Ideas; and they are all produced from God through the same stages. And strictly speaking, when he says *all things*[25] he means the Ideas, for the rest are included in these. *The second around the Second. The third around the Third.* Zoroaster posited three princes of the world, the lords of three orders: Ohrmazd, Mithra, and Ahriman.[26] These Plato calls God, Mind and Soul.[27] The three orders, however, he placed in the divine species: the Ideas, Reasons, and Seeds. The first therefore, that is the Ideas, revolve around the First, that is, around God, since they were given to the Mind by God, and they lead back to Him the Mind to which they were given. *The second around the Second:* that is, the Reasons around the Mind, because they pass through the Mind into the Soul and direct the Soul toward the Mind. *The third around the Third:* that is, the Seeds of things around the Soul, for they pass through the Soul into Nature, that is, into that power of procreation, and again they join Nature to the Soul. In the same way the Forms descend from Nature into Matter. But Plato does not include these[28] in the stated sequence[29] because since Dionysius had inquired about the divine things, Plato cited as divine the three orders pertaining to incorporeal species, but he left out the Forms of bodies. And Plato did not wish to call God the "First" King but the *King of all,* lest, if he said, "First," he might perhaps appear to be grouping Him in some kind of numerical order and equality of status with the subordinate rulers. Nor did he say that only the first things are *around* Him, but *all things,* lest we think that God is the governor of only a certain order rather than *of all things.*

The human soul wishes to understand what those things are. Skillfully, after those three splendors of the divine beauty shining in the three circles, he added the love of the soul for them. For it is from there that the ardor of the soul is kindled. It is certainly appropriate that the divine should desire the divine.[30]

By looking at those things which are related to itself. Since human cognition arises from the senses, we are often accustomed to judge divine things by those things which we regard as most impressive in bodies: by the powers of corporeal things we judge God's power; by their orderliness, His wisdom; by their usefulness, God's goodness.[31] But Plato calls the Forms of bodies *related to* the soul, as if next of kin. For the Forms of bodies are located on the next level below the soul.

But none of these proves adequate. Forms of this kind neither exist sufficiently, nor do they sufficiently represent divine things to us. For the true things are the Ideas, Reasons, and Seeds. But the Forms of bodies seem to be shadows of things, rather than true things. But just as the shadow of a body does not represent the exact and clear shape of the body, so bodies do not represent the proper nature of things divine.

Around the King Himself and the things which I have mentioned, nothing is of that kind. For in what way can mortal things be like immortal or false like true? *And what is after this the soul says,* that is, the soul, as long as it judges divine things by mortal, speaks falsely of divine things, and does not pronounce divine things but mortal ones.

Chapter 5

The divine beauty shines through all things
and is loved in all things

Moreover, in order that we may include many things in a few words, the Good is certainly said to be that supereminent existence itself of God. Beauty is a certain act or ray from it penetrating through all things:[32] first into the Angelic Mind, second into the Soul of the whole, and the other souls, third into Nature, fourth into the Matter of bodies. It adorns the Mind with the order of the Ideas. It fills the Soul with the series of the Reasons. It supports Nature with the Seeds. It ornaments Matter with the Forms. But just as a single ray of the sun lights up four bodies, fire, air, water, and earth, so a single ray of God illuminates the Mind, the Soul, Nature, and Matter. And just as anyone who sees the light in those four elements is looking at a ray of the sun itself and, through that ray is turned to looking at the supreme light of the sun, so anyone who looks at and loves the beauty in those four, Mind, Soul, Nature, and Body, is looking at and loving the splendor of God in them, and, through this splendor, God Himself.

Chapter 6

On the passion of lovers

Hence it happens that the passion of a lover is not extinguished by the sight or touch of any body. For he does not desire this or that body, but he admires, desires, and is amazed by the splendor of the celestial majesty shining through bodies. For this reason lovers do not know what they desire or seek,[33] for they do not know God Himself, whose secret flavor infuses a certain very sweet perfume of Himself into His works. By which perfume we are certainly excited every day. The odor we certainly smell; the flavor we undoubtedly do not know. Since, therefore, attracted by the manifest perfume, we desire the hidden flavor, we rightly do not know what we are desiring and suffering.

Hence it also always happens that lovers fear and worship in some way the sight of the beloved.[34] Let me even say, although I fear that some one of you will blush when you hear these things, that even brave and wise men, I say, have been accustomed to suffer in the presence of the beloved, however inferior. Certainly it is not anything human which frightens them, which breaks them, which seizes them. For a human power is always stronger in braver and wiser men. But that splendor of divinity, shining in the beautiful like a statue of God, compels lovers to marvel, to be afraid, and to worship.

For the same reason, on account of the presence of the beloved, a lover spurns riches and honors and considers them worthless. For it is fitting that divine things be preferred to human things. It also repeatedly happens that someone wishes to transfer himself into the person of the beloved. And not wrongly, for he wants and tries to become a god instead of a man. And who would not exchange a man for God?

It also happens that those who have been trapped by love alternately sigh and rejoice. They sigh because they are losing themselves, because they are destroying themselves, because they are ruining themselves. They rejoice because they are transferring themselves into something better. They are also alternately hot and cold, like those whom a tertian fever attacks. They are cold rightly, because they are deserted by their own warmth, and they are also hot since they are enflamed by the splendors of the celestial ray. Timidity follows cold: courage, heat. Therefore they also seem alternately timid and bold. Moreover, some of the stupidest men are rendered more intelligent by loving. For who does not see very clearly with the help of a heavenly ray? But let these words suffice about love itself, and about beauty, its origin, and about the passions of lovers.

Chapter 7

On the two origins of love and the double Venus

Next the two kinds of loves should be discussed briefly. According to Plato,[35] Pausanias says that Cupid is the companion of Venus. And he thinks that there must necessarily be as many Cupids as there are Venuses. He mentions two Venuses, whom twin Cupids likewise accompany. One Venus he certainly calls Heavenly, but the other Vulgar. That Heavenly Venus was born of Uranus,[36] without any mother. The Vulgar Venus was born of Jupiter and Dione.[37]

The Platonists call the supreme God Uranus because just as heaven, that sublime body, rules over and contains all bodies, so that supreme God is exalted over all spirits. But the Mind they call by several names. For they sometimes call it Saturn, sometimes Jupiter, sometimes Venus.[38] For that Mind exists, lives, and understands. Its being they were accustomed to call Saturn; its life, Jupiter; its intelligence, Venus. The World Soul also we call, in the same way, Saturn, Jupiter, and Venus: insofar as it understands the celestial things, Saturn; insofar as it moves the heavenly things, Jupiter; insofar as it procreates lower things, Venus.

The first Venus, which is in the Mind, is said to have been born of Uranus without a mother, because *mother*, to the physicists, is *matter*. But that Mind is a stranger to any association with corporeal matter. The second Venus, which is located in the World Soul, was born of Jupiter and Dione. "Born of Jupiter"—that is, of that faculty of the Soul itself which moves the heavenly things, since that faculty created the power which generates these lower things. They also attribute a mother to that second Venus, for this reason, that since she is infused into the Matter of the world, she is thought to have commerce with matter.

Finally, to speak briefly, Venus is twofold. One is certainly that intelligence which we have located in the Angelic Mind. The other is the power of procreation attributed to the World Soul. Each Venus has as her companion a love like herself. For the former Venus is entranced by an innate love for understanding the Beauty of god. The latter likewise is entranced by her love for procreating that same beauty in bodies. The former Venus first embraces the splendor of divinity in herself; then she transfers it to the second Venus. The latter Venus transfers sparks of that splendor into the Matter of the world. Because of the presence of these sparks, all of the bodies of the world seem beautiful according to the receptivity of their nature. The beauty of these bodies the human soul perceives through the eyes. The soul again possesses twin powers. It certainly has the power of understanding, and it has the power of procreation. These twin powers are two Venuses in us, accompanied by twin loves. When the beauty of a human body first meets our eyes, our intellect, which is the first Venus in us, worships and esteems it as an image of the divine beauty, and through this is often aroused to that. But the power of procreation, the second Venus, desires to procreate a form like this. On both sides, therefore, there is a love: there a desire to contemplate beauty, here a desire to propagate it. Each love is virtuous and praiseworthy, for each follows a divine image.

What, therefore, does Pausanias censure in love? Indeed I shall tell you. If anyone, through being more desirous of procreation, neglects contemplation or attends to procreation beyond measure with women, or against the order of nature with men, or prefers the form of the body to the beauty of the soul, he certainly abuses the dignity of love. This abuse of love Pausanias censures. He who properly uses love certainly praises the form of the body, but through that contemplates the higher beauty of the Soul, the Mind, and God, and admires and loves that more strongly. And he uses the office of procreation and intercourse only as much as the natural order and the civil laws laid down by the prudent prescribe. About these things Pausanias speaks at greater length.

Chapter 8

On simple and reciprocal love. Exhortation to love

So, my friends, I encourage and entreat you to embrace love with all your strength, as a thing which is undoubtedly divine. And do not be frightened by what they say Plato said about a certain lover: "That lover," he said, "is a soul dead in its own body and living in a foreign body."[39] Also, do not be disturbed by what Orpheus sang about the bitter and wretched lot of lovers.[40] For how these things are to be understood, and how one can remedy them, I shall inquire next, if you don't mind; listen carefully.

Plato calls Love a bitter thing.[41] And not wrongly, because anyone who loves, dies. And Orpheus calls him *gluchupichron*, that is, "bittersweet."[42] Certainly, since love is a voluntary death. Insofar as it is voluntary, sweet. And whoever loves, dies. For his attention, oblivious of himself, is always turned to the beloved. If he does not think about himself he certainly does not think *in* himself. And therefore a soul thus affected does not function *in* itself, since the special function of the soul is thought itself. He who does not function in himself does not exist in himself either. For these two, function and existence, are equivalent to each other. Neither is there existence without function, nor does function go beyond existence itself. Nor can anyone function where he does not exist, and wherever he exists, he functions. Therefore the soul of a lover does not exist in itself because it does not function in itself. If it does not exist in itself, it also does not live in itself. He who does not live is dead. Therefore anyone who loves is dead in himself. But at least he lives in another?[43] Certainly.

There are two kinds of love: one love is simple, the other reciprocal.[44] Simple love is where the beloved does not love the lover. There the lover is completely dead. For he neither lives in himself, as we have already sufficiently proved, nor does he live in the beloved, since he is rejected by him. Where, then, does he live? Possibly in the air, or water, or fire, or earth, or in some brute body? By no means. For a human soul does not live in a body other than human. Perhaps it may lead its life in some other body of a man not loved? Certainly not that either. For if it does not live in that body where it most fiercely desires to live, how will it live in another? Therefore he who loves another, but is not loved by the other, lives nowhere. Therefore the unloved lover is completely dead. Nor will he ever revive unless indignation should revive him.

But where the beloved responds in love, in him at least the lover leads a life. Here certainly a strange thing happens. Whenever two men embrace each other in mutual affection, this one lives in that; that one, in this. Such men exchange themselves with each other; and each gives himself to the other in order to receive the other. How they give themselves up while they forget themselves, I see. But how they receive each other I do not understand. For he who does not have himself will much less possess another. Rather each has himself and has the other. Certainly this one has himself, but *in* that one. That one also possesses himself, but in this one. Certainly while I love you loving me, I find myself in you thinking about me,[45] and I recover myself, lost by myself through my own negligence, in you, preserving me. You do the same in me.

And this again seems amazing. For after I have lost myself, if I recover myself through you, I have myself through you; if I have myself through you, I have you before and more than I have myself, and I am closer to you than to myself, since I approach myself in no other way than through you as an intermediary.

In this certainly, the power of Cupid differs from the violence of Mars.[46] Certainly dominion and love differ thus. The ruler possesses others through himself; the lover recovers himself through another, and the further each of the two lovers is from himself, the nearer he is to the other, and dead in himself, revives in the other. But in reciprocal love there is only one death, a double resurrection. For he who loves dies in himself once, when he neglects himself. He revives immediately in the beloved when the beloved receives him in loving thought. He revives again when he finally recognizes himself in the beloved, and does not doubt that he is loved. O happy death which two lives follow! O wondrous contract in which he who gives himself up for another has the other, and does not cease to have himself! O inestimable gain, when two become one in such a way that each of the two, instead of being only one, becomes two, and, as if he were doubled, he who had one life, with only one death intervening, now has two lives. For a man who dies once and revives twice has acquired for a single life a double, for a single self two selves.

There is certainly a very just vengeance in reciprocal love. A murderer ought to be punished by death. Who would deny that a man who is loved is a murderer, since he separates the soul from the lover? Again, who would deny that the beloved likewise dies when he likewise loves the lover? When one person returns to another, and the other to him, the soul he has received—this indeed is due restitution. Each man by loving gives up his own soul, and by loving in return restores the foreign soul through his own. Therefore, out of justice itself, whoever is loved ought to love in return. But he who does not love his lover must be held answerable for murder. No, rather a thief, murderer, desecrator. Money is possessed by the body, the body by the soul. Therefore he who steals a soul, by which the body as well as the money are possessed, steals at the same time the soul, the body, and the money. Hence it happens that like a thief, murderer, and desecrator, he is punishable by a triple death, and being completely abominable[47] and impious, he can be killed by anyone with impunity, unless he himself should, of his own accord, carry out that law, namely, that he love his lover. In which case with him who dies once, he likewise dies once and with him who revives twice, he likewise revives twice.

In the above arguments it has been shown that the beloved ought to love his lover in return. But that he not only ought to but must is proven in the following way. Likeness generates love.[48] Likeness is a certain nature which is the same in several things. For if I am like you, you also are[49] necessarily like me. Therefore the same likeness which compels me to love you also forces you to love me. Moreover, the lover removes himself from himself and gives himself to the beloved. Therefore the beloved takes care of him as his own possession. For one's own things are always the dearest to one. There is also the fact that the lover engraves the figure of the beloved on his own soul. And so the soul of the lover becomes a mirror in which the image of the beloved is reflected. For that reason, when the beloved recognizes himself in the lover, he is forced to love him.

The astrologers[50] think that there is a special reciprocity of love between those at whose birth there was an interchange of the lights, that is, of the sun and the moon. That is, if at my birth the sun were in Aries and the Moon in Libra, and at yours the sun were in Libra and the moon in Aries. Or those for whom the same or similar sign and the same or similar planet was in the ascendant. Or those for whom favorable planets looked[51] on the angle of ascendance in the same way. Or those for whom Venus was situated in the same house of birth and in the same grade.

The Platonists add, or those whose life the same or certainly a similar daemon governs. The natural and moral philosophers say that likeness of complexion, nourishment, education, habit, or opinion is the cause of like affection. Finally where several of these causes occur together, there the interchange of love is found to be very strong. Where they all occur together, there the passion of Damon and Pythias, or Orestes and Pylades, rises up again.

Chapter 9

What lovers seek

In conclusion, what do they seek when they love reciprocally? They seek beauty. For love is the desire of enjoying beauty.[52] But beauty is a certain splendor attracting the human soul to it. Certainly beauty of the body is nothing other than splendor itself in the ornament of colors and lines. Beauty of the soul also is a splendor in the harmony of doctrine and customs. Not the ears, not smell, not taste, not touch, but the eye perceives that light of the body. If the eye alone recognizes, it alone enjoys. Therefore the eye alone enjoys the beauty of the body. But since love is nothing else except the desire of enjoying beauty, and this is perceived by the eyes alone, the lover of the body is content with sight alone. Thus the desire to touch is not a part of love, nor is it a passion of the lover, but rather a kind of lust and perturbation of a man who is servile. Moreover, that light and beauty of the soul we comprehend with the Intellect alone. Therefore he who loves the beauty of the soul is content with the perceiving of the Intellect alone. Finally, among lovers beauty is exchanged for beauty. A man enjoys the beauty of a beloved youth with his eyes. The youth enjoys the beauty of the man with his Intellect. And he who is beautiful in body only, by this association becomes beautiful also in soul. He who is only beautiful in soul fills the eyes of the body with the beauty of the body. Truly this is a wonderful exchange. Virtuous, useful, and pleasant to both. The virtue certainly is equal to both. For it is equally virtuous to learn and to teach. The pleasure is greater in the older man, who is pleased in both sight and intellect. But in the younger man the usefulness is greater. For as superior as the soul is to the body, so is the acquisition of beauty of the soul superior to that of the body. This finishes the speech of Pausanias; now let us interpret the speech of Erixymachus.[53]

Notes

1. That is, that God governs everything in threes, and accordingly creation takes place in three stages. In the back of Ficino's mind may be the discussion of the Trinity and creation in Aquinas *ST.* 1-1. Q.45. Art.6-7.

2. Vergil *Eclogues* 8.75.

3. The cosmic motions of emanation and reversion described in this and the following chapters are described in Pseudo-Dionysius *De div. nom.* 4.7-16, but Dionysius's

source (and probably one of Ficino's as well) is Proclus *Elements of Theology* 14–39.

4. Orpheus *Hymn* 15 (To Zeus) 7 (Abel, p. 66); Ficino may be citing this text from Plato *Laws* 4.716a.

5. For the application of these three terms, *pulchritudo–amor–voluptas*, to the iconography of the three Graces, see Edgar Wind, *Pagan Mysteries in the Renaissance* (New York, 1968), pp. 36–52.

6. Pseudo-Dionysius *De div. nom.* 4.14.712d. Hierotheus is mentioned by Dionysius as a pupil and friend of his and the author of some "Erotic Hymns." See F. S. Marsh, *The Book of the Holy Hierotheos* (London, 1927), especially pp. 232–46.

7. That is, not because it is exhausted but because it is satisfied.

8. Pseudo-Dionysius *De div. nom.* 4.1.693b; 4.4.697b–c.

9. Plato *Republic* 6.508a–509b.

10. The technical terminology here is from Aquinas's treatise on creation, but the ideas are not. See Aquinas *ST.* 1.1. Q.44. Art.2; Q.45. Art.1; and Q.75. Art.5.

11. Orpheus *Frag.* 6 (Abel, pp. 147–48). Ficino gives a Latin translation in *Opera*, p. 934. The fragment is preserved in Eusebius *De. praep. evang.* 13.2. Another text of the same poem is preserved in Abel's *Frag.* 5.

12. Ficino is here apparently working from Plotinus *Enneads* 5, but his basic account of the cosmic motions of emanation and reversion is also influenced by Proclus *Elements of Theology* 14–39 and 56–64.

13. That is, divisible and mobile.

14. That is, in every direction outward from the center.

15. That is, it constitutes one point in every radius which radiates from it.

16. That is, to and from.

17. That is, in every radius as well as at the center of the circumference.

18. The concept of a nucleus, epitome, apex, or unity-point of every class of being Ficino apparently derived from Plotinus *Enneads* 5.5.4. See also Ficino's VII.13 (p. 169) below. As applied to the human soul, the concept leads to Ficino's stressing the Mens or intellect as the divine nucleus of the soul, an idea which is also discussed by Hermes in *Pimander* 10 (pp. 199–205 of Scott's trans.).

For the background of the related concept of the *summum animae, scintilla animae,* or *apex mentis*, see the references cited by Maurice Gandillac in "Le platonisme au XIIe et au XIIIe siècle" in *Association Guillaume Budé. Congrès de Tours et Poitiers* (Paris, 1954), pp. 266–85; including especially, Endre von Ivanka, "Apex mentis, Wanderung und Wandlung eines stoischen Terminus," *Zeitschrift für katholische Theologie* 72 (1950) : 129–76; and R. P. Reypens's article "Ame" in *Dictionnaire de spiritualité* (Paris, 1933), 1 : 434–67. One of many statements of the idea which Ficino might have known is Bonaventure's: "In the human soul the inmost part is also the highest part, as is evident in the fact that it is by virtue of its highest part that the soul is most like God, and likewise by virtue of its inmost part, and the more the soul turns inward, the more it ascends and is united" (*Commentary on the Sentences* 2.8).

19. The distinction between intellect and will is a standard scholastic doctrine. See Aquinas *ST.* 1–1. Q.82. Art.3–4.

20. Ficino is here attempting to coordinate Platonic cosmology with Aristotelean psychology. The three parts of the soul, according to Aristotle, are the rational, sensitive,

and vegetative parts. The medieval Platonists identified Nature with the World Soul. But Ficino says that, when he uses the term *Soul*, he means the rational and sensitive soul, and when he uses the term *Nature*, he means the vegetative soul.

21. That is, the mobility.

22. That is, reason and sensation.

23. This paragraph is repeated in the opening of V.4 below.

24. Plato *Letters* 2.312e. King Dionysius the younger succeeded his father in 367 B.C. as Tyrant of Syracuse. Ficino could have found an interpretation of this letter in Plotinus *Enneads* 5.1.8 or in Proclus *Platonic Theology* 2.8, 9. Bessarion cites the same letter, and probably from the same sources. See Mohler, ed., *In calumniatorem*, 1.2.4, pp. 15–16.

25. That is, in the first sentence of the quotation.

26. Plutarch *De Iside et Osiride* 369e–370d.

27. Plato *Timaeus* 30b.

28. That is, the Forms.

29. That is, Plato does not say, "The fourth things around the Fourth." See Michael Allen, "Ficino's Theory of the Five Substances...," *JMRS* 12 (1982) : 19–44.

30. That is, that the soul should want to understand divinity.

31. On power, wisdom, and goodness as attributes of God see Aquinas *ST*. 1–1. Q.39, esp. Art.8.

32. For the sun analogy developed here see Plotinus *Enneads* 5.3–12; but the sun analogy is a commonplace in other Platonists as well.

33. Plato *Symposium* 192c.

34. Plato *Symposium* 192b.

35. Plato *Symposium* 180d.

36. See p. 44, n.22.

37. The classical account of the birth of Venus from the sea is that of Hesiod *Theogony* 188–206. Venus is described as the daughter of Dione by Homer *Iliad* 5.370.

38. In this section Ficino appears to take the Venus allegory from Plotinus *Enneads* 3.5.2, but the attribution of mythological names to the three subdivisions of each hypostasis is probably derived from Proclus (e.g., see his *Platonic Theology* 6.11).

39. Ficino elsewhere (*Opera*, p. 613) attributes this idea to Plato's *Phaedrus*, but it is not in that dialogue or in the *Symposium* either; it is in Aquinas *ST*. 1–2. Q.28.2–3. This section probably owes something also to the physiology of the exchange of spirits described in VII.4.

40. Vergil *Georgics* 4.454–506.

41. Possibly Plato *Philebus* 47e, where love is classed as a pain instead of a pleasure.

42. Orpheus *Frag.* 316 (Abel, p. 272; known only from this passage in Ficino).

43. This discussion is probably based on Aquinas's section on "mutual indwelling," in *ST*. 1–2. Q.28.2.

44. Cf. V.9, below.

45. The Italian translation shows that in the Latin text (p. 157, line 1) the comma should be put after *amantem*, not after *amo*.

46. This obviously inserted comment evidently refers to Plato *Symposium* 196d and is an example of Ficino's effort to disguise his treatise as a Commentary.

47. For Marcel's *informis* (p. 157, last line) read *infamis*. The whole of this playful

discussion on rejection as a form of murder is evidently directed at Giovanni Cavalcanti, who is, ironically, the speaker.

48.   For the background of this idea, see especially Aquinas *ST.* 1-2. Q.27.3 and Proclus *Elements of Theology* 32.

49.   For Marcel's *est* read *es.*

50.   This section, to the end of the chapter, is one of the astrological passages added to the work about 1475.

51.   For Marcel's *aspexerit* read *aspexerint.*

52.   In the Oxford manuscript of the Commentary (fol. 16^v), Ficino calls attention here, by a marginal note, to a passage on this subject in a poem of Cristoforo Landino:

> For since love is a desire stricken by beauty, it
> loves beauty and takes pleasure in beautiful sights.
> Whatever is good is beautiful, and everything evil
> is ugly. Thus love enjoys the good and avoids the evil.

See *Carmina omnia* of Landino, ed. Alessandro Perosa (Florence, 1939), p. 162:

> Namque amor a pulchro cum sit perculsa cupido,
> Pulchrum amat et pulchris gaudet imaginibus,
> At quodcumque bonum, pulchrum est, turpe omne nefandum:
> Sic bona deposcit, sic mala vitat amor.

53.   Marcel (p. 160) moves this sentence to the beginning of the next chapter.

Speech III

Chapter 1

Love is in all things and for all things

ACCORDING TO THE opinion of our Erixymachus,[1] there seem to be three things which we should discuss, in order. First, that love is present in all things and extends through all things. Second, that he is the creator and preserver of all works that are according to nature.[2] Third, that he is the master and lord of all of the arts.

Certainly in nature three grades of things are considered: superior, inferior, and equal.[3] Those which are above are the causes of the inferior; those which are below are the works of the superior; things which are equal are endowed among themselves with the same nature. Now the causes love their own works as parts and images of themselves. The works, on the other hand, also desire their causes as their preservers. But things which are located in the same rank are drawn to each other mutually by reciprocal love, as if they were similar parts of one and the same body.[4] Thus, God rules and governs the angels with a certain benevolence; and the angels, together with God, rule and govern the souls; and the souls, with those,[5] the bodies. In this is clearly perceived the love of superiors for inferiors.

Again, bodies are both most eagerly joined to their souls and most unwillingly separated from them. Our souls desire the bliss of the heavenly things. The heavenly things blissfully worship the majesty of the supreme divinity. And this is the feeling of love of inferiors for the superior.

Similarly, all the parts of fire willingly cohere with each other. Again the parts of earth, water, and air cohere with each other; and in any species of animals, animals of the same species always accept each other in mutual association. Here is seen the love for equal and similar things.

For who, therefore, will doubt that love for all things is innate in all things? And that is what Dionysius the Areopagite signified in the book *On The Divine Names* according to the opinion of Hierotheus, in these words:

> *Love, whether we have called it divine or angelic or spiritual or animal or natural, we understand to be a certain grafted and mixing virtue*[6] *which certainly moves superior things to the care of inferior things, also reconciles equals to social intercourse with each other, and lastly, urges any inferior things to turn toward greater and higher things.*[7]

This is what he said.

Chapter 2

Love is the author and preserver of all things

But that second point of our speech, in which love is called the creator and preserver of all things, is proved in the following way. The desire to propagate one's own perfection is a certain type of love. Absolute perfection is in the supreme power of God. This perfection the divine Intellect contemplates. And from there the divine Will desires to propagate the same perfection outside itself. Out of this love of propagation, all things are created by Him. Therefore our Dionysius says, "Divine Love did not permit the King of all things to remain in Himself without issue."[8] The same instinct for propagation is infused into all things by that first author. Through this instinct the holy spirits move the heavens and distribute their gifts to all inferior beings. Through this, the stars scatter their light through the elements. Through this, fire moves air by communicating its own heat, air moves water, and water, earth. And vice versa, earth attracts water to itself, and water air, and air fire; and all herbs and plants, desiring to propagate their own seed, bear things like themselves. Brute animals also, and men, are led to procreate progeny by the enticements of the same desire.

But if Love creates all things, it also preserves all things. For the function of creating and preserving always belongs to the same thing. Certainly like things preserve like things. But love attracts like to like.[9] Individual pieces of earth adhere to other pieces of earth like themselves because of reciprocal, joining love. Also the whole earth descends toward the center of the world, which is like itself, because of a longing for that. Similarly, drops of water move toward each other, and, with the whole body of water, toward a place appropriate to them. The parts of air and fire do the same. And also these two elements are drawn to a celestial region congruous and similar to them by love of that region. The heaven,[10] also, as Plato says in the book *The Statesman*,[11] is moved by innate love. For the whole soul of heaven is present in all of the points of heaven at once. Therefore, the heaven, desirous of enjoying the soul, for that reason runs, in order that it may enjoy the whole soul everywhere, through all of its parts. Moreover, it flies very fast insofar as it can be done, to be present all at once wherever the soul is all at once. In addition to this, the concave surface of each larger sphere is the natural place of the convex surface of the next smaller sphere. And because any particle of the latter sphere corresponds equally to any particle of the former, any one particle of the smaller sphere desires to touch all the particles of the larger. If the heaven were motionless, single particles would touch single particles, not any one, all. By running, it nearly achieves what it could not achieve standing still. And it runs very fast in order that as far as possible any particle may touch all the others at almost the same time.

Finally, all things are preserved by the unity of their parts; with the dispersion of their parts things die. But their mutual love brings about the unity of their parts. This may be seen in the humors of our bodies and in the elements of the world; in a concord of these, as Empedocles the Pythagorean says,[12] both the world and our body consist; in a discord, they are destroyed. But a concord among them an exchange of peace and love produces. Hence, Orpheus: "You alone, O Love, rule the reins of all these things."[13]

Chapter 3

Love is the master and governor of the arts

It remains, after these things, that we explain in what way he is the master and governor of all the arts. That he is certainly the master of the arts we shall understand if only we shall consider that no one can ever discover or learn any art unless the pleasure of learning and the desire of discovering move him, and unless he who teaches loves his students, and the students thirst very eagerly for that learning. Moreover he is rightly called governor. For, whoever greatly loves both works of art themselves and the people for whom they are made executes works of art diligently and completes them exactly. In addition to these points there is the fact that artists in all of the arts seek and care for nothing else but love.

Let us for the present briefly run through the arts which Erixymachus mentions in Plato:[14]

For what else does *Medicine* consider but how the four humors of the body may become and remain mutual friends; what foods and drinks and other needs of living or healing nature loves and desires? Here also, through a certain similitude, Erixymachus touches on those two loves, heavenly and vulgar, which Pausanias had distinguished above.[15] For a temperate complexion of the body has a moderate love and for moderate and fitting things. An intemperate has an opposite love, and for opposite things. The former love, of course, is to be indulged; the latter never submitted to.

In *Gymnastic* exercise also, one must find out what habits of the body, what kinds of exercise and what postures the body loves and demands.

In *Agriculture* one must find out what soil requires what seeds or what care; or what method of cultivation is desired by all the plants.

In *Music* the same thing is observed, whose artists investigate what numbers love what numbers either more or less. They find the least love between one and two and between one and seven.[16] Between one and three, four, five, or six, they find a stronger love. Between one and eight the strongest. Musicians make acute and grave tones, which are different by nature, more friendly to each other, by means of certain intervals and modes. From this derive the composition and sweetness of harmony. They also temper slower and faster motions to each other in such a way that they become very good friends, and produce rhythm and harmony.[17] But there are said to be two kinds of musical melody. For one is ponderous and steady. The other is delicate and playful. Plato, in the books on the *Republic* and *Laws*,[18] judges the former to be beneficial to users and the latter harmful. In the *Symposium*[19] he assigns to the former the Muse Urania, to the latter Polyhymnia. Some people love the first type; others, the second. The love of the former people should be tolerated, and the sounds which they desire should be permitted; but the appetite of the latter people should be resisted. For the love of the former is heavenly; of the latter, vulgar.

There is a certain friendship among the stars and the four elements which *Astronomy* considers. In these are found those same two loves, in a sense. For the moderate love is in them when they very temperately harmonize together with reciprocal powers. And the immoderate love is when some one of them loves itself too much and forsakes the others in some way. From the former derive pleasant temperature of air, tranquility of water, fertility of earth, and health of animals. From the latter derive opposite things.

Finally, the power of prophets and priests seems to consist principally in this, that it teaches us what offices of men are pleasing to God, how men become friends to God, and what kind of love and charity is to be shown to God, to country, to parents, and to others, both living and dead.

In the rest of the arts, it is possible to infer the same thing, and to conclude summarily that Love is in all things, for all things. That he is the author and preserver of all things, and the lord and master of all the arts.

The god Orpheus rightly called him *clever, double-natured, holding the keys of all things*.[20] For in what sense he is *double-natured* you have heard first from Pausanias, and then from Erixymachus. For what reason he is said by Orpheus to hold the *keys of the world*, we can understand sufficiently from the above. Certainly as we have shown, this desire for propagating one's own perfection, which is innate in everything, explains the latent and implicit fecundity of everything, while it makes seeds develop into an embryo, and draws out the powers of each thing from its heart, and conceives offspring, and, by opening these offspring as though with certain keys, brings them into the light. On this account all the parts of the world, because they are the works of one artist, parts of the same machine, and like each other in being and life, are bound to each other by a certain reciprocal love; so that love may rightly be called the eternal knot and link of the world, and the immovable support of its parts, and the firm foundation of the whole machine.

Chapter 4

No part of the world hates another part

If this is so, no parts of this work[21] can be inimical among themselves in any way. For fire does not flee water out of hatred of water, but out of love for itself, lest it be extinguished by the coldness of the water. Nor does water extinguish fire out of hatred of fire; but it is led by a certain desire for multiplying its own cold to create water like itself out of the body of the fire. For, since every natural desire tends toward good and none toward evil, the aim of water is not to extinguish fire, which is evil, but to propagate water like itself, which is good. If water could accomplish this without the destruction of fire, it certainly would not extinguish fire.

The same principle is applied about other things which seem opposite and inimical. Certainly the lamb does not hate the life and form of the wolf, but is fearful of his own destruction, which is occasioned by the wolf. Nor does the wolf kill and devour the lamb out of hatred for him, but out of love for himself. Nor does man hate man, but the vices of man. Nor do we envy the stronger or smarter their gifts out of hatred for them, but out of solicitude for ourselves, fearing lest we completely succumb to them. Therefore nothing prevents love from being in all things and penetrating through all things.

Therefore let us without doubt fear this so great god because he is everywhere, and occupies the inner chambers of all things, like a powerful lord whose rule we cannot escape, like a very wise judge from whom our thoughts cannot hide. Because he is the creator and preserver of all things, let us venerate him as a father; let us revere him as a protector and refuge. Because he instructs us in each of the arts, let us follow him as a teacher. By him as our author we exist and live. Through him as our preserver we endure perpetually. By him as protector and judge we are governed. By him as teacher we are taught and trained to live well and happily.

Notes

1. See last sentence of preceding chapter.

2. That is, of all things in the physical world. The Italian translation says "of all natural things."

3. The whole of Speech III (except for the first part of chap. 3) is based on Pseudo-Dionysius *De div. nom.* 4.10–16, but the source behind the Pseudo-Dionysius is Proclus *Elements of Theology* 23–39 and 155.

4. Supplied from the Italian translation.

5. That is, with God and the angels.

6. As the Italian translation shows, what this phrase means is "a certain instinct for joining and uniting."

7. Pseudo-Dionysius *De div. nom.* 4.15. 713a, b. On Hierotheus, see p. 59, n.6 above.

8. Pseudo-Dionysius *De div. nom.* 4.10.708b.

9. Cf. Plato *Lysis* 214.

10. Throughout this passage, I use the term *The heaven* in the singular because it is singular (*celum*) in Ficino, but what he means is "The heavens," that is, the rotating spheres of the fixed stars, the planets, and the elements of air and fire.

11. Plato *The Statesman* 269d.

12. I have not been able to locate any such discussion as that to which Ficino refers. See Diels, *Die Fragmente der Vorsokratiker* (Berlin, 1938), 1 : 308–72; and Denis O'Brien, *Empedocles' Cosmic Cycle* (Cambridge, 1969). The allusion here is probably a quotation from Proclus, but the idea is a commonplace association with Empedocles.

13. Orpheus *Hymn* 58 (To Eros) 8 (Abel, p. 89). By "these things" are meant "things in this world."

14. *Symposium* 186b–187d.

15. Cf. above, II.7.

16. The term "numbers" refers to intervals in the octave scale. *One, two,* and *seven* are the first, second, and seventh notes. Thus the passage explains that intervals of thirds, fourths, fifths, sixths, and octaves are more euphonious than seconds or sevenths.

17. As the Italian translation (*concordia grata*) shows, the phrase *rhythm and harmony* (*rhytmum concinnitatemque*) is a hendiadys, one of Ficino's favorite figures. Another example is "composition and sweetness" in the previous sentence.

18. Plato *Republic* 3.398c–399; *Laws* 7.800d.

19. Plato *Symposium* 187e.

20. Orpheus *Hymn* 58 (To Eros) 4 (Abel, p. 89).

21. That is, of the physical world.

Speech IV

Chapter 1

Plato's text on the ancient nature of man is described

WITH THESE WORDS our familiar put an end to his speech. After him followed Cristoforo Landino,[1] a man excellent in learning, whom we knew chiefly in our times as an Orphic and Platonic poet, setting out to interpret the obscure and involved opinion of Aristophanes, as follows.

Although Giovanni Cavalcanti, through his care in disputation, has saved us from long digressions, nevertheless the opinion of Aristophanes, because it is wrapped in very obscure language, still requires some explanation and light.

More than the other gods, says Aristophanes, Love is especially generous to mankind; a guardian, protector, and physician to men. First one should notice what the nature of men formerly was, and what its passions were.[2] Nor was it formerly what it is now, but very different. In the beginning there were three genders of human beings, not only two, as now, male and female, but also there existed a certain third, composed of both. Moreover, the appearance of every person was whole, and round, having the back and sides in a circle, four hands and legs matching the hands, likewise two faces, joined on a round neck, and exactly alike. The male gender was born from the sun, the female from the earth, and the bi-sexual from the moon. Whence they were of proud spirit and robust body. Therefore they tried to fight with the gods and ascend into heaven. For this reason Jupiter cut each one of them lengthwise, and made two out of one, like those who cut hard-boiled eggs lengthwise with a hair. And he threatened that if ever again they were seen to rage in pride against the gods, he would divide them again in the same way. After the nature of men was divided in this way, each half-person desired its other half. Therefore they ran to each other, and throwing their arms about each other, embraced each other, trying to be returned to their former condition. On that account they would have perished of hunger and inactivity if God had not added a means of intercourse.

Hence certainly a reciprocal love is innate in men, the conciliator of their original nature, striving to make one out of two and to heal the nature of men. For each of us is half of a man, just as the little fish which are called *psettae*, or goldfish, being sliced, from one become two. But each human half seeks its own half. And so whenever his own half meets someone, of whichever sex he may be desirous, he is most violently aroused, clings to it with burning love, and does not even for a moment permit being separated from it. And so the desire and longing for the whole to be restored receives the name of love. This, for the present time, helps us greatly while it leads each of us to his own formerly lost half, and for the future, inspires the highest hope in us who worship God piously, that by restoring us to our former condition and healing us He will make us most blessed.

Chapter 2

Plato's opinion about the ancient nature
of man is explained

Aristophanes tells these things and many other things like wonders or portents, behind which, as if behind veils of some kind, divine mysteries must be supposed to lie. For it was the custom of the ancient theologians[3] to conceal their holy and pure mysteries in the shadows of metaphors, lest they be defiled by the profane and impure. But we do not think that all the things which are described in the figures above (and in others) apply precisely to the meaning. For even Aurelius Augustine[4] says that not all the things that are represented in figures must be thought to mean something. For many things are added for the sake of order and connection, on account of the parts that do mean something. Only by the ploughshare is the earth turned, but in order that this can be done, other parts too are joined to the plough. Therefore the sum of what is intended to be explained by us is as follows:[5]

> Men formerly had three sexes: masculine, feminine, and mixed, the sons of the sun, the earth, and the moon. And they were whole. But on account of pride, when they wished to equal God, they were cut in two; if they are proud again, they are to be split in two parts again. The division having been made, half is drawn to half by love, in order that a restitution of wholeness may be effected. This achieved, the race of men will be blessed.[6]

The sum of our interpretation[7] will be this:

Men, that is, the souls of men, formerly, that is, when they are created by God, are whole, they are provided with two lights, one innate and the other infused, in order that by the innate light they may perceive inferior and equal things, and by the infused, superior things. They wished to equal God. They turned themselves toward the innate light alone. Hence they were divided. They lost the infused splendor when they were turned toward the innate light alone, and they fell immediately into bodies. If they become more proud, they will be divided again, that is, if they trust too much to the natural power, that innate and natural light which remains will be extinguished in some measure. They had three sexes: male born of the sun; female, of the earth; and mixed, of the moon. Some received the splendor of God as courage, which is male; others as Temperance, which is female; others as Justice, which is mixed. These three virtues in us are the daughters of three others which God possesses. But in God those three are called sun, earth, and moon; but in us male, female, and mixed. The division having been made, half is drawn to half by love. When souls, already divided and immersed in bodies, first have come to the years of adolescence, they are aroused by the natural and innate light which they retained (as if by a certain half of themselves) to recover, through the study of truth, that infused and divine light, once half of themselves, which they lost in falling. This once recovered, they will be whole, and blessed with a vision of God. This, therefore, will be an abridgment of our interpretation.

Chapter 3

Man is the soul itself, and the soul is immortal

Since the body is composed of matter and quantity, and it pertains to matter to receive, and to quantity to be divided and extended; and since reception and division are passive experiences, the consequence is that the body is by nature subject only to passive experience[8] and corruption. Even if some action appears to be suitable to the body, the body acts not inasmuch as it is a body, but inasmuch as there is in it a certain power in some measure incorporeal, and a quality, like the heat in a mass of fire, or the cold in the matter of water, or the complexion in our body. From these qualities certainly the operations of bodies arise. For fire heats not because it is long or wide or deep, but because it is hot. Nor does a more spread-out fire heat more (on the contrary, because of its dispersion, less), but only one which is hotter. Since, therefore, bodily actions take place by virtue of powers and qualities, and since powers themselves and qualities are not composed of matter and quantity (though they exist in matter and quantity), it follows that to be passive pertains to the body, but to act pertains to something incorporeal.

Certainly these powers are indeed instruments of bodily operation, but they themselves are by no means in themselves sufficient for operation because they are not sufficient for existence. For what lies *in* another and cannot sustain itself obviously depends upon another. For this reason the qualities, because they are necessarily sustained by the body, are made and ruled by some higher substance which neither is a body, nor lies in a body. This higher substance is the soul, which, though present and dwelling in bodies, sustains itself, and gives bodies the quality and power of complexity through which, as through organs, the soul carries out various operations in and through the body.

Hence, Man is said to procreate, nourish, grow, run, stand, sit, speak, make works of art, feel, and understand. But all these things the soul itself does. And for this reason the soul will be Man. If we say that *Man* procreates, grows, and nourishes, then the soul, as father and creator of the body, begets, feeds, and nourishes. If *Man* stands, sits, and speaks, the soul supports the parts of the body, and bends and vibrates. If *Man* makes or runs, the soul extends the hands and turns them at will, or moves the feet. If *Man* feels, the soul, through the instruments of the senses, as though through windows and doors, perceives external bodies. If *Man* understands, the soul by itself, without any bodily instrument, arrives at the truth. Therefore all the things that *Man* is said to do the soul itself does; the body merely suffers them. Therefore Man is the soul alone; the body is merely a work and instrument of Man. The more especially because the soul carries out its most important action, namely, intelligence, without any instrument of the body, since it understands incorporeal things through the intelligence, whereas through the body only corporeal things are known.

Thus if the soul *does* anything by itself, it certainly *exists* and *lives* by itself, for that which operates without the body lives without the body. If it exists by itself, a certain proper being is appropriate to it, a being not common to the body; therefore the soul can take the name of *Man* as proper to itself, independent of the mass of the body.

Since each of us throughout our entire life is called "*man*," at any age,[9] then surely this name seems to signify something that remains fixed. The body is perpetually in flux, changed by growing, shrinking, continuous disintegration, liquefaction, and alternate heat and cold. The soul always remains the same, which its search for truth clearly shows us, and its never-changing will for the Good, and its firm preservation of memory. Who,[10] therefore, will be so foolish as to attribute the appellation of *Man*, which is firmly fixed in us, to the body, which is always flowing and everywhere changed, rather than to the most stable soul? From these things it can be clear that, when Aristophanes said *men*, he meant our souls, in the Platonic way.

Chapter 4

That the soul was created furnished with two lights
and why it descends into the body

Further, immediately after the soul is born from God, it turns toward Him as its parent by a certain natural instinct, just as a fire created on earth by the power of higher things is immediately directed toward the higher things by an impulse of nature. Having turned toward Him, the soul is illuminated by His rays. But this first splendor received in the substance of the soul, which was previously formless in itself, becomes dimmer and, contracted to the soul's capacity, becomes proper and natural to it. Since this first light is the soul's equal, the soul can see, by it, both itself and things which are inferior to itself, that is, all bodies, but it cannot see God or things above itself. But soon, having become closer to God through this first spark, it receives another, brighter light by which it recognizes heavenly things also.

It therefore has a double light. One natural or innate, the other divine and infused. With these joined together, as though with two wings, it is able to fly through the heavenly region. And if it always used that divine light, it would always cleave to the divine things; the earth would be empty of rational animals. But it has been decreed by divine Providence that the soul should be mistress of itself, and be able to use sometimes both lights at once and sometimes one. Hence it happens that the soul, under the guidance of nature, being turned toward its own light, and neglecting the divine light, pays attention to itself and to its own powers which look after the making of the body, and it desires to carry out these powers in making bodies. Weighed down, as they say,[11] by this desire, it descends into the body, where it exercises its powers of procreating, moving, and sensing, and with its presence adorns the earth, the lowest seat of the world. This region must not lack reason, in order that no part of the world be destitute of the presence of rational animals, just as its author, in whose image the world was made, is entirely reason. But our soul fell into the body when, neglecting the divine light, it used its own light alone and began to be content with itself. Only God, to whom nothing is lacking, above whom there is nothing, remains content with Himself, sufficient to Himself. Therefore the soul made itself equal to God when it wished to be content with itself alone, as if it could be sufficient to itself no less than God.

Chapter 5

In how many ways the soul returns to God

Aristophanes says that this pride was clearly the cause of the soul, which was born whole, being *split*, that is, with regard to its twin lights; after this it used one but neglected the other. Plunged into the abyss of the body as though into the river Lethe,[12] and forgetting itself for a time, it is seized by the senses and lust, as though by police and a tyrant.

But when the body has matured, and the instruments of the senses have been purged, with learning contributing, the soul wakes up a little. Here the natural light shines forth and searches out the order of natural things. By this investigation the soul perceives that there is some architect of this huge machine. And it desires to see and possess Him, but He is perceived only by the divine splendor.[13] For this reason the soul's intellect is very strongly goaded, by the prodding of its own light, to recover the divine light. But this instigation and appetite is true love, under the guidance of which one half of the man desires the other half of the same man, because the natural light, which is one half of the soul, tries to kindle again in the soul that divine light, which is called the other half of the same soul, formerly neglected. And that is what Plato says in the letter to Dionysius: *The human soul desires to understand what the divine things are by looking at those things which are related to itself.*[14]

But when God infused His own light into the soul, He adapted the light above all to this: that it might lead men to bliss, which consists in the possession of Him. To this we are led by four virtues: Prudence, Courage, Justice, and Temperance.[15] Prudence first shows us bliss; those other three virtues, like three paths, lead to bliss. And so God tempers his own spark variously in various souls to this end, that under the direction of Prudence some seek their author again through the offices of Courage, others through the offices of Justice, and others through the offices of Temperance. Certainly some, thanks to this gift, undergo dangers and death with a brave heart, for the worship of God, for integrity, or for fatherland. Others arrange life so justly that they neither themselves do harm to anyone nor, insofar as possible, permit it to be done by others. Others master the appetites by vigil, fast, and work. These certainly proceed by three paths, but they all strive to arrive at the same end of bliss which Prudence shows them.

Accordingly those three virtues are also contained in the Prudence of God Himself. Enflamed with a desire for them, the souls of men seek to arrive at them, by exercising them, and then to cleave to them and possess them eternally.

The Courage of men we call masculine because of its hardness and boldness. Temperance we call feminine because of a certain restrained and cooler habit of desire and its soft nature. Justice we call mixed. Feminine certainly inasmuch as because of its innocence it brings harm to no one. But masculine inasmuch as it does not permit harm to be done to others, and with very severe judgment levies punishment upon wicked men.

But because it is proper to the male to give and to the female to receive, for that reason we call the sun male, since it receives light from none and gives to all. The moon giving and receiving—receiving from the sun it gives to the elements—we call mixed. And the earth, since it certainly receives from all and gives to none, we call female. Therefore sun, moon, earth; Courage, Justice, Temperance are rightly signified by the names masculine, mixed, feminine. And in order to allow a more excellent appellation to God, we call these virtues in Him sun, moon, earth; in ourselves we call them masculine sex, mixed, and feminine. And to those in whom that divine light from the sun of God was infused at their birth with a disposition of Courage we say that a masculine light has been granted. To those in whom the moon of God with a disposition of Justice, a mixed. To those from the earth of God, with a disposition of Temperance, a feminine.

As soon as we turned to the natural light, we neglected that infused and divine light. Therefore the one having been disdained, we have kept the other. Where we keep one-half of ourselves, we have lost the other half. But, at a certain age, prompted by the natural light, we all certainly desire the divine, but being different, we proceed to the attainment of it in a different way: with Courage, those who originally received light with a quality of Courage from God's Courage. Others with Justice, or similarly Temperance. Finally, each seeks that half of himself as he had received it, and some, certainly through the masculine light of God, once lost, now recovered, wish to enjoy the masculine Courage of God; others likewise through the mixed light, the mixed virtue; others through the feminine, in the same way.

These actually achieve so great a reward who, after their natural spark has shone forth in them in maturity, decide that the natural light is not sufficient for judging divine things, lest, by the standard of the natural spark, they attribute the passions of souls or bodies to divine majesty and think that that divine majesty is not superior to bodies or souls. In this certainly many are said to have erred. Those who having trusted, in their investigation of divine things, in the natural power, either have said that God does not exist, like Diagoras; or have doubted it, like Protagoras, or have judged God to be a body like the Epicureans, the

Stoics, and the Cyrenaics, and many others; or a kind of soul, like Marcus Varro and Marcus Manilius, and several others.[16] These men, being impious, not only have not recovered their divine light, formerly neglected, but also have spoiled their natural light by abusing it. That which is spoiled is not wrongly thought to be broken and split. Therefore the souls of those who, being proud and swollen with arrogance, trust their own powers, are divided again, as Aristophanes says, since even the natural light which was left them they darken with false opinions and extinguish with wicked habits.

And so they use the natural light properly who, recognizing that it is maimed and mutilated, think it sufficient in some measure for judging natural things. But thinking that they need a more sublime light for things which are above nature, they prepare themselves, by a certain very thorough purging of the soul, in such a way that the divine light may again shine for them, by whose rays they will judge rightly about God, and will be restored to that original wholeness.

Chapter 6

Love leads souls back to heaven; it distributes
degrees of bliss; it bestows eternal joy

Make propitious to yourselves, distinguished guests, by every kind of sacrifice, this god who, Aristophanes says, is kind to the human race above the other gods. Invoke him with pious prayers; embrace him with all your heart. By his beneficence he first leads souls to the heavenly table, laden with ambrosia and nectar; then he assigns every soul to a seat; finally he keeps them there sweetly for eternity. For no one returns to heaven except those who have pleased the King of the Heavens. They please Him who love Him exceedingly. Certainly, to know Him truly in this life is completely impossible. But to love Him truly in whatever way He is known is both possible and easy. Those who know God do not yet please Him unless they love Him when they know Him. Those who know Him and love Him are loved by God, not because they know Him, but because they love Him.[17] For we do not embrace with love those who have known us, but only those who have loved us. For many of those who know us we regard as enemies. Therefore what restores us to heaven is not knowledge of God but love.

Moreover, the order of those banqueting at the heavenly table corresponds to the various degrees of the lovers. For those who have loved God more excellently enjoy more excellent feasts there. Certainly, those who through works of Courage have worshipped the Courage of God enjoy that itself. But those who have worshipped Justice enjoy Justice. Likewise Temperance, those who have worshipped Temperance. And so the various souls enjoy the various Ideas and Reasons of the divine mind according to the various raptures of their love. But they all enjoy the whole God because He is whole in all the Ideas. But they possess the whole God more excellently who perceive Him in a more excellent Idea. But each possesses that virtue of God which he has loved in life.[18] Therefore Envy, as Plato says in the *Phaedrus*,[19] is absent from the divine chorus. For, since the most pleasing of all things is to achieve the beloved thing, anyone lives content and satisfied in possessing that which he loves. Certainly if two lovers become possessed of their hearts' desires, each will be content with the possession of his own beloved, and will not even have any worry whether the other possesses a more beautiful beloved. Therefore by the beneficence of Love it is brought about that among the various degrees of bliss each is content with his own portion without any envy.

It also happens that souls enjoy the same feasts eternally without any satiety. For, neither foods nor wines suffice to please the guests unless hunger and thirst allure them to eat, and the pleasure lasts only as long as the appetite. But who will deny that appetite is a kind of love? Therefore an eternal love by which the soul is always drawn toward God brings it about that the soul always enjoys God as a new spectacle. The same Goodness of God that also makes the lover blessed always kindles this love in the soul.

Therefore, to sum up briefly, we shall praise three benefits of Love: that by restoring us, formerly divided, to a whole, he leads us back to heaven; that he assigns each to his own seat, and makes all content in that distribution; that, all distaste removed, by a certain love of his own he perpetually kindles pleasure as if new in the soul and renders it blessed with enticing and sweet fruition.

Notes

1. On Ficino's friend Landino (1424–1504), the commentator on Dante and author of the *Disputationes Camaldulenses*, see Kristeller, *Suppl.*, 2 : 327–28. A short marginal

note on Landino in Ficino's hand appears in the Oxford manuscript of the *De amore*, fol. 21ʳ; printed by Marcel, p. 167, n.1.

2. Ficino is not here talking about the *emotions*; *passiones* may best be rendered as "experiences" (i.e., what happened to the nature of Man).

3. Hermes Trismegistus *Asclepius* 1.1.

4. St. Augustine *De trinitate* 15.9.

5. That is, the only part of the fable of Aristophanes which Plato intended for us to interpret allegorically is the following.

6. This is not, as it appears to be, a quotation but an abstract of Plato *Symposium* 189e–193b.

7. Ficino's allegorization of the fable is based on Aquinas's distinction between innate and infused virtues (*ST*. 1–2. Q.63), developed in IV.4, 5 and VI.12, 13, below. In his own translation, Ficino calls them "natural" and "supernatural." It is noteworthy that Ficino does not use an alternative Orphic allegorization which he probably knew about in Damascius *De principiis* 123. See Ruelle, ed. (Paris, 1889), 1 : 317–19. Although this passage purports to give a phrase-by-phrase commentary on the *Symposium*, the phrases are those of Ficino's paraphrase, not of Plato's text.

8. This chapter is probably based on Proclus *Elements of Theology* 80 and 184–88.

9. This section is based on Plato *Symposium* 207d–208b, part of the discourse of Diotima in the speech of Socrates.

10. For Marcel's *Quid* read *Quis*.

11. Plato *Phaedrus* 248c. The two "lights" described in this chapter are reason (the human, "natural" light) and intuition (the Divine, infused light), but Ficino deliberately keeps the distinction metaphorical and mixes the metaphor of the two lights (from *Republic* 6.508e–509b) with that of the two wings of the soul in the *Phaedrus*, as well as with the Thomist distinction (*ST*. 1–2. Q.62–63) between innate and infused virtues.

12. Plato *Republic* 10.621.

13. As the Italian translation ("supernatural light") shows, Ficino means by "divine splendor" merely the infused light of the soul, as opposed to its natural light.

14. Plato *Letter* 2.312e. See II.4, above.

15. In the following section Ficino combines several different ideas:

   (a) The four classical virtues, from Plato, Aristotle, and Cicero. See especially *Symposium* 196c–d.

   (b) The special status of Prudence, as discussed by Aquinas in *ST*. 1–2. Q.57.4–5, 58.5, and 61.2.

   (c) The distinction between human virtues and their divine counterparts in Aquinas *ST*. 1–2. Q.61, 62 and in Plotinus *Enneads* 1.6.

   (d) The distinction between habitual and infused virtues in Aquinas *ST*. 1–2. Q.63.

   (e) The triplet sun, moon, and earth as male, mixed, and female from the fable of Aristophanes (*Symposium* 190b).

16. This sentence is derived from Cicero's *De natura deorum* 1.2. Diagoras of Melos was a contemporary of Socrates; his atheism is satirized in *The Clouds* and *The Frogs* of Aristophanes. Protagoras of Abdera (c. 485–410 B.C.) was a Sophist; he appears in

Plato's dialogue the *Protagoras*. Epicurus (342–270 B.C.) was a materialist. The Cyrenaics were the followers of Aristippus of Cyrene (c 435–356 B.C.), a hedonist. Varro (116–27 B.C.) was a friend of Cicero. Manilius (1st century A.D.) was an astronomer and astrologer. This paragraph repeats ideas found in Ficino's two early tracts on God (1453? and 1458). See Kristeller, *Studies*, pp. 64–67 and *Suppl.*, 2 : 128–41.

17.   The first part of this chapter is based on *Phaedrus* 247d–e.

18.   The clarification "in life" is supplied from the Italian translation.

19.   Plato *Phaedrus* 247a; also *Timaeus* 29e.

Speech V

Chapter 1

Love is most blessed because
he is beautiful and good

Carlo marsuppini, a sweet pupil of the Muses, following the poet Landino, approaches the speech of Agathon thus. Our Agathon thinks that Love is the most blessed god because he is the most beautiful and the best.[1] What things are required for this, that he be the most beautiful, and likewise what things are required that he be the best, Agathon carefully enumerates. In these enumerations he describes Love himself. Finally, after he has told what Love is, he lists the benefits given by him to the human race. And this is the sum of his disputation. It is important for us first to investigate for what reason Agathon said, in order to show him blessed, that he is very beautiful and good, or what difference there is between goodness and beauty.

In the *Philebus*[2] Plato says that the blessed is that which lacks nothing. And that is that which is perfect in every part. But there is a certain internal perfection and an external one. The internal we call goodness, the external, beauty. Therefore that which is completely good and beautiful we call blessed, since it is "perfect in every part." This distinction we certainly observe in all things. Certainly in precious stones, as the natural philosophers say, a certain very temperate internal combination of the four elements produces an external sparkle. Moreover, an innate fecundity in the roots and stems clothes herbs and plants with the most attractive variety of flowers and foliage. And in animals a healthy complexion of humors produces a pleasing appearance of lines and colors. Likewise the virtue of the soul seems to display a certain very virtuous beauty in words, gestures, and deeds. The heavens also their sublime substance bathes in a very brilliant light.

In all these things the internal perfection produces the external. The former we can call goodness, the latter, beauty. For this reason, we say that beauty is a certain blossom of goodness, by the charms of which blossom, as by a kind of bait, the hidden internal goodness attracts beholders. But since the cognition of our intellect takes its origin from the senses,[3] we would never be aware of and never desire the goodness itself hidden in the heart of things if we were not attracted to it by the visible signs of external beauty. In which fact is apparent the truly wonderful usefulness of this beauty and of its companion love.

Through these things I think it has been sufficiently shown that there is as much difference between goodness and beauty as there is between a seed and a flower, and that just as the blossoms of plants, having originated in seeds, also produce seeds themselves, so this beauty, the blossom of goodness, as it originates from goodness, so it also leads lovers to goodness. This, indeed, is what that hero of ours has fully demonstrated above.[4]

Chapter 2

How love is pictured, and with what parts of the
soul beauty is recognized and love is generated

After this, Agathon enumerates at greater length how many things are required for the beautiful appearance of this god. *Love,* he says, *is young, tender, agile, well-proportioned, and glowing.*[5] But for our part we must ask first what these qualities contribute to beauty, and second, how they should be interpreted when they are applied to this god.

Men possess both reason and sensation.[6] Reason by itself grasps the incorporeal Reasons of all things. Sensation, through the five instruments of its body, perceives the images and qualities of bodies: colors through the eyes; through the ears sounds; odors through the nose, through the tongue taste, and through the nerves the simple qualities of the elements, such as heat, cold, and the rest. Therefore, as far as the question before us is concerned, six powers of the soul are counted as pertaining to cognition: reason, sight, hearing, smell, taste, and touch. Reason is assigned to supreme divinity, sight to fire, to air hearing, to the odor of vapors smell, to water taste, touch to earth. For reason investigates heavenly things, and does not have a seat of its own in any part of the body, just as divinity also does not have a particular seat in any part of the world. Sight is located in the highest part of the body, just as fire is located in the highest region of the world, and by its nature perceives light, which is characteristic of fire. Hearing, following sight in the same way that pure air follows fire, takes in sounds, which both originate in broken air, and through the interval of the air glide into the ears. Smell is assigned to the moist air, and to vapors composed of air and water for this reason, because, being placed between the ears and the tongue, as though between air and water, it easily apprehends and greatly esteems those vapors which result from the mixture of air and water. Such are the odors of herbs, flowers, and the fruits which are sweetest to the nose. Who would hesitate to compare taste to the liquids of water, since taste succeeds smell, as water succeeds thicker air, and, bathed in the continuous liquid of the saliva, is pleased most vehemently by drink and moist flavors? Likewise, who would hesitate to assign touch to earth, since it comes into being through all the parts of the earthly body, is completed in the nerves, which are very earthly, and easily touches things which have solidity and weight, qualities which earth gives to bodies?

Hence it also happens that touch, taste, and smell perceive only things which are very near them, and suffer greatly in their perceiving, although the sense of smell seems to detect things more remote than do touch and taste. Hearing, on the other hand, perceives things at a greater distance and is not hurt so much. Sight looks out still further and does instantaneously what the ears do in time. For lightning is seen before thunder is heard. Reason perceives the most remote things. For it perceives not only those things which are in the world and the present, as sensation does, but also those which are above the heaven, and those which have been or will be.

From these things it can be apparent to anyone that of those six powers of the soul, three pertain more to the body and matter (touch, taste, and smell) whereas the other three (reason, sight, and hearing) pertain to the spirit. For this reason those three which incline more toward the body agree with the body more than with the soul. And those things which are perceived by those senses, since they move the body, which is congruous with themselves, scarcely reach as far as the soul, and they please the soul very little because they are very little like it. But the three higher powers, which are very far removed from matter, agree with the soul much more, and they perceive those things which move the body very little, but the soul a great deal. Certainly odors, flavors, heat, and the like either harm the body a great deal, or help it, but they present little either to the admiration or to the censure of the soul, and are only moderately desired by it. On the other hand, the reason of incorporeal truth, colors, shapes, and sounds move the body either not at all or with difficulty and very little. But they greatly sharpen the edge of the soul for digging, and they attract its desire to themselves.

The food of the soul is truth. The eyes contribute greatly to finding it and the ears to learning it. Therefore, those things which pertain to reason, sight, and hearing the soul desires for its own sake, as its proper food. But those things which move the other three senses are more necessary to the body, either for nourishing, or comforting, or procreating. Thus the soul seeks those things, not for its own sake, but for the sake of another, namely the body. But we are said to *love* those things which we desire for our own sakes but not those which we desire for the sake of something else. Therefore we rightly say that love pertains only to knowledge, shapes, and sounds. And therefore only that grace which is found in these three, virtue of the soul, shape, and sound, because it greatly *provokes* the soul, is called *kallos*, that is a provocation, from *kaleo*, which means I *provoke*.[7] But *kallos* in Greek means *pulchritudo* in Latin.[8]

Pleasing to us indeed is a true and excellent habit of soul; pleasing the shape of a beautiful body; pleasing a harmony of sounds. And since the soul values these three, as being related to itself and in some measure incorporeal, very much more highly than it does the other three,[9] it is fitting that it should seek them more eagerly, embrace them more ardently, and admire them more greatly. And this grace itself, whether of virtue, shape, or sound, which calls the soul to it and seizes it, through reason or sight or hearing, is most rightly called beauty. And these are those three Graces, about whom Orpheus thus: Aglaia, Thalia, and rich Euphrosyne—that is, Splendor, Viridity, and Abundant Joy.[10] That

grace and beauty of the soul which consists in brightness of truth and
virtue he calls *Splendor*. Pleasantness of shape and color he calls *Viridity*,
for this flourishes most in the greenness of youth. Finally, that pure,
powerful, and perpetual pleasure which we experience in musical
melody he calls *Joy*.

Chapter 3

Beauty is something incorporeal

Since these things are so, it is necessary for beauty to be something common to virtue, shape, and sounds.[11] For we certainly would not call any
of these three "beautiful" in the same way, unless a single definition of
beauty were present in all three. Hence it happens that the Reason itself
of beauty cannot be a body, since, if beauty were corporeal, it would not
be applicable to the virtues of the soul, which are incorporeal. And
beauty is so far from being a body that not only the beauty which is in
the virtues of the soul cannot be corporeal, but also that which is in
bodies and sounds. For although we call certain bodies beautiful, they
are nevertheless not beautiful by virtue of their matter, in itself. For one
and the same body of a man may be handsome today, but tomorrow,
through some disfiguring misfortune, ugly, as if it were one thing to be a
body and another to be handsome. Nor are bodies beautiful by virtue of
their quantity in itself. Since some tall bodies and some short ones seem
beautiful, and often the large seem ugly and the small attractive, and
vice versa, the small ugly, and the large very handsome. It also sometimes happens that there is a similar beauty in some large bodies and
some small ones. Therefore, if beauty is changed by some misfortune,
even though very often the quantity remains the same, and if, conversely, beauty remains the same, even though the quantity is changed in
some way, and if beauty seems the same in both large and small things,
certainly these two, beauty and quantity, must be completely different.

But even if the beauty of some body were in some measure corporeal,
in the sheer density of its body, it would nevertheless not please the beholder by virtue of its being corporeal. For the beauty of any person
pleases the soul not insofar as it lies in external matter, but insofar as an
image of it is comprehended or grasped by the soul through the sight.
That image cannot be a body, either in the sight or in the soul, since

both of these are incorporeal. For in what way could the small pupil of
the eye take in the whole heaven, so to speak, if it received it in a corporeal way? In no way, obviously. But the spirit receives in a point the entire breadth of a body, in a spiritual way and in an incorporeal image.
The soul likes only that beauty which it has taken in. Though this beauty may be an image of an external body, it is nonetheless incorporeal in
the soul. Therefore it is an incorporeal beauty which pleases the soul.
What pleases is that which is attractive to someone. What is attractive,
this finally is beautiful. Whence it happens that love refers to something
incorporeal, and beauty itself is a certain spiritual image of a thing
rather than a corporeal attractiveness.

There are some who think that beauty consists in a certain arrangement of all the parts, or, to use their own terms, in symmetry and proportion,[12] together with a certain agreeableness of colors. The opinion
of these people, however, we do not accept, because since such an arrangement of parts exists only in composite things, no simple things
would be beautiful. Now pure colors, lights, a single voice, the splendor
of gold, the gleam of silver, knowledge, the soul, all of which are simple,
we call beautiful, and they please us as wonderfully as if they were truly
"beautiful."

In addition to this is the fact that that "proportion" includes all of the
parts of a composite body, and does not exist in individual parts, but in
all of them. And so, the individual parts in themselves will not be beautiful. But the "proportion" of the whole construction arises out of all the
parts. Whence something very absurd follows, that things which are not
beautiful of their own nature give birth to beauty.

It also repeatedly happens that even though the proportion and size of
the parts remain the same, the body does not please as much as before.
Certainly the shape of your body is the same today as it was last year,
but its grace is not the same. Nothing grows old more slowly than
shape. Nothing grows old more quickly than grace. From this it is
clearly established that beauty and shape are not the same thing. We
also often see a more correct arrangement of the parts and size of the
members in a certain one than in another. Yet the other, for we know
not what reason, being judged more beautiful by us, is loved more
dearly. By this we seem to be warned sufficiently that we should consider beauty to be something other than an arrangement of parts.

The same reason warns us not to suppose that beauty is agreeableness of colors. For often the color is brighter in an old person, but the grace is greater in a young person. And in equals[13] it sometimes happens that the one who surpasses the other in color is nevertheless surpassed by the other in grace and beauty.

Nor would anyone dare assert that beauty is a certain combination of shape and colors. For in that case neither knowledge nor sounds (which lack both shape and color), nor colors and lights (which have no definite shape) would be judged worthy of love.

Moreover the desire of anyone is quenched after he has that which he desired. Certainly hunger and thirst are satisfied by food and drink. Love is not satisfied by any seeing or embracing of a body. Therefore love does not seek any nature of a body; it certainly does seek beauty. Whence it happens that it cannot be anything corporeal.

From all these arguments the conclusion is that for those who are aroused by love and thirst for beauty it is necessary, if they wish to quench their burning thirst by drinking this liquid, to seek the very sweet humor of this beauty by which their thirst is kindled elsewhere than in the river of matter or in the streams of quantity, shape, or any colors. Where, finally, will you turn, O wretched lovers? Who kindled the burning flames of your heart? Who will extinguish so great a fire? This is the work, this the labor.[14] I shall tell you immediately, but listen.

Chapter 4

Beauty is the splendor of the divine countenance

The divine power, supreme over all things, as soon as the Angels and the Souls[15] are born from Him, gently infuses into them, as His offspring, that ray of His, in which there is a fecund power of creating all things. This imprints the arrangement and order of the whole world much more exactly in these,[16] because they are nearer to Him, than in the matter of the World.[17] For this reason this whole picture of the world which we see shines more clearly in the Angels and the Souls. For in them there is a picture of each sphere, the sun, moon, the other stars, the elements, stones, plants, and each of the animals. In the Angels, these pictures are called by the Platonists Archetypes or Ideas; in the Souls they are called Reasons or Concepts; in the Matter of the World they are called Forms or Images. They are certainly bright in the World, brighter in the Soul, and brightest in the Angelic Mind. Therefore the single face of God shines successively in three mirrors, placed in order: the Angel, the Soul, and the Body of the World. In the former, as nearer to God, the image shines most brightly. In the second, more remote, more dimly. In the latter, most remote, if you compare it to the others, most dimly. Then the holy Angelic Mind, hampered by no duty to a body, turns back to itself. There it sees that face of God imprinted in its own breast. It immediately admires what it has seen. It cleaves passionately to it forever. The grace of that divine face we call beauty. The Angel's passion, clinging inwardly to the face of God, we call Love.

O that the same thing might happen to us! But our soul, created in a condition such that it is surrounded by an earthly body, inclines to the function of procreating. Weighed down by this inclination, it neglects the treasure hidden in its own heart.[18] Then wrapped in its earthly body, the soul serves the use of the body for a very long time. To this work it always accommodates sensation, and also reason more often than it should. Hence it happens that it does not notice the glow of the divine countenance shining eternally within itself until, when the body is mature, and the reason has been awakened, it considers by contemplation the face of God shining in the machine of the world, and manifest to the eyes. Through this contemplation it is led to behold the face of God which shines within itself. But since the face of a parent is pleasing to the children, it is necessary for the face of God the Father to be most pleasing to souls. The splendor and grace of this face—to repeat the same thing very often—whether in the Angel or in the Soul, or in the Matter of the World, is to be called universal beauty. And the impulse toward that is to be called universal love.

That this beauty is everywhere incorporeal we do not doubt. For no one doubts that it is not a body in the Angel and in the Soul. That it is also incorporeal in bodies we both have shown above and at present understand chiefly from this, that the eye sees nothing else except the light of the sun, for the shapes and colors of bodies are never seen unless they[19] are illuminated with light.[20] They themselves do not come to the eyes with their matter. Nevertheless it seems to be necessary that they be in the eyes in order to be seen by the eyes. And so the one light of the sun, imprinted with the colors and shapes of all the bodies illuminated by it, presents itself to the eyes. The eyes, with the help of a certain ray of their own, perceive the light thus imprinted: they see both the perceived light itself and all the things which are imprinted in it. Therefore this whole order of the world which is seen is perceived, not in the manner in which it exists in the matter of bodies, but in which it exists in the light infused into the eyes. Since in this light it is separated from matter, it is necessarily devoid of body.

Which is also clearly apparent from this, that the light itself cannot be a body, since it fills the whole world instantaneously from east to west, penetrates the body of air and water everywhere without obstruction, and is nowhere soiled when it is mixed with filthy things. But these things do not in any way correspond with the nature of bodies. For the body does not move instantaneously, but in time. Nor can one body penetrate another without damage to itself or the other or the destruction of both. And two bodies which are mixed together infect each other with a mutual contagion. Which we see in the mixing of water and wine, fire and earth. Therefore, since the light of the sun is incorporeal, whatever it receives it receives in the manner of its own nature. Therefore it receives the colors and shapes of bodies in a spiritual way. And in this same way it is itself seen when it is received by the eyes. Whence it happens that all this beauty of the World, which is the third face of God, presents itself as incorporeal to the eyes through the incorporeal light of the sun.

Chapter 5

How love is born, and hate,
or that beauty is incorporeal

From all these things[21] it follows that every grace of the divine countenance, which is called universal beauty, is incorporeal, not only in the Angel and in the Soul, but also in the sight of the eyes. Stricken with admiration, we not only love this countenance as a whole, but also its parts. This is the origin of particular love for particular beauty. Thus we are attracted to a certain man as a part of the world order, especially when the spark of the divine beauty shines brightly in him. This affection arises from two causes. Not only because the image of the paternal countenance pleases us, but also because the appearance and figure of a well-constructed man correspond most closely with that Reason of Mankind which our soul received from the author of all things and still retains. Whence, if the image of the external man received through the senses and passing into the soul disagrees with the figure of Man which the soul possesses, it instantaneously displeases and is regarded with hate as being ugly. If it agrees, it immediately pleases, and is loved as being beautiful. Whence it happens that some people whom we meet immediately please or displease us, and we do not know the cause of this feeling; certainly, since the soul, preoccupied with its service to the body, never pays any attention to those Forms within it. But by a certain natural and hidden[22] incongruity or congruity, it happens that the external form of a thing, striking with its image the Form of the same thing depicted in the soul, either disagrees or agrees with it, and moved by this hidden opposition or attraction, the soul either hates or loves the thing itself.

The pattern for the creating of Man which that divine power implanted in the Angel and in the Soul was certainly complete. But in the Matter of the World, which is very far removed from that Artificer, the constitution of Man degenerates from that perfect pattern of him: in better disposed matter it turns out more like the pattern; in other matter, more unlike. That which turns out more like corresponds to and squares with the Soul's Reason as it does with God's Power and the Angel's Idea. The soul approves this correspondence. Certainly in this correspondence itself beauty consists; and in this approval, the feeling of love consists. But since Idea and Reason are alien to the matter of the body, the constitution of Man is judged to be like them, not on the basis of matter or quantity, but rather on the basis of something incorporeal. To the degree that it is like them, it corresponds. To the degree that it corresponds, it is beautiful. Therefore body and beauty are different.

If anyone asked in what way the form of the body can be like the Form and Reason of the Soul and Mind, let him consider, I ask, the building of the architect.[23] In the beginning the architect develops a Reason or Idea, as it were, of the building in his soul. Then he builds, as nearly as possible, the kind of house he has conceived. Who will deny that the house is a body and that it is very much like the architect's incorporeal Idea, in the likeness of which it was built? Furthermore, it must be judged as being like the architect[24] more on account of a certain incorporeal design than on account of its matter. Therefore go ahead; subtract its matter if you can (and you can subtract it mentally), but leave the design. Nothing of body, nothing of matter will remain to you.

On the contrary, the design which came from the artist and the design which remains in the artist will be completely identical. You may do the same in any body of a man. You will find that its form, corresponding to the Reason of the Soul, is simple and devoid of matter.

Chapter 6

How many things are required that
a thing be beautiful and that
beauty is a spiritual gift

Finally, what is the beauty of the body?[25] Act, vitality, and a certain grace shining in itself through the influence of its own Idea. This splendor does not descend before the matter has been appropriately prepared. But the preparation of the living body consists of these three things: Arrangement, Proportion, and Aspect.[26] Arrangement means the distances between the parts, Proportion means quantity, and Aspect means shape and color. For in the first place it is necessary that all the parts of the body have their natural position: that the ears be in their place, and the eyes and nose, etc., and that the eyes be at equal distances near the nose, and likewise both ears be equally distant from the eyes. Nor does this equality of distances pertaining to Arrangement suffice unless there is added a Proportion of the parts, which gives to every part a moderate size, preserving the proper proportion of the whole body,[27] so that three noses placed end to end will fill the length of one face, the semi-circles of both ears joined together will make the circle of the open mouth, and the joining of the eyebrows will also amount to the same; the length of the nose will match the length of the lip, and likewise of the ear. The twin circles of the eyes will equal the one opening of the mouth; eight heads will make the length of the body; this same length the spread of the arms to the side and likewise of the legs and feet will also measure.

In addition, we believe that Aspect is necessary, in order that artful drawings of lines and wrinkles, and the splendor of colors, may enhance the Arrangement and Proportion of the parts.

And these three, although they exist in matter, cannot be any part of the body. The Arrangement of the parts is certainly not a part, for the Arrangement is present in all the parts, and no part is found in all the parts. There is in addition the fact that Arrangement is nothing other than an appropriate interval between the parts. But what do we mean by "interval" if not the distance between the parts? Finally, distance is either nothing, and an utterly empty vacuum, or a certain drawing of lines. But who would call lines (which lack breadth and depth, which are necessary to the body) bodies? Likewise, Proportion is not quantity but a boundary of quantity. But boundaries are surfaces and lines and points, which, since they lack the thickness of depth, are not considered bodies. Aspect also we locate not in matter but in the pleasing harmony of lights, shadows, and lines. From all these things it is clear that beauty is so alien to the mass of body that it never imparts itself to matter itself unless the matter has been prepared with the three incorporeal preparations which we have mentioned.

The basis of these is a temperate complexion of the four elements, so that our body may be much like heaven, the substance of which is temperate, and will not rebel, through some excess of humors, against the soul's shaping of it. For in this way both the heavenly splendor will easily shine in a body which is like heaven, and that perfect Form of Man which the Soul possesses will turn out more clearly[28] in matter which is pacified and obedient. Moreover, sounds are arranged to receive their beauty in almost the same way. For the Arrangement of those is an ascent from a low note to the octave, and thence a descent. Proportion is a proper progression through third, fourth, fifth, and sixth intervals, and also full tones and half-tones. Aspect is the sonorous intensity of a clear note.

At any rate by means of these three,[29] as if by elements of some kind, bodies which are composed of many parts, such as plants and animals, and a combination of several sounds, are prepared to receive beauty. But simpler bodies, such as the four elements, stones and metals, and also single sounds are sufficiently prepared for it by a certain inner temper, richness, and clarity of their own nature. The soul is prepared for it by its own nature, especially in this, that it is both a spirit and a mirror, as it were, next to God, a mirror in which, as we have said above, the image of the divine countenance is reflected. Therefore just as absolutely nothing need be added to gold in order for it to look beautiful, but smutches of earth, if any cling to it, must be removed, so the soul needs no additions in order that it appear beautiful, but its worry and anxious solicitude about the body must be put aside; its perturbation of desire and fear must be dispelled; then the natural beauty of the soul will shine out immediately.[30]

Finally, lest my speech digress too far, let us conclude briefly from what has been said above that beauty is a certain lively and spiritual grace infused by the shining ray of God, first in the Angel, and thence in the souls of men, the shapes of bodies, and sounds; a grace which through reason, sight, and hearing moves and delights our souls; in delighting, carries them away, and in carrying them away, inflames them with burning love.

Chapter 7

On the painting of love

The poet Agathon, in the manner of the ancient poets, clothes this god in human form, and paints him as attractive, like men: *Young, tender, flexible or agile, well-proportioned, and glowing.*[31] Why these? Certainly these are preparations for a beautiful nature rather than beauty itself. For, of these five parts, the first three signify the temperate complexion of the body, which is the first foundation; the other two represent Arrangement, Proportion, and Aspect.

Natural philosophers have shown that the sign of a temperate constitution is soft and firm smoothness of the tender flesh.[32] Where heat exceeds too much, the body is dry and hairy; where cold exceeds, the skin is stiff; where dryness, hard and rough; where moisture, loose, flabby, uneven, drawn. Therefore a smooth and firm tenderness of the body shows that the body's constitution in the four humors is well-balanced. This is why Agathon called Love *soft, delicate,* and *tender.*

Why *young*? Because this temperateness is possessed through the kindness not only of nature, but also of age.[33] For with the passage of time, as the finer parts of the humors are dissipated, only the coarser parts remain: when the fire and air have been exhaled, an excess of water and earth prevails.

But why *agile and flexible*? So that you may understand that love is fit and ready for all motions, lest you perhaps suppose that when he said *soft*, he meant the effeminate, weak, and unfit softness of water. For that is contrary to a balanced complexion.

After these Agathon added *well-proportioned*, that is, properly formed in the Arrangement and Proportion of parts. He also added *glowing*, that is, shining in the attractive Aspect of colors. Having explained these preparations, Agathon did not say what the rest was. For it is up to us to understand that after these preparations occurs the advent of grace.[34]

These five parts[35] seem to be meant in the way we have said, with respect to the figure of Man, but in a different way with respect to the potency of love, for they refer to its force and quality. Love is said to be *young* for the reason that the young are usually caught by love, and those who are caught in his traps desire the youthful age. *Soft* because gentle natures are more easily caught. And those who are caught, even though formerly wild, are rendered tame. *Agile and flexible* because it flows in secretly, and flows out in the same way. *Well-proportioned* and *well-shaped* because it desires shapely and well-ordered things and avoids the opposite. *Glowing* because it influences the character of Man at the blooming and glowing age, and it desires blooming things. Since Agathon explains these things at length, let it suffice to have touched on them briefly.

Chapter 8

On the virtue of love[36]

Also the things which Agathon says about the four virtues,[37] in order to show the goodness of Love, are to be interpreted in this way. Love is affirmed as *just* for this reason, that where love is pure and true, there is an interchange of good will which admits no insult or injury. So great is the power of this charity that it alone is able to preserve the human race in tranquil peace, which neither prudence nor fortitude, nor the power of arms, of laws, or of eloquence, without good will, can bring about.

Moreover, he calls it *temperate* because it conquers the base desires. For, since love seeks beauty, which consists in a certain order and temperance, it scorns cheap and intemperate appetites; it always shrinks from sinful actions. This you heard enough about in the beginning from the hero. And where the desire for this[38] rules, all other desires are disdained.

He added *courageous*. For what is more courageous than boldness? And who fights more boldly than the lover for his beloved? *Than the*

other gods,[39] that is, Mars surpasses the other planets in courage, because
he makes men braver. *Venus dominates him.* For when Mars is located in
the corners of the heaven, in either the second or the eighth house of a
nativity, he threatens evils to the person being born, but Venus often
shackles, so to speak, the malignancy of Mars, by coming into conjunction or opposition with him, or by receiving him or by watching him
from the trine or sextile aspect. Again, when Mars dominates at the
birth of a man, he bestows greatness of soul and irascibility. If Venus
comes near, she does not impede that virtue of magnanimity given by
Mars, but she does restrain the vice of irascibility. Here she seems to
make Mars more gentle and thus to *dominate* him. *But Mars never dominates Venus.* Because if she was the ruler of one's life,[40] she grants the
passion of love. If Mars comes near, he renders the impulse of Venus
more ardent by his own heat, so that if at someone's birth Mars was in a
house of Venus, such as Libra or Taurus, on account of the presence of
Mars, he who was born then will be burned by the most passionate
loves. *Mars also follows Venus; Venus does not follow Mars,* since boldness
is a follower of love, not love of boldness. For men are not ensnared by
love from the fact that they are brave, but very often, from the fact that
they are wounded by love, they become very bold, and fearlessly undergo any dangers, for the sake of the beloved. Finally, the most obvious
proof of love's courage, surpassing all things, is the fact that all things
obey love, but he himself obeys no one. Certainly the heavenly beings
love, and animals and all bodies; likewise the brave and the wise, rich
men and the greatest kings bow their necks to the rule of love. But love
is subject to none of these. For the bribes of the rich do not buy love,
nor can the threats and violences of the powerful force us to love or
cease loving. For love is free, and arises of its own accord in free will,
which not even God constrains, who decreed from the beginning that it
would be free. Whence it happens that love, which gives power to all
things, escapes the violence of all things. So great is the freedom of this
that although the other passions or skills and functions of the soul usually seek some reward which is different from themselves, love is content
with itself as its own reward, as if there were no other reward except love
which is worthy of love. For he who loves, loves love primarily. For he
wishes chiefly from his beloved that he love his lover in return.

   He is also most wise. In what sense love is the creator and preserver of
all things and the master and lord of all of the arts is, I think, sufficiently

stated in the speech of Erixymachus[41] and it is in these things that the wisdom of love is shown.

From all these things, it is concluded that Love is most blessed for the reason that he is the most beautiful and the best. That he is the most beautiful is certain from the fact that he takes delight in the most beautiful things, as being like himself. He is also the best, on account of the fact that he makes lovers best, and he who makes others best, must necessarily be the best.

Chapter 9

On the gifts of love

What Love is, has appeared from that discussion of ours.[42] What it is, from the above words of Agathon. What gifts[43] it bestows is easily deduced from what has been said. For one love is simple, another is reciprocal. The simple love renders whomever it seizes prudent in foresight, keen in disputation, eloquent in expression, magnanimous for things to be done, witty for jests, ready for games, and very brave for serious things.

Reciprocal love brings security by dispelling dangers, peace by removing dissension, and happiness by avoiding misery. For where there is reciprocal charity, there are no plots. There all things are common. There lawsuits, robberies, murders, and battles cease. That this tranquility is bestowed by reciprocal love not only upon animals, but also upon the heavens and elements, Agathon mentions here, and it was also shown at greater length above, in the speech of Erixymachus.[44] At the end of this speech[45] Love is said to soothe with his song the minds of gods and men, which anyone will clearly understand who remembers that it was shown above that love is in all things and is extended to all things.

Chapter 10

Love is both older and younger than the other gods

But before I make an end, gentlemen, I shall answer as best I can three questions which arise in Agathon's disputation.[46] For first, it is asked why Phaedrus and that Love was older than Saturn and Jupiter, whereas Agathon said that he was younger. Second, what Plato means by "The Reign of Necessity" and "The Rule of Love." Third, which gods invented which arts during the reign of love.

God, the father of all things, created those Minds, his ministers, which move Saturn, Jupiter, and the other planets, through a certain love of propagating His own seed, and through the kindness of providence. Again the Minds, from the moment they are born, recognizing their parent, love Him. That love by which the celestial beings are created we call "older" than they; but that with which the creatures love their creator we call "younger." Moreover, the Angelic Mind did not receive from its Father the Ideas of the planet Saturn and the others until the Mind was turned toward His countenance by innate love. Again, after it received them,[47] it loved the gift of its parent more strongly. Thus therefore the love of that Angel for God is partly older than the Ideas, which are called *gods*,[48] and partly also younger. Therefore Love is the beginning and end, the first and the last of the gods.

Chapter 11

Love reigns before necessity

But, to answer the second question, it must be said to reign before Necessity[49] for the reason that the divine love[50] gave to all things born from it their origin. In this[51] no violence of Necessity is involved. For, since it has nothing above itself, it does whatever it pleases, not constrained but freely. The Mind, on the other hand, which follows that, since that plants it, necessarily comes up. The former therefore produces out of love; the latter proceeds out of necessity. There begins the domination of Love; here, that of Necessity. The latter,[52] although it is born from the supreme goodness of God and is for this reason good, nevertheless, because it proceeds outside God, necessarily degenerates from the infinite perfection of its parent. For the effect never receives the whole goodness of its cause. Certainly in this necessary proceeding but also degenerating[53] of the effect consists the reign of necessity. But the Mind, from the moment it is born, as we have said, loves its author. Here the reign of Love resurges again. For by love it[54] is raised toward God and by love God illuminates it after it turns toward Him. But here again the power of necessity slips in. Since that light descending from

God is certainly not received by the mind (in its own nature dark) with as much brightness as is given by God. For it is forced to receive according to the capacity of its own nature. Therefore, through the violence of the receiving nature the light becomes dimmer. To this Necessity the principate of Love succeeds again. For that, kindled by this first splendor of God, turns back more ardently to Him, and, aroused by this mere spark, as it were, of light, desires the whole plenitude of light. Hence also God, by the kindness of his providence, in addition to that first natural light, also bestows a divine light. And thus the power of Love and the power of Necessity alternately succeed each other. This succession certainly takes place in divine things according to the hierarchy of being;[55] in other things according to intervals of time. In such a way, however, that Love is the first and last of all.

About the Soul also and the other things which are made by God, with respect to these two rules,[56] it must be judged in the same way. Therefore, if we are speaking absolutely, the rule of Love is older than that of Necessity, since the power of the former begins in God, and the power of the latter begins in created things. But if we are speaking about the things created by God, the reign of the tyrant Necessity precedes that of Love, since things themselves proceed by necessity, and in proceeding, degenerate before they turn toward their father with love.

Orpheus sings about these two rules in two hymns. The rule of Necessity in the *Hymn to Night*, thus: "Heavy Necessity holds sway over all things." And the reign of Love in the *Hymn to Venus*, thus: "You rule the three Fates and create all things that are in the heavens, on the earth, and in the sea."[57] Orpheus divinely set forth two reigns, and compared them with each other, and he put Love before Necessity when he said that the former rules the three Fates, in whom Necessity consists.

Chapter 12

In what way, in the reign of Necessity,
Saturn castrated Uranus, but
Jupiter bound Saturn

But in what way during the reign of Necessity, the inferior gods are said here[58] by Agathon to castrate or bind their parents, we understand easily from what has been said above. For these[59] are not to be interpreted

that the Angelic Mind divides and dismembers within itself God Himself, but the gift[60] which is given to it by God. A little while ago[61] we
proved sufficiently that the gifts of God necessarily degenerate from
their highest perfection in the spirit which receives them. Whence it
happens that that fertility of nature, certainly whole in God, but in the
Angel diminished and in some measure mutilated, is justly said to have
been castrated. This is certainly said to happen during the reign of
Necessity because it happens necessarily, at the wish of neither the giver
nor the receiver, but by that necessity by which the effect cannot equal
its cause. For thus Saturn, that is, the Angel, seems to castrate Uranus,
that is, the supreme God. Also, Jupiter, that is, the World Soul, seems
to bind Saturn, that is, to confine to narrower limits, within itself
through the insufficiency of its own nature, the power which it has
received from the Angel. For the power of the former is greater than
that of the latter.[62] Therefore, the power which in the former, because of
its breadth, seems unshackled and unbound, in the latter, because of its
narrowness, seems bound and restricted. I omit what the astrologers
think, that the malice of the planet Saturn is usually checked when it is
in conjunction, reception, or opposition, or in trine or sextile aspect to
Jupiter.[63] But so much for these matters. Let us descend to the third
question.

Chapter 13

Which gods give which arts to men

Agathon thinks that the arts were given to the human race by the
gods[64] on account of love: ruling, by Jupiter; archery, prophecy, and
medicine, by Apollo; bronze work, by Vulcan; weaving, by Minerva;
and finally music, by the Muses. Twelve gods preside over the twelve
signs of the Zodiac: over Aries, Pallas; over Taurus, Venus; Apollo over
Gemini; over Cancer, Mercury; over Leo, Jupiter; over Virgo, Ceres;
over Libra, Vulcan; over Scorpio, Mars; Diana over Sagittarius; Vesta
over Capricorn; over Aquarius, Juno; and over Pisces, Neptune. By
these all the arts are handed down to our race. The signs confer their
powers for each of the arts upon the body, and the gods who preside
over them, upon the soul. So Jupiter, through Leo, renders man fit for
the governing of gods and men, that is, for managing excellently both
divine and human[65] affairs. Apollo, through Gemini, shows us proph-

ecy,[66] medicine, and the skill of the bow; Pallas, through Aries, the skill of weaving; Vulcan, through Libra, the bronze trade; and the others, the rest of the arts. But because they generously bestow their gifts upon us through the kindness of providence,[67] we say that they give them at the instigation of love.

Moreover, we think that from the swift and orderly revolution of the heavens originates musical harmony; that eight tones are produced by the motions of the eight spheres, and a ninth, a kind of harmony, is produced from all of them. And so we call the nine sounds of the heavens, from their musical harmony, the nine Muses. Our soul was endowed from the beginning with the Reason of this music, for the celestial harmony is rightly called innate in anything whose origin is celestial. Which it later imitates[68] on various instruments and in songs. And this gift likewise was given us through the love of divine providence. Therefore, distinguished friends, let us love this god because he is most beautiful; because he is the best, let us imitate him; because he is most blessed, let us worship him, so that by his mercy and bounty he may grant us possession of his own beauty, goodness, and bliss.

Notes

1. Plato *Symposium* 195a.
2. Plato *Philebus* 20d, 21. The distinction between goodness and beauty as internal and external is probably from Aquinas *ST.* 1-2. Q.27.1.
3. See VI.6.
4. See above, I.4.
5. Plato *Symposium* 195c.
6. In this section Ficino leaves Aquinas and turns to an argument which he found in Plotinus *Enneads* 1.6.1 (and also in Chalcidius's *Commentary on the Timaeus* 267). Ficino's argument begins by stating that there are six "powers of the soul": reason and the five senses. He then draws a parallel between the five senses and a different set of five: the four elements and the vapors. He then eliminates the three most corporeal senses on the ground that they service the body only. In this way he leaves only reason, sight, and hearing as eligible for perception of things spiritual. Cf. I.4 above.
7. Cf. Plato *Cratylus* 416c-d. I owe this reference to Professor Kristeller.
8. The Greek noun *kallos*, like the Latin noun *pulchritudo*, means "beauty."
9. That is, the pleasure of touch, taste, and smell.
10. Orpheus *Hymn* 60 (The Graces) 3 (Abel, p. 90). On the three Graces, see especially Edgar Wind, *Pagan Mysteries in the Renaissance*, 2d ed. (New York, 1968), chap. 2-3. Cf. Ficino, *Opera*, pp. 845-46.
11. This section, which is based on Plotinus *Enneads* 1.6, is expanded in Ficino's commentary on Plotinus's *Liber de Pulchritudine* (see *Opera*, pp. 1573-578). For the conflict

between Plotinus and Proclus on Beauty, see Ficino's translation of a passage from Proclus's *Commentary on I Alcibiades* (*Opera*, pp. 1908–909) and Oskar Walzel, "Von Plotin, Proklos und Ficinus," *DVLG* 19 (1941) : 407–29.

12. This definition was an Aristotelean commonplace; see *Poetics* 7.8 and *Metaphysics* 13.4, but similar definitions were also available in Vitruvius *Archit.* 3.1 and Alberti's *Della statua*. Ficino criticizes the definition here, but he comes close to using the definition himself in II.9.

13. That is, people of the same age.

14. Vergil *Aeneid* 6.129.

15. That is, the Angelic Mind and the World Soul.

16. That is, the ray imprints on the Angelic Mind and the World Soul.

17. That is, the World Body.

18. The idea that the Nature of God is to be learned by looking inward, not outward, is common in Augustine, but Ficino doubtless also knew passages on this subject in Proclus (*Commentary on I Alcibiades* [1–21] and in Plotinus [*Enneads*, 1.6 and 5.3.1–2]). Ficino is not much interested in the concept in the *De amore* (see VI.19 below), but he does become more interested in the idea later. See especially the Preface to the *Theologia platonica*.

19. In the Latin original, these pronouns are all neuter plural, referring to bodies (*corpora*). In the Italian translation, they are all masculine plural, referring to shapes and colors (*le figure e li colori*).

20. The importance of the sun as an external aid to the human soul in vision is here symbolic of the necessity of divine grace to the perception of beauty, the concept outlined in chap. 6 below. The discussion of the nature of vision itself was probably suggested by Plotinus *Enneads* 5.5.7. See also the section on that subject in Chalcidius *Commentary on the Timaeus* 236–48.

21. That is, from what has been said in V.2–4. In this chapter he paraphrases Plotinus *Enneads* 1.6.2–3 and 5.3.3.

22. The distinction which Ficino is trying to express here is the distinction between conscious and sub-conscious comparison of the visual image of an object with the pre-conceived idea of it. What he means by "hidden" we call "sub-conscious."

23. Ficino's example of the architect is from Plotinus *Enneads* 1.6.3. The analogy of the artist's conception is also present in Plato (*Republic* 10.596b–599e), but the example given there is that of the carpenter and a couch.

24. That is, like the architect's idea for the building.

25. This chapter is an effort to reconcile two Platonic theories of beauty: Proclus's view that beauty is an arrangement (see I.4 above) and Plotinus's view that it is a quality in which things participate (Plotinus 1.6.1). Ficino's solution, borrowed in part from Aquinas's conception of grace (*ST.* 1–2. Q.62) is to say that both Proclus and Plotinus are right: beauty is a quality (grace) conferred upon (received by) an object after it has been "arranged" in a certain way. A similar idea is expressed in Hermes *Asclepius* 1.3c; Plato *Republic* 6.508e–509b, and Plotinus *Enneads* 5.9.2. Ficino repeats the idea in V.13 below, where he cites the passage in the *Republic*. It should be noticed, however, that the saving qualification is added only at the beginning and end of the chapter. The body of the chapter is a detailed exposition of the old theory of beauty as arrangement and was

probably written earlier.

26. A possible source of the three terms *ordo*, *modus*, and *species* is St. Augustine's *De natura boni* 23.23 (in turn related to the Book of Wisdom 11.20). But see also St. Bonaventure's *De reductione artium ad theologiam*, cited by Richard McKeon in "Rhetoric in the Middle Ages," *Speculum* 17 (1942) : 24.

27. For the history of theories of proportion of this sort, see Erwin Panofsky, "Die Entwicklung der Proportionslehre als Abbild der Stilentwicklung," *Monatshefte für Kunstwissenschaft* 14 (1921) : 188–209; and William S. Story, *The Proportions of the Human Figure* (London, 1864).

28. The soul's shaping of the body is like stamping a mold on a piece of clay. The mold is the soul's innate *idea* of Man, and the clay is the unshaped matter of the body. The mold will produce a truer copy if the clay is soft and malleable.

29. That is, Arrangement, Proportion, and Aspect. The argument quietly shifts here, for these qualities have been described previously as components of beauty, whereas now they are to be described as merely pre-conditions for beauty, which is a quality infused from without.

30. Cf. Plotinus *Enneads* 1.6. I owe this reference to Professor Kristeller.

31. *Symposium* 195b–196b. As elsewhere, Ficino is here only abstracting the text, though he italicizes his phrases as though they were direct quotations. Ficino's term *nitidus*, "glowing," apparently refers to Plato's phrase *chroas de kallos*, "beauty of skin" or beauty of complexion, though in his translation of the passage (p. 325a of the Lyons, 1590 edition of the *Opera Platonis*), Ficino renders the phrase *Coloris decorem*, "beauty of color."

32. Throughout this paragraph Ficino speaks of *the flesh* and *the body*, but what he is actually talking about is only the condition of the skin.

33. That is, the previously discussed balance among the four humors is a function of age as well as of the individual constitution.

34. That is, as was said above, Arrangement, Proportion, and Aspect are merely preparations; Beauty is granted by grace after the preparations have been completed.

35. That is, Agathon's five adjectives.

36. The Latin *virtute* Ficino translates *virtù*; hence Marcel's translation, *puissance* "power." The chapter deals, however, with the relation of love to the four classical virtues, and the word *virtute* therefore must mean *virtue* or *virtues*.

37. Plato *Symposium* 196b–e. Again, Ficino abstracts rather than quotes.

38. That is, for beauty.

39. Ficino is commenting on a phrase in which Agathon says that love overcomes Mars, "who is mightier than all the rest" (Plato *Symposium* 196d). Ficino's Italian translation punctuates this passage differently.

40. That is, if she was the dominant planet at the nativity. This explanation is based on the Italian translation.

41. See above, III.3.

42. See above, II.7. The difference between *Quid amor sit* in this sentence and *Qualis sit* in the following sentence is that the former refers to love's genealogy and the latter to its character. The references to reciprocal love, murder, etc., in the next paragraph suggest that this section was originally part of II.8.

43. The concept of divine gifts recurs often in the *De amore*. It has two principal roots: Aquinas *ST*. 1-2. Q.68, and Proclus *Elements of Theology* 18 and 56-58.

44. See II.8 above. For the argument that love promotes morality see also I.4 above.

45. That is, of the present speech, Agathon's (Plato *Symposium* 197e).

46. The material for this chapter comes from Plotinus *Enneads* 5.8.13.

47. That is, after the Angelic Mind received the Ideas from God.

48. There is an extra point to this comment, lost in English; it is to call attention to the similarity in Italian between *Idee* (Ideas) and *Iddii* (gods). As the playful plurals (Angels and Souls) and blind pronouns also show, this chapter is written in the esoteric style.

49. The question of the precedence of Necessity and Love is from Orpheus's *Hymn to Night*, as Ficino acknowledges below (see p. 100); but cf. also Plato *Symposium* 197b. Ficino's exposition is probably based on Proclus *De providentia et fato* 5-9, but with a glance at Plotinus *Enneads* 5.4.1-2. Also relevant is one of the works which Ficino had translated in preparation for translating Plato, the *De fato* of Plutarch, the text of which was present in Cosimo's manuscript containing Alcinous: *Introduction to Platonism* and the Hermetic *Pimander*. The problem of the relation of Platonic emanationism to the Christian doctrine of Providence and free will was one of the principal issues debated by renaissance apologists for Platonism.

50. That is, God. In this and the next four sentences my translation keeps the esoteric style of the original, but the meaning would be clearer if I had translated all the pronouns "it" and "that" as He and Him, referring to God.

51. That is, in God's love.

52. That is, the Angelic Mind.

53. The fact that degeneration is an element in the creative process is stated by Proclus in *Elements of Theology* 75.

54. That is, the Angelic Mind.

55. The Latin text here reads *naturae origine*, but this is probably a scribal error for *naturae ordine*, since Ficino himself translates it "the order of nature." Elsewhere the Latin phrase is *ordo naturae* or *naturae ordine*. "The order of nature" is not a temporal sequence but the hierarchy of being, in which the higher always governs the lower creature. The phrase is explained in this way by Pico in his *Commento*. Ficino's main authorities on the hierarchy of being were Proclus's *Elements of Theology* and two imitators of Proclus, the author of the *Liber de causis* and the Pseudo-Dionysius. The standard modern authority on the subject is A. O. Lovejoy, *The Great Chain of Being* (Cambridge, Mass., 1948).

56. That is, of Love and Necessity.

57. Orpheus *Hymn* 3 (To Night) 11 (Abel, p. 60) and *Hymn* 55 (To Venus) 5 (Abel, p. 87). See also Plotinus *Enneads* 5.8-13. The last clause of this sentence, omitted by Marcel because it is not found in the Vatican manuscript, appears in one manuscript and in all of the printed editions after Basel, 1532: "quae in caelo sunt, et quae in terra, et quae in mari."

58. Plato *Symposium* 195c.

59. That is, the words of Agathon.

60. For Marcel's *minus* read *munus*.

61. V.11.

62. In this and the following sentence the Italian translation identifies "the former" as Saturn and "the latter" as Jupiter.

63. This sentence is present only in the Oxford manuscript (fol. 41^v) but in a hand which Bembo says is Ficino's.

64. Plato *Symposium* 197a–b. On the concept of the cosmic gifts, see VI.4.

65. Ficino translates this phrase "spiritual and temporal."

66. In the Italian translation Ficino omits prophecy. For possible reasons in contemporary circumstances, see Donald Weinstein, *Savonarola and Florence* (Princeton, 1970).

67. Ficino translates, "through the kindness of their providence."

68. That is, the human soul, during its life in the body, imitates the music of the spheres.

Speech VI

Chapter 1

Introduction to a disputation on love

HERE CARLO MARSUPPINI ended. Then Tommaso Benci, a devoted imitator of Socrates, with willing spirit and cheerful countenance undertook to comment on the Socratic words.[1]

Our Socrates, he said, who was judged by the oracle of Apollo to be the wisest of all the Greeks,[2] used to say that he professed the art of love more than any other art, as if it were primarily on the basis of mastery of this art that Socrates or anyone else should be judged "the wisest." He used to say that he had received this art not from the natural philosophers, Anaxagoras, Damon, or Archelaus, not from the professors of rhetoric, Prodicus of Chios or Aspasia, and not from the musician Connus,[3] from all of whom he had learned many things, but from Diotima, a prophetess, on an occasion when she was inspired by the divine spirit.[4] But certainly in my opinion Socrates said this in order to show that only by divine inspiration can men understand what true beauty is, what legitimate love is, and in what way one ought to love. So great is the power of the amatory faculty! So great its sublimity.

Therefore stay away from these heavenly feasts, stay away, I say, you profane people, who are covered with earthly filth, who are completely enslaved to Bacchus and Priapus,[5] and who trample the heavenly gift of love in the dirt and mud, like swine. But you virtuous guests, and all others dedicated to Diana and Pallas,[6] who rejoice in the freedom of a guiltless soul, and in the endless pleasures of the intellect, you are welcome to come and listen carefully to the divine mysteries revealed to Socrates by Diotima.

But before you hear Diotima, a certain disagreement must be settled which has arisen between those who have discussed love above and those who are about to discuss it. For the previous speakers have called love beautiful, good, blessed, and a god. Socrates and Diotima deny this, and they place love midway between the beautiful and the ugly, the good and the bad, the blessed and the wretched, god and man. We think that both of these opinions are true, but each for a different reason.

Chapter 2

Love is midway between beauty and ugliness,
and between god and man

A lodestone puts into iron a certain quality of its own by which the iron is first made like the lodestone, and then drawn to it.[7] To the extent that this attraction originates in the stone, and attracts toward the stone, it may certainly be called a stonish attraction; but to the extent that it occurs in the iron, it is just as much ironish as it is stonish. However, that attraction is certainly not present in the matter of the iron in its natural state but only after it has been treated by the quality of the stone, so the attraction has some attributes of both lodestone and iron.

Fire also, to speak more openly, by its own quality, that is by heat, kindles flax; the flax, raised by the quality of heat, flies up toward the upper region of Fire.[8] To the extent that this ascending is caused by fire and moves toward Fire, we may clearly call it fiery. But to the extent that the ascending is in the flax (not in its natural state, of course, but only after it has been ignited), we may say that it partakes of both natures, of flax as well as of fire, and is equally flaxen and fiery.

A man's appearance, which is often very beautiful to see, on account of an interior goodness fortunately given him by God, can send a ray of its splendor through the eyes of those who see him and into their soul. Drawn by this spark as if by a kind of hook, the soul hastens toward the drawer. Because this drawing, which is love, derives from the beautiful, good, and blessed, and is directed toward the same, we do not hesitate to call it the beautiful, the good, the blessed, and a god, following the opinion of Agathon and the others above. But because it is in a soul already kindled by the presence of that beautiful ray, we are forced to call it an emotion which is halfway between the beautiful and the not beautiful. For obviously a soul which up to now has received no image at all of a beautiful thing does not yet love that thing, because it is unknown. On the other hand he who possesses a beauty entirely is not bothered by the pangs of love. For who longs for something that he already possesses? It follows that the soul catches fire with burning love only when it has found some attractive image of a beautiful thing and is incited by that foretaste to full possession of that beauty. Therefore, since the soul of a lover partly does possess the beautiful object, and partly does not possess it, the soul is obviously partly beautiful and partly not beautiful. And thus because of this mixture, we say that love is a certain emotion halfway between the beautiful and the not beautiful, participating in both. Certainly it was for this reason that Diotima, to come back now to her, called love a *daemon*. Because, just as the daemons are midway between heavenly things and earthly things, so love occupies the middle ground between formlessness and form. This middle region of love between the unformed and the beautifully formed nature Giovanni has explained sufficiently in his first and second speeches.

Chapter 3

On the souls of the spheres and the daemons

But how the daemons inhabit the middle region between heaven and earth, learn thus from the words of Diotima in this *Symposium*, of Socrates in the *Phaedrus* and *Philebus*, and of the Athenian stranger in the *Laws* and *Epinomis*.[9]

Plato thinks that the whole machine of this world is ruled and moved by a single soul, because the whole body of the world is a single body (composed of all of the four elements) of which the parts are the bodies of all living things. For the little body of each living thing is a piece of the World Body, and is composed not of a whole element (fire, air, earth, or water), but of certain parts of these elements.[10] Therefore to the same extent that a whole is more perfect than a part, the World

Body is more perfect than the body of any individual living thing. Certainly it would be an absurdity if an imperfect body could possess a soul but a perfect body could neither possess a soul nor be alive.[11] For who is so distracted as to say that a part is alive but the whole is not? Therefore, the whole World Body is alive, since the bodies of living things, which are its parts, are alive.

The soul of the Universe[12] must be single, just as its matter is single and its structure is single. Therefore, since, according to Plato[13] there are twelve spheres in the Universe (eight heavens[14] and the four elements below the heavens), and since these twelve spheres are separate from each other, and are different in appearance, motion, and property, they must have twelve souls, all different in appearance and power. Therefore the soul of the one prime Matter must be single, but the souls of the twelve spheres must be twelve.

Who will deny that the elements earth and water are alive, since they give life to the creatures born from them? But if these lower orders of the Universe are alive and full of living things, why would not air and fire, which are higher parts of the Universe, also be alive and have living things in them? And likewise the eight heavens? The heavenly creatures, which are the stars, and the creatures of earth and water we certainly can see; but the creatures of fire and air we cannot see because we cannot see the pure element of fire or air. But there is one difference. In the element of earth there are two kinds of creatures, brute and rational. The same is true of water; since water is a higher element than earth, it too must possess some rational creatures[15] no less than the element of earth does. But the ten highest spheres, on account of their sublimity, are inhabited by nothing but rational creatures.

The Soul of the World, that is of prime Matter, and the souls of the twelve spheres and the stars the Platonists call *gods*[16] because they are very close to the Angelic Mind and the Supreme God. The creatures which inhabit the region[17] of ethereal fire, located under the moon, and the regions of pure air and humid air (next to water), the Platonists call *daemons*. But those which inhabit earth, and are rational, the Platonists call *men*. The gods are both immortal and impassible; men are both mortal and passible; daemons are of course immortal but are also passible.[18]

The Platonists do not attribute to daemons the passions of the body, but only certain passions of the soul which somehow cause them to like

good men and dislike bad ones. Daemons involve themselves very closely and zealously in taking care of the affairs of lower creatures, especially
human beings. Because of this service, all daemons seem good. Some
Platonists[19] and Christian theologians have said that there are some
other daemons which are evil, but for the present we shall not argue
about the evil daemons.

The good daemons, who are our guardians, Dionysius the
Areopagite[20] usually calls by the proper name *angels, rulers of the lower
world*; this differs very little from the opinion of Plato. Moreover, those
souls whom Plato calls *gods*, or the *souls of the spheres and stars*, we can
call *angels, or ministers of God*, as Dionysius does. This, too, does not dis-
agree with Plato, for the reason that, as is apparent in the tenth book of
the *Laws*,[21] Plato does not in the least enclose souls of this kind within
the confines of their spheres in the way that he confines the souls of
earthly creatures to their bodies. Rather he asserts that the heavenly
souls are endowed with such great power by the supreme God that they
are able at the same time to enjoy the sight of God, and without any effort or trouble control and move the spheres of the universe according
to the will of their father, and, by moving the spheres, easily govern
lower things. Thus the difference between Plato and Dionysius is only a
matter of words rather than of opinion.

Chapter 4

On the seven gifts which are bestowed upon men
by God through intermediary spirits

The Ideas of all things, which the divine Mind contains, the inferior
gods are said to serve; the gifts[22] of those gods, the daemons are said to
serve. For from the highest to the lowest, all things go through interme-
diaries in such a way that the Ideas, which are conceived by the divine
Mind, bestow their gifts upon men through the mediation of the gods
and the daemons. Of these gifts seven are preeminent: acuity of contemplation, power of governing, animosity, clarity of the senses, ardor in
love, subtlety in interpreting, and fecundity in procreating.

The power of these gifts God first contains in Himself. Then He distributes the power of these gifts to the seven gods who move the seven
planets (and are called angels by us). He does this in such a way that

each god receives one gift in preference to the others. The gods then pass on the gifts to the seven classes of daemons which are subject to them, one gift to each class in particular. The daemons transfer them to men.

Certainly God infuses these gifts into souls[23] as soon as they are born from Him. As they fall from the Milky Way, through Cancer, into the body, they are wrapped in a special transparent astral body;[24] swathed in this wrapping, they are then enclosed in earthly bodies. For the order of nature requires that the perfectly pure soul is not able to descend into this most impure body until the soul receives a certain mediating and pure covering. This covering, since it is coarser than the soul, but purer and finer than the body,[25] is regarded by the Platonists as the most appropriate link between the soul and its earthly body.

And hence it happens that the souls of the planets reinforce and strengthen in our souls (and their bodies in our bodies) the powers of those seven gifts which are given to us[26] by God from the very beginning and continuously thereafter. For the same purpose there is an equal number of kinds of daemons which stand midway between the heavenly beings and men. The gift of contemplation Saturn strengthens by means of Saturnian daemons.[27] The power of governing and ruling Jupiter strengthens with the help of Jovian daemons. Greatness of soul, Mars, through Martian daemons. Clarity of the senses and of opinion (whence comes prophecy), the Sun, with the help of Solar daemons. Love, Venus inspires through Venerean daemons. Skill in speaking and interpretation, Mercury promotes, through the influence of Mercurial daemons. Finally, Luna encourages the function of procreation with the assistance of Lunar daemons.

The planets distribute the powers for these gifts to all men, but especially to those over whom they have domination because of the disposition of the heavens at their conception and at their birth. Since these gifts are divinely infused in us, they are obviously virtuous. Nevertheless they can sometimes seem sinful in us on account of abuse; this is obvious in our exercise of governance, animosity, love, and procreation.

The instinct of love (lest we digress too far) we have received from the supreme God, and from Venus, who is called a goddess, and from Venerean daemons. Since it descends from God, it must be called a god; since it is strengthened by daemons, it must be called a daemon. Therefore it is rightly called by Agathon a god, by Diotima a daemon, a Venerean daemon, as I say.

Chapter 5

On the order of the Venerean daemons
and how they shoot love

The Venerean daemon is a three-fold love. The first is placed by the Platonists in the heavenly Venus, that is, in the intelligence itself of the Angelic Mind. The second in the vulgar Venus, that is, in that power of procreation which the World Soul possesses. These two are called daemons for the reason that they are midway between formlessness and form, as we have mentioned above and will explain more fully a little later. The third order is of the daemons who are the companions of the planet of Venus. Of these also we posit a three-fold order. Some are assigned to the element of fire, others to that of the purest air, others to that of thicker and cloudy air. All are called *heroes*,[28] that is, *lovers*, from the Greek word *heros*, which means *love*.

The first shoot the arrows of love into those men in whom bile, the choleric and fiery humor, dominates. The second, into those in whom blood, the airy humor. The third into those in whom phlegm and black bile, the watery and earthy humors, dominate. Not only all men, but especially four kinds of men, are wounded by Cupid's arrows. For Plato points out in the *Phaedrus*[29] that souls which are followers of Jupiter, Apollo, Mars, and Juno (that is, Venus) are wounded the most. And that being disposed to love from the very beginnings of their creation, they are accustomed to love especially those men who are born under the same stars. Hence Jovians are strongly affected by Jovians, Martians by Martians, and similarly the others by the others.

Chapter 6

How we are caught by love

What I shall explain about one example, understand about the other three.[30] Any soul which falls into its earthly body under the domination of Jupiter conceives for itself during its descent a certain pattern for making a man corresponding to the star of Jupiter. This pattern the soul is able to imprint very exactly on its astral body because that is very well disposed to receive it.[31] If the soul finds[32] on earth a seed which is similarly well disposed, the soul then imprints on that seed a third image[33] which is very much like the first and second, but if not, then not so much like.[34]

It frequently happens that two particular souls will have descended, although at different intervals of time, nevertheless both under the domination of Jupiter; and one of them, having found on earth a suitable seed, will have shaped its body in very close conformity to those earlier ideas;[35] but the other, on account of the unsuitableness of its matter, will have begun the same work, certainly, but will not have carried it out with such close correspondence to its pattern. The former body will be more beautiful than the latter. Both, because of a certain similarity of nature, will please each other, but the one which is thought the more beautiful of the two will please more. This is how it happens that everyone loves most, not those who are the most beautiful, but those who are his own, that is, similarly born,[36] even if they are less beautiful than many others.

Therefore those who, as we have said,[37] are born under the same star are so constituted that the image of the more beautiful of them, penetrating through the eyes into the soul of the other, matches and corresponds completely with a certain identical image which was formed in the astral body[38] of that soul as well as in its inner nature from its creation. The soul thus stricken recognizes the image before it as something which is its own. It is in fact almost exactly like the image which this soul has long possessed within itself, and which it tried to imprint on its own body, but was not able to do. The soul then puts the visual image beside its own interior image, and if anything is lacking in the former as a perfect copy of the Jovial body, the soul restores it by reforming it. Then the soul loves that reformed image as its own work. This is how it happens that lovers are so deceived that they think the beloved more beautiful than he is. For in the course of time they do not see the beloved in the real image of him received through the senses, but in an image already reformed by the lover's soul, in the likeness of its own innate idea, an image which is more beautiful than the body itself. Moreover, every day they want to see that body from which the image first emanated. For although the soul preserves within itself an image of the body even when the body is absent, and that image is almost enough for it, the spirit (which is the instrument of the soul) and the eye do not preserve it.

Certainly three things seem to be in us: the soul, the spirit, and the body.[39] The soul and the body, which are by nature very different from each other, are joined by means of the spirit, which is a certain very thin and clear vapor produced by the heat of the heart from the thinnest part of the blood. Spread from there[40] through all parts of the body, the spirit receives the powers of the soul and transmits them to the body. It also receives through the organs of the senses images of external bodies, images which cannot be imprinted directly on the soul because incorporeal substance, which is higher than bodies, cannot be formed by them through the receiving of images. But the soul, being present to the spirit everywhere,[41] easily sees the images of bodies shining in it, as if in a mirror, and through those judges the bodies. And this cognition is called by the Platonists sensation. While looking at these, by a power of its own, it conceives within itself images like them but much purer[42] still. This kind of conceiving we call imagination or fantasy.[43] Images conceived here[44] are stored in the memory. By these the eye of the soul[45] is often aroused to contemplate the universal Ideas of things which it contains in itself. And for this reason at the same time that the soul is perceiving a certain man in sensation, and conceiving him in the imagination, it can contemplate, by means of the intellect, the reason and definition common to all men through its innate Idea of humanity; and what it has contemplated, it preserves. Therefore, since the soul can preserve in the memory the image of a handsome man once it has conceived and reformed that image within itself, the soul would be satisfied to have seen the beloved only once. But the eye and the spirit, which, like mirrors, can receive images of a body only in its presence, and lose them when it is absent, need the continuous presence of a beautiful body in order to shine continuously with its illumination, and be comforted and pleased. Therefore, on account of their poverty, the eye and the spirit require the presence of the body, and the soul, which is usually dominated by them, is forced to desire the same thing.

Chapter 7

On the birth of love

But now let us return to Diotima. When, for the reasons we have given, she had restored Love to the ranks of the daemons, she explained its origin to Socrates in the following way:

On the birthday of Venus, while the gods were feasting, Porus, the son of Counsel, drunk with nectar, lay with Penia in the garden of Jupiter. From this union was born Love.[46]

On the birthday of Venus, that is, when the Angelic Mind and the World Soul (which we call Venuses, for the reason which we have given elsewhere)[47] were born from the supreme majesty of God.

While the gods were feasting, that is, while Uranus, Saturn, and Jupiter were enjoying their respective powers. For at the time when the intelligence in the Angel and the power of procreating in the World Soul, powers which we rightly call twin Venuses, first came into being, the supreme God, whom they[48] call Uranus, was already in existence; moreover, existence and life, which we call Saturn and Jupiter, already existed in the Angelic Mind; and also in the World Soul there already existed the knowledge of the superior things and the moving of the celestial bodies, which powers, again, we call Saturn and Jupiter.

Porus and Penia mean plenty and poverty respectively.

Porus, the son of Counsel, that is, the ray of the supreme God. Certainly God is called Counsel, and the fountain of Counsel, because He is the truth and goodness of all things, by whose splendor every counsel becomes true, and toward acquiring whose goodness every counsel tends.

The garden of Jupiter means the fertility of the Angelic life, into which, when that *Porus*, that is, the ray of God, descends, once united with *Penia*, that is, the previous poverty of this,[49] he creates love. In the beginning the Angel exists and lives through God. With reference to these two, existence and life, the Angelic Mind is called Saturn and Jupiter. It has in addition the power of understanding, which we think is Venus. This power is of its own nature formless and dark unless it is illuminated by God, like the eye's power before the arrival of the sun. This darkness we think is *Penia*, a lack, as it were, or deficiency of light. Finally, that power of understanding, turned by a certain natural instinct toward its parent, receives from Him the divine ray, which is *Porus*, or plenty. In this ray, as though in a kind of seed, the Reasons[50] of all things are contained. By the flames of this ray that natural instinct is kindled. This fire, this desire, rising out of the former darkness and the light added to it, is love, born of poverty and plenty.

In the garden of Jupiter, that is, born under the shadow of life. Certainly, since immediately after the vigor of life, arises a desire to understand.[51] But why do they introduce *Porus* as *drunk with nectar*? Because he overflows with the dew of the divine vitality.

Why is love partly rich and partly poor? Because we are not accustomed to desire that which we completely possess or that which we completely lack. For since everyone seeks that which he does not have, if a person possesses the whole thing, what more can he want? But also, since no one wants things which are unknown to him, anything that we love must necessarily have been known to us beforehand in some way. And not only known, for we usually dislike many of the things which are known to us, but considered good for us or pleasing. And not even that seems to be enough to produce an ardent benevolence: we must, in addition, be convinced that we can easily attain the anticipated pleasure. Therefore anyone who loves something certainly does not yet possess it completely in itself, but through the activities of his soul he knows about the thing, judges it pleasing, and believes that he can attain it. This knowing, judging, and hope are a kind of present anticipation, as it were, of an absent good. For he would not desire it unless it pleased him, and it would not please him unless it had been pre-tasted in some way. Therefore, since lovers certainly partly have what they desire but partly do not have it, love is not inappropriately mixed of a certain poverty and plenty.

It is certainly for this reason that that heavenly Venus, aroused by her first taste of the divine ray, is carried by love toward the complete plenitude of the whole light; in this effort clinging to her parent more efficaciously, she immediately shines with His full glory, and those disordered Reasons of things, which before were entangled in the ray which we call *Porus*, now are put in order through that clinging power of Venus and, being separated, shine out more clearly.

But just as the Angel is to God, so the World Soul is to the Angel and to God. For turning itself toward the higher beings, the World Soul likewise receives a ray from them, is kindled, and begets a love which participates in both plenty and poverty. Hence, adorned with the Forms of all things, by their model, it moves the heavens, and through its power of procreating creates forms like them in the Matter of the elements.

Here[52] again we see the double Venus. One Venus clearly is the power of the Soul to understand superior things, but the other is its power to create inferior things. The former power certainly is not peculiar to the Soul but is an imitation of the contemplation of the Angelic Mind; the latter power, however, is peculiar to the nature of the Soul. For this reason whenever we place only one Venus in the World Soul, we mean its own special power which is its own Venus. Whenever two, we mean one which it has in common with the Angel and another which is peculiar to the Soul itself.

Therefore, let there be two Venuses in the World Soul, the first heavenly and the second vulgar. Let both have a love: the heavenly for contemplating divine Beauty, the vulgar for procreating the same in the Matter of the World.[53] For such beauty as the former sees, the latter wishes to pass on as well as it can to the machine of the World. Or rather both are moved to procreate beauty, but each in its own way. The heavenly Venus strives, through its intelligence, to reproduce in itself as exactly as possible the beauty of the higher things; the vulgar Venus strives, through the fertility of its divine seeds, to reproduce in the Matter of the World the beauty which is divinely conceived within itself. The former love we sometimes call a god for the reason that it is directed toward divine things; but we usually call it a daemon since it is midway between lack and plenty. The other love we always call a daemon since it seems to have a certain affection for the body, and to be more inclined toward the lower region of the world. Which[54] is certainly foreign to God but appropriate to the nature of daemons.

Chapter 8

In all souls there are two loves,
but in ours there are five

But these twin Venuses and twin loves are present not only in the World Soul but also in the souls of the spheres, of the stars, of daemons, and of men. And since, in the normal sequence of the natural order, all individual souls are related to that first Soul, it follows that the loves of all individual souls must similarly be related to the World Soul's love, in such a way that they derive from it in some way. That is why Diotima used to call individual loves simply "daemons," but the love of the World Soul "the great daemon" which, hanging over all things throughout the whole universe, does not permit hearts to sleep, but everywhere wakens them to loving.

But in us are found not two loves only, but five. The two extreme loves are certainly daemons. The middle three are not daemons but passions. Certainly in the intellect of man there is an eternal love of seeing the divine beauty, thanks to which we pursue both the study of philoso-

phy and the practice of justice and piety. There is also in the power of
procreation a certain mysterious urge to procreate offspring. This love
too is eternal; by it we are continuously driven to create some likeness of
that celestial Beauty in the image of a procreated offspring. These two
eternal loves in us are daemons which Plato predicts will always be present in our souls, one of which raises us to things above; the other presses
us down to things below. One is a *kalodaemon*, that is, a good daemon;
the other is a *kakodaemon*, that is an evil daemon. In reality both are
good, since the procreation of offspring is considered to be as necessary
and virtuous as the pursuit of truth. But the second is called evil because, on account of our abuse, it often disturbs us and powerfully di-
verts the soul from its chief good, which consists in the contemplation of
truth, and twists it to baser purposes.

Between these loves in us there are three which will more properly be
called emotions or passions rather than daemons, since they are not
uniformly strong in the soul, as the other two are, but begin, grow, decrease, and cease. Of these, one is equidistant from both extremes. The
other two are inclined toward one extreme or the other. Moreover,
when the figure of some body meets the eye, and through the eyes penetrates into the spirit, if that figure, on account of the preparation of its
matter, corresponds closely to the figure which the divine Mind contains in its Idea of the thing, it immediately pleases the soul since it corresponds to those Reasons which both our intellect and our power of
procreation preserve as copies of the thing itself, and which were originally received divinely.[55] Hence a three-fold love arises, as we have said.
For we are born or brought up inclined and disposed toward the contemplative, active, or voluptuous life.[56] If we are disposed to the contemplative life, we are immediately elevated by the sight of bodily beauty to
the contemplation of spiritual and divine beauty. If to the voluptuous
life, we descend immediately from sight to the desire to touch. If to the
active and moral life, we continue in the mere pleasure of seeing and
conversing. Those of the first type are so intelligent that they rise to the
heights; those of the last type are so stupid[57] that they sink to the bot-
tom; and those of the middle type remain in the middle region.

Thus every love begins with sight. But the love of the contemplative
man ascends from sight to intellect. That of the voluptuous man descends from sight to touch. That of the active man remains in sight. The
love of the contemplative man turns toward the highest daemon rather

than toward the lowest; that of the voluptuous man is directed toward the lowest daemon rather than toward the highest; and that of the active man keeps an equal distance from both. These three loves are given three names. The love of the contemplative man is called divine; that of the active man, human; that of the voluptuous man, bestial.

Chapter 9

Which passions are present in lovers
because of the mother of love

Thus far we have said that Love is a daemon, born of plenty and poverty, and divided into five types. We shall next discuss, following the words of Diotima, what kinds of passions arise in lovers as a result of love's having this nature.

Since, she says, Love was born on the birthday of Venus, he follows and worships Venus and is seized by a desire for the beautiful, since Venus herself is very beautiful. Because he is the son of Poverty, he is dry, thin, and squalid, barefooted, humble, without a home, without a bed, and without any cover: sleeping on doorsteps, on the road, under the sky; and finally, he is always needy. Because he is the son of Plenty, he lies in wait for the beautiful and the good. He is manly, bold and high-strung, impetuous, a crafty and keen-scented hunter,[58] always laying new traps, devoted to prudence, eloquent, philosophizing all of his life, a sorcerer, an enchanter, powerful, a magician, and a sophist. He is neither entirely immortal in nature nor mortal. But he sometimes is born and lives in the same day (when he is flourishing). Sometimes he dies and revives again, on account of the nature of his father. What is procured leaks away. For this reason love is never either poor or rich. He is also located midway between wisdom and ignorance.[59]

This is what Diotima says. We shall explain these things as briefly as we can. Although these characteristics are present in all kinds of loves, they nevertheless seem clearer in the three middle kinds, because these are more manifest to us.

Since Love was born on the birthday of Venus, he follows Venus; that is, since he was born among those celestial spirits whom we have called Venuses, he leads the souls of men up to celestial things.

And he is seized by a desire for the beautiful since Venus herself is very beautiful; that is, he kindles souls with a desire for the supreme and divine beauty since he himself was born among those spirits which, being nearest to God, are lighted supremely by the beauty of God, and to those same rays lift us.

Moreover, since the life of all animals and plants, and the fertility of the earth, consists in moisture and warmth, in order to show Love's poverty, Diotima implied that both are lacking in him, moisture as well as warmth, when she said *he is dry,* and *thin, and squalid.* For who does not know that arid and dry things are those which moisture forsakes? Likewise, who would say that pallor and squalor come from anything else than a lack of sanguine heat? Moreover, in a long-lasting love mortals become pale and thin. Certainly the power of nature does not usually suffice for two tasks at once. The entire attention of a lover's soul is devoted to continuous thought about the beloved. And to this all the force of the natural complexion is directed. For this reason the food in the stomach is not digested perfectly. Whence it happens that the greater part is eliminated as superfluous wastes; the smaller part, and that indeed raw, is drawn to the liver. There, too, for the same reason, it is badly digested. For this reason only a little crude blood is dispersed from there through the veins. As a consequence, all parts of the body become thin and pale because of the scarcity and crudity of food.

Moreover, wherever the continuous attention of the soul is carried, there also fly the spirits, which are the chariots, or instruments[60] of the soul. The spirits are produced in the heart from the thinnest part of the blood. The lover's soul is carried toward the image of the beloved planted in his imagination, and thence toward the beloved himself. To the same place are also drawn the lover's spirits. Flying out there, they are continuously dissipated. Therefore there is a need for a constant source of pure blood to replace the consumed spirits, since the thinner and clearer parts of the blood are used up every day in replacing the spirits. On that account, when the pure and clear blood is dissipated, there remains only the impure, thick, dry, and black. Hence the body dries out and grows squalid, and hence lovers become melancholics. For from dry, thick, and black blood is produced melancholy, that is, black bile, which fills the head with its vapors, dries out the brain, and ceaselessly troubles the soul day and night with hideous and horrible images. This, we have read, happened to the Epicurean philosopher Lucretius on account of love; shaken first by love and then by madness, he finally laid hands on himself.[61]

These things were accustomed to happen to those, who, having abused love, converted what is a desire for contemplation into a desire for embrace. For we tolerate more easily the desire to see than the longing to both see and touch. When ancient physicians observed these things, they said that love was a passion very close to the disease of melancholy. And the physician Rhazes[62] taught that it was cured by coitus, fasting, inebriation, and walking. And not only does love render men thus[63] but conversely those who are thus by nature are more susceptible to love. And people are thus in whom bile (which they call choler) or black bile (which they call melancholy) dominates the other humors. Bile is hot and dry; black bile is dry and cold. The former takes the place of fire in the body of animals; the latter, of earth. Therefore melancholics are considered arid or dry, in the likeness of earth, and cholerics are squalid and pale, in the likeness of fire. Cholerics, because of the force of the fiery humor, are carried into love headlong. Melancholics love more slowly because of the sluggishness of the earthy humor, but because of the stability of that humor, after they have been caught, they continue for a long time. Therefore Love is rightly described as *dry* and *squalid*, since men who are thus are accustomed to indulge in love more than others. This, we think, comes chiefly from the fact that cholerics are burned up by the heat of the bile; the melancholy are gnawed away by the sharpness of the black bile. Aristotle asserted this in the seventh book *On Ethics*.[64] And so a nagging humor always torments both[65] and drives them to seek some strong and continuous relief from the continuous annoyance of their humors. The pleasures of music and love are of this kind. For we can devote our energy to no other pleasures so continuously as to the charms of music and voices and the attractions of beauty.[66] The rest of the senses are quickly satiated. But sight and hearing are gratified longer by even the weakest voice or the blankest picture. And not only are the pleasures of these senses more lasting, but they are also more akin to the human complexion. For what is more appropriate to the spirits of the human body than the voices and figures of men? Especially of those who are pleasing not only through similarity of nature, but also through grace of beauty. For this reason choleric and melancholy men pursue as the only remedy and solace of their vexatious complexions, the pleasures of song and beauty. And for this reason they are more susceptible to the charms of Venus. And Socrates, whom Aristotle judged a melancholic,[67] confessed that he was the most inclined to the art of love of all men. And we can judge the same thing of the melancholy Sappho, as she herself testifies.[68] And even our Vergil (whom his portrait shows to have been a choleric), although chaste,[69] was nevertheless much disposed to loving.

Bare-footed. Diotima pictured Love thus since a lover is so much occupied with matters of love that in the other affairs of life, public as well as private, he does not proceed as cautiously as he should, but, without any anticipation of dangers, is rashly carried anywhere. For this reason in his travels he encounters frequent dangers, not unlike those who do not protect their feet with leather. Whence they are hurt by frequent thorns and pebbles.

Humble. Plato's Greek word *chamaipetes* means *on the ground* or *low-flying.* For he sees that repeatedly, on account of the abuse of love, "lovers live without common sense, and through their trivial preoccupations great causes fail."[70] Lovers give themselves up to beloveds so far that they try to be changed into them altogether, and to reproduce them in themselves in words as well as deeds. But who would not become effeminate from constant imitation of boys and girls? Who would not turn out to be a boy or a girl?

Without a home. The soul itself is the home of human thought; the spirit is the home of the soul; and the body is the home of this spirit. There are three inhabitants; there are three homes. Giving up its natural home, each of these inhabitants goes into exile. For every thought is devoted not to the discipline and tranquility of its own soul, but to the service of the man beloved. And the soul abandons the service of its own body and spirit and tries to leap across into the body of the beloved. But while the soul is hurrying elsewhere, the spirit, which is the chariot of the soul, is also flying out elsewhere, in sighing. And thus thought leaves its home, the soul leaves its home, and the spirit leaves its home. The first departure is accompanied by madness and restlessness; the second, by weakness and the fear of death; and the third, by nervousness, trembling, and sighing. On this account love is deprived of its own Lares, its natural seat, and its hoped-for rest.

Without a bed and without any cover. For he has no place to rest, and nothing to cover himself with. For since all things seek their own origin, the little blaze of love, kindled in the appetite of the lover by the sight of a beautiful body, tries to fly back into that same body. By which impulse certainly it carries with it in flying out both the desired and the desirer. O cruel lot of lovers! O life more wretched than any death, unless perhaps your soul, snatched out of its own body by this violence of love, will also[71] neglect the image of the beloved and betake itself to the temple of the divine splendor, where at last it will find rest, where it will be satisfied.

Likewise, who will deny that Love wanders *without cover* and naked? For who can conceal Love, whom a wild, ox-like, fixed stare betrays, whom stammering speech reveals, and redness or paleness of face, frequent sighs, shaking of the parts,[72] perpetual complaining, inappropriate praises, sudden indignation, boasting, flirting,[73] petulance, groundless suspicion, and obsequious devotions, all give away? For just as in the sun and fire, light accompanies the heat of its ray, so external evidences accompany the internal fire of love.

Sleeps on doorsteps. The doors of the soul seem to be the eyes and ears. For through these, many things are brought into the soul, and the feelings and habits of the soul clearly shine out through the eyes. Lovers spend most of their time in looking at appearances and listening to voices. Rarely does their intellect concentrate upon itself. More often it wanders out through the eyes and ears. That is why lovers are said to *sleep on doorsteps.*

And they are said to lie *on the road*[74] for the beauty of the body ought to be a road by which we begin to ascend to higher beauty. But those who debase themselves in wicked lusts, or even merely occupy themselves more than they should with ogling, seem to remain *on the road* itself, and not to set out for its terminus.

Under the sky. Right. For being completely preoccupied with a single thing, lovers pay no attention to responsibilities. Thus, leading their life by chance, they are exposed to all the dangers of fortune, just as those who lead their life naked under the sky are exposed to all storms.

Because of the nature of his mother, he is *always needy.* Clearly since the first origin of love was from need, and what is natural cannot be completely extirpated, love is *always needy,* always thirsty. For as long as there is anything left to be obtained, the fire of love burns. When the whole is completely possessed, with the cessation of need, desire ceases rather than endure without need.

Chapter 10

What are the gifts of lovers
on account of the father of love

These follow the mother of Love, Poverty; but the opposite, his father, Plenty. But what the opposites are, anyone will know, the above being understood. He was described above as simple, careless, *humble*, and unarmed. Here are brought in the opposites of these. For he is called *crafty*, a *hunter*, *keen-scented*, a trapper, a lyer-in-wait, *devoted to prudence*, a philosopher, *manly* and *bold*, *impetuous*, *eloquent*, a *magician*, and a *sophist*.[75] The same love which makes a lover careless and indolent in other affairs makes him clever and *crafty* in affairs of love, so that in marvelous ways he goes bird-catching for the beloved's favor, whether he snares him with traps, or captures him with attentions, or appeases him with eloquence, or soothes him with song. The same madness which had made him flattering in his attention, the same madness, I say, supplies arms: ferocity to those incensed against the beloved, and confidence and invincible strength to those fighting for him.

Love, as we have said, takes its origin from sight. Sight is midway between intellect and touch; hence the soul of the lover is always being pulled in opposite directions, and thrown alternately backwards and forwards. Sometimes a desire for caressing arises, but sometimes a chaste desire for heavenly beauty, and now that and now this conquers and leads him. In those who have been brought up virtuously and are strong in sharpness of intelligence, the latter wins; in others, more often the former. Those who debase themselves in the excrements of the body are rightly considered to be *dry*, *naked*, *humble*, unarmed, and dull. *Dry* because they are always consuming but are never filled. *Naked*, because, being rash, they are subject to all dangers, and being shameless and unrefined, they are held in disrepute. *Humble* because they think about nothing high, nothing great. *Unarmed* because they succumb to shameful desire. *Dull* because they are so stupid that they do not know where love is leading them, and they remain *on the road*, and do not arrive at the goal.

But the opposite seem oppositely affected, for since they feed on solid goods of the soul, they are better satisfied; and since they love more quietly, they preserve their modesty.[76] They neglect the shadowy beauty of the body and are raised higher: protected as if by armament, they drive vain lusts away from themselves, and they subject the senses to reason. Since they are the cleverest and most prudent of all, they philosophize in such a way as to walk among the shapes of bodies very cautiously as if they were footprints or odors; by following these they wisely track down the sacred beauty of the soul, and of the divine things, and by hunting thus prudently they happily attain what they desire.

Certainly this great reward of Love derives from his father, Plenty, since the ray of beauty which is both Plenty and the father of love, has the power to be reflected back to what it came from, and it draws the lover with it. But it descends first from God, and passes through the Angel and the Soul as if they were made of glass; and from the Soul it easily emanates into the body prepared to receive it. Then from that body of a younger man it shines out, especially through the eyes, the transparent windows of the soul. It flies onward, through the air, and penetrating the eyes of an older man, pierces his soul, kindles his appetite, then leads the wounded soul and the kindled appetite to their healing and cooling, respectively, while it carries them with it to the same place from which it had itself descended, step-by-step indeed, first to the body of the beloved, second, to the Soul, third, to the Angel, and finally to God, the first origin of this splendor. This is the useful hunt; this is the happy bird-catching of lovers. This is certainly the kind of hunting which a certain familiar of our Socrates attributed to him in Plato in the *Protagoras*. For he asks, "Where have you been, O Socrates? I suppose of course that you are returning from that hunting to which the virtuous character of Alcibiades always excites you?"[77]

Besides this, she[78] calls Love a *sophist* and a *magician*. A *sophist* Plato defines, in the dialogue *Sophist*,[79] as an ambitious and crafty debater who, by the subtleties of sophistries, shows us the false for the true, and forces those who dispute with him to contradict themselves in their speeches. This lovers as well as beloveds endure at some time or other. For lovers, blinded by the clouds of love, often accept false things for true, while they think that their beloveds are more beautiful, more intelligent, or better than they are. They contradict themselves on account of the vehemence of love, for reason considers one thing, and concupiscence pursues another. They change their counsels at the command of the beloved; they oppose themselves in order to comply with others. Also the beautiful are often trapped by the craftiness of lovers, and those who have previously been obstinate become compliant.

But why do we think that Love is a *magician?* Because the whole power of magic consists in love. The work of magic is the attraction of one thing by another because of a certain affinity of nature. But the parts of this world, like the parts of a single animal, all deriving from a single author, are joined to each other by the communion of a single nature. Therefore just as in us the brain, lungs, heart, liver, and the rest of the parts draw something from each other, and help each other, and sympathize with any one of them when it suffers, so the parts of this great animal, that is all the bodies of the world, similarly joined together, borrow and lend natures to and from each other. From this common relationship is born a common love; from love, a common attraction. And this is the true magic. Thus fire is drawn upward by the concavity of the sphere of the moon, because of a congruity of nature; air, by the concavity of fire; earth is drawn downward by the center of the world; water also is drawn by its region. Thus also the lodestone draws iron, amber draws chaff, and sulphur, fire; the sun turns many flowers and leaves toward itself, and the moon, the waters; Mars is accustomed to stir the winds, and the various plants also attract to themselves various kinds of animals. In human affairs also, "his own pleasure draws each."[80] Therefore the works of magic are works of nature, but art is its handmaiden. For where anything is lacking in a natural relationship, art supplies it through vapors, numbers, figures, and qualities at the proper times. Just as in agriculture, nature produces the crops, but art makes the preparations. The ancients attributed this art[81] to daemons because the daemons understand what is the inter-relation of natural things, what is appropriate to each, and how the harmony of things, if it is lacking anywhere, can be restored. Some are said to have been either friends,[82] through some similarity of nature, such as Zoroaster and Socrates, or their beloveds, through worship, such as Apollonius Tyaneus and Porphyry.[83] For this reason signs, voices, and portents from daemons are said to have come to them, when they were awake, or oracles and visions when they were asleep. They seem to have become magicians through the friendship of the daemons, just as the daemons are magicians through understanding the friendship of things themselves. And all nature, because of mutual love, is called a magician. Moreover, anyone who is beautiful bewitches us with his youthful eyes. Men charm and win men over to themselves through the powers of eloquence and the measures of songs, as if by certain incantations. Moreover, they drug and capture them with worship and gifts exactly as though with enchantments. Therefore no one can doubt that love is a magician, since the whole power of magic consists in love, and the work of love is fulfilled by bewitchments, incantations, and enchantments.

He is neither entirely mortal nor also immortal. Not mortal, since two loves, those two which we called daemons, are present in us permanently. *Not immortal* since the three middle loves change every day, grow, and decrease. Moreover, in the appetite of men, from the beginnings of life, there is an inextinguishable innate fervor which does not permit the soul to rest, and always forces it to devote itself zealously to some definite thing. The temperaments of men are diverse, and one does not live by a single vow. Whence that continuous ardor of concupiscence, which is natural love, impels some to the study of letters, others to music or painting, others to virtue of conduct, or the religious life, others to honors, some to making money, many to the pleasures of the stomach and of Venus, and others to other things, and also the same man to different things at different ages. And so this fervor is called both *immortal* and *mortal*. *Immortal* because it is never extinguished and it changes its object rather than die. *Mortal* because it does not always concentrate on the same object, but seeks new pleasures, either because of a change in its own nature or because of satiety rising from long frequenting of the same thing; and that which has almost expired in one thing revives in some measure in another. It is also called *immortal* for the reason that a figure once loved is always loved. For, as long as it remains the same in the same man, it is loved in him himself. But when it has left him, there is no longer the same figure in him which you loved originally. This new figure[84] you do not love, of course, because you had not loved it previously; but you do not cease loving that previous figure. This is the only difference: that you previously saw that figure in another, but now you see it only in yourself; you always love this same figure fixed forever in your memory, and whenever it presents itself to the eyes of your soul, it burns you with love. For this reason whenever we meet a person whom we used to love, we are shaken; either the heart jumps or palpitates, or the liver melts, or the eyes blink, and the face turns various colors on seeing him. For his presence brings up to the eyes of the soul the figure lying hidden in the mind,[85] and, as if by blowing, rekindles the fires slumbering under the ashes.[86] This is why Love is called *immortal*. But he is also said to be *mortal*, for this reason, that although the beloved's features remain fixed forever in the breast, nevertheless they do not present themselves to the eyes of the mind all the time. On that account our benevolence seems to kindle and re-kindle by turns.

In addition to these things is the fact that neither animal nor human love can ever exist without hate.[87] Who would not hate one who took his soul away from him? For as liberty is more pleasant than anything else, so servitude is more unpleasant. And so you hate and love beautiful men at the same time; you hate them as thieves and murderers; you are also forced to love and revere them as mirrors sparkling with the heavenly glow. What can you do, O wretch? Where to turn, you do not know; alas, O lost soul, you do not know. You would not want to be with this murderer of yourself, but you would not want to live without his blessed sight. You cannot be with this man who destroys you, who tortures you. You cannot live without him, who, with wonderful enticements, steals you from yourself, who claims all of you for himself. You want to flee him who scorches you with his flames. You also want to cling to him, in order that by being very near him who possesses you, you may also be near yourself. You seek yourself outside yourself, O wretch, and you cling to your captor in order that you may sometime ransom your captive self. You would certainly not want to love, O madman, because you would not want to die. You would also certainly not want not to love since you think that service must be rendered to an image of heavenly things. Therefore, through this alternation it happens that love is at every moment drying up and growing green again, so to speak.

It is also placed by Diotima *midway between wisdom and ignorance.* Moreover, love pursues things which are beautiful. The most beautiful of all things is wisdom. Therefore it seeks wisdom. He who seeks wisdom does not possess it completely. For who seeks things that he possesses? Nor also does he lack it altogether. For he is wise in this one thing at least, that he recognizes his own ignorance. But he who does not know that he is ignorant is ignorant of things themselves as well as of his own ignorance; and he does not seek knowledge which he does not know he lacks. Therefore love of wisdom, since it partly lacks wisdom and is partly wise, is located between wisdom and ignorance.

This, says Diotima, is the condition of love. But the nature of the beautiful itself, that is of the supreme Beauty, is that it is *delicate, perfect,* and *blessed*.[88] *Delicate* in that, by a certain sweetness of its own, it allures to itself the appetite of all things. *Perfect* in that, when the things which it has attracted approach, it illuminates them with its own rays and perfects them. *Blessed* in that it fills the illuminated objects with eternal goods.

Chapter 11

What is the usefulness of love from its definition

But after Diotima has explained what the origin of love is, and what love itself is, she now reveals what is its object and what benefits it entails for men. Certainly we all want to have belongings, and not only to have them, but to have them permanently. But the individual belongings of mortals are moved around and wear out, and they would soon all disappear if new ones were not made every day in place of those which pass away. Therefore, in order to keep our possessions permanently, by whatever means, we try to reproduce those which pass away. Reproduction is effected through procreation. Hence the instinct for procreation is innate in all things. But since procreation renders mortal things like divine things in continuity, it is certainly a divine gift. Since divine things are beautiful, ugly things are their opposite, but beautiful things are like divine things and have an affinity with them. Therefore, procreation, a divine function, is easy and natural to perform with a beautiful object, but the reverse with the opposite. That is why the urge to procreate is attracted to the beautiful and shuns the opposite.

What is the love of men, you ask? What purpose does it serve?[89] It is the desire for procreation with a beautiful object in order to make eternal life available to mortal things. This is the love of men living on earth; this is the goal of our love. For within the period itself that any single creature is said to be alive and to be the same, as from childhood to old age, although it is said to be the same, nevertheless it never really contains in itself the same things, but is always becoming new, as Plato says,[90] and losing the old, as with his hair, flesh, bones, blood, and the whole body completely. And this happens not only in the body, but also in the soul. Customs, habits, opinions, desires, pleasures, pains, and fears are continually changing, nor does any of these remain the same or even similar; certainly the original ones are destroyed, and new ones take their places. But what is even more remarkable is that, in the realm of knowledge too, not only does some disappear and some rise up, and we are not always the same with respect to knowledge; but almost the same thing happens to any one piece of knowledge. For meditation or reminiscence is a recovering, as it were, of lost knowledge. For forgetting seems to be a departing of knowledge. But meditation, by always providing a new memory in place of the departing one, preserves knowledge so that it seems to be the same. Certainly by this means are preserved whatever things are mutable in the soul or the body, not because they remain forever completely the same (for that is peculiar to divine things), but because whatever wastes away and departs leaves behind something new and like itself. Certainly by this remedy mortal things are rendered like immortal ones.

Therefore in both parts of the soul, both in that which belongs to cognition and in that by which the body is ruled, there is an innate love of procreation for preserving life eternally. The love which is in the latter part, the part designed to govern the body, causes us from the moment of our birth to take food and drink, so that from these nutrients humors may be generated to replace what continuously drains out of the body. By this regeneration the body is nourished and grows. When the body reaches maturity, that same love of procreation stimulates the semen and provokes the urge to procreate offspring, so that what is unable in itself to last forever, may last forever, perpetuated in offspring like itself.

Correspondingly the love of procreation which is assigned to the cognitive part of the soul causes the soul to desire truth as its proper food, by which, in its own way, it is nourished and grows. And if anything escapes the soul through forgetfulness, or lies inert through inactivity or neglect, by diligence in recall and meditation, the love of procreation regenerates it, so to speak, and thus it restores to the mind what had either perished through forgetfulness, or had grown inactive through laziness. Once the soul is mature, the love of procreation inspires it with a burning desire to teach and to write, so that by propagating its knowledge, either in writings or in the minds of students, the knowledge and truth of a teacher may remain among men eternally. And in this way, thanks to love, both the body and the soul of any man seem to be able to survive in human affairs forever after death.

Both kinds of love seek the beautiful. Certainly the love which rules and governs the body tries to feed its charge with foods as tasty, delicious, and beautiful as possible, and to procreate handsome offspring by a beautiful woman. Similarly, the love which pertains to the soul tries to imbue it with the most elegant and pleasing learning, and to spread knowledge like its own by writing in an elegant and beautiful style, and to reproduce it, by teaching, in some very beautiful soul, that is to say, which is pure, intelligent, and excellent. Certainly we cannot see the soul itself. And for this reason we cannot see its beauty. But we can see the body, which is the shadow and image of the soul. And so, judging by its image, we assume that in a beautiful body there is a beautiful soul. That is why we prefer to teach men who are handsome.

Chapter 12

On the two loves, and that the soul
is born endowed with truth

About the definition of love we have now said enough. But now let us explain what the distinction is, in Plato's dialogue on love, between the fertility of the soul and that of the body.

"*In all men,*"[91] he says, *the body is pregnant or fertile, and the soul is pregnant.*[92] The seeds of all of the body's own things are implanted in it from the beginning. Hence at appropriate intervals of time the teeth come through, hair appears, a beard develops, and the seeds of procreation begin to flow. If the body is fecund or fertile with seeds, the soul, which is more excellent than the body, is much more fertile, and it possesses the seeds of all of its own things from the beginning. Therefore the soul long ago was allotted the Reasons of the customs, arts, and disciplines, and from them, if the soul is properly attended to, it will bring its own progeny into the world at the proper time. That the soul possesses innate Reasons of all its own things we know from its desires, its seeking, its finding, its judging, and its comparing.

Who will deny that the soul immediately from a tender age desires the true, the good, the virtuous, and the useful? But no one desires things which are unknown to him. Therefore there are in the soul some notions of those things even before it desires them, through which, as Forms or Reasons of the things themselves, it judges them to be desirable.

The same thing is shown by the soul's seeking and finding. If in a crowd of men Socrates looks for Alcibiades, and if he is ever to find him, it is necessary that there be some picture of Alcibiades in Socrates' mind, in order that he may know what man he is looking for rather than the others, and in order that he may be able to distinguish Alcibiades, when he finds him, from the others in a group of many men. And so the soul would not look for those four things, and it would never find them, unless it had some notion of them, that is, of truth, goodness, virtue, and utility, through which it could seek them, with some chance of finding them, and when it found what it had been seeking, could recognize them and distinguish them from their opposites.

And we can prove it not only from desire, from seeking, and from finding, but also from judgment. For anyone who judges someone to be a friend or an enemy is not ignorant of what friendship or enmity is. Similarly by what means could we judge many things true or false, good or bad, as we are accustomed to do, every day, and judge them correctly, if truth and goodness were not in some way already known to us? Or again, how could so many people, even though untrained in these arts, so often rightly approve or disapprove works of architecture, music, painting, and the other arts, and also the inventions of philosophers, if some Form or Reason of those things were not given to them by nature?

The principle of comparison also shows us the same thing. For anyone who compares honey with wine and pronounces one sweeter than the other is not ignorant of what the sweet taste is. And anyone who compares Speusippus and Xenocrates[93] with Plato and decides that Xenocrates looks more like Plato than Speusippus does, must certainly know the appearance of Plato. In the same way, since we can judge correctly that among several good things, one is better than another, and since one thing seems better or worse than another by virtue of its greater or lesser participation in the Good, it is necessary for us not to be ignorant of the Good. Moreover, since we often judge very accurately which, among many different opinions of philosophers, or anyone else, is more like the truth and more probable, it must be that we do not lack some conception of truth, in order that we may not be ignorant of which opinions are more like it. On this account some men are said to have become very learned even in boyhood, others with no teacher at all, and many others from a few rudiments of knowledge shown to them by their teachers. This could never have happened, as we have said, except with Nature[94] helping a great deal. Socrates clearly proved this to the boys Phaedo, Theaetetus, and Meno;[95] and he showed them that boys can respond correctly in any subject if someone questions them properly, obviously because they are endowed by nature with the Reasons of all the arts and disciplines.

Chapter 13

In what way the light of truth is in the soul

But in what way Reasons of this kind exist in the soul seems to be ambiguous in Plato. If one reads the books which Plato wrote in his youth, the *Phaedrus*, *Meno*, and *Phaedo*,[96] one will perhaps think that they are painted on the substance of the soul, as it were, like pictures on a wall, a view which has been alluded to often above, both by me and by you. For Plato seems to imply this there.[97] But in the sixth book on the *Republic*[98] that divine man explains the whole thing, and he says that the light of the intellect for understanding all things is the same God himself, by whom all things are made. For he compares the sun and God to each other in this way: as the sun is to our eyes, so God is to our intellects. The sun creates our eyes and gives them the power of seeing, which would be useless and sunken in eternal darkness if the light of the sun were not there, painted with the colors and shapes of objects, in which light the eye sees the colors and shapes of objects. The eye does not see anything except light. However, it seems to see various objects, because the light which pours into it is charged with various shapes of external objects. The eye certainly can look at this light reflected in objects, but it cannot bear[99] to look at the light itself at its source.

In the same way[100] God creates the soul and gives it the intellect, which is the faculty of understanding. The intellect would be empty and dark unless the light of God were present to it, in which it sees the Reasons of all things. Thus the intellect understands by means of the light of God, and it actually knows only that divine light itself. However it seems to know different things because it perceives the divine light in the form of the various Ideas and Reasons of things. When anyone sees a man with his eyes, he creates an image of the man in his imagination and then ponders for a long time, trying to judge that image. Then he raises the eye of his intellect to look up to the Reason of Man which is present in the divine light. Then suddenly from the divine light a spark shines forth to his intellect and the true nature itself of Man is understood. And it happens in the same way with all other things. And so we understand all things through the light of God. But the pure light itself and its source we cannot see in this life. The whole fertility of the soul clearly consists in this: that in its inner being shines that eternal light of God charged with the Reasons and Ideas of all things; the soul can turn to this light whenever it wishes, through purity of life and intense concentration of desire, and when it has so turned, it shines with the sparks of the Ideas.

Chapter 14

Whence comes love for males, whence for females

Just as the human body is pregnant, according to Plato,[101] so the soul is pregnant, and both are stimulated to childbearing by the incitements of love. But some, either by nature or by education, are better fitted for progeny of the soul than of the body, and others, certainly the majority, the opposite. The former follow heavenly love, the latter, vulgar. For this reason the former naturally love males and certainly those already almost adult rather than women or boys,[102] since in them[103] sharpness of intellect flourishes more completely, which, on account of its more excellent beauty, is most suitable for receiving the learning which they[104] wish to procreate. The others the opposite,[105] motivated by the pleasure of sexual intercourse, and the achievement of corporeal reproduction. But since the reproductive drive of the soul, being without cognition, makes no distinction between the sexes,[106] nevertheless, it is naturally aroused for copulation whenever we judge any body to be beautiful; and it often happens that those who associate with males, in order to satisfy the demands of the genital part, copulate with them. Especially those at whose birth Venus was in a masculine sign and either in conjunction with Saturn, or in the house of Saturn, or in opposition to Saturn.[107] But it should have been noticed that the purpose of erections of the genital part is not the useless act of ejaculation, but the function of fertilizing and procreating; the part should have been redirected from males to females.

We think that it was by some error of this kind that that wicked crime arose which Plato in his *Laws*[108] roundly curses as a form of murder. Certainly a person who snatches away a man about to be born must be considered a murderer no less than one who takes from our midst a man already born. He who destroys a present life may be bolder, but he who begrudges light to the unborn and kills his own unborn sons is more cruel.

Chapter 15

Above the body is the soul;
above the soul, the Angel;
above the Angel, God[109]

So much for the twin fertility of the soul, and the twin loves. Next let us discuss the steps by which Diotima takes Socrates from the lowest things to the highest. She leads him back from the body to the soul, from the soul to the Angel, and from the Angel to God. That these four grades of things must exist in nature may be proved as follows:

Every body is moved by something else; it cannot move itself of its own nature, since it cannot do anything by itself. But on account of the presence of the soul, the body seems to move by itself, and on account of the soul it seems to be alive. And certainly when the soul is present, the body does move itself, in some sense, but when the soul is absent, the body is moved only by something else, being a thing which does not possess this ability of itself; but the soul properly possesses the power of moving itself. For the soul lends the power of self-motion to anything in which the soul is present. What the soul lends to other things by its own presence it must first itself possess, and much more than they do. The soul is therefore superior to bodies, inasmuch as what can move itself by virtue of its own essence must in that respect be superior to those things which achieve self-motion not of themselves, but only through the presence of others. When we say that the soul moves "by itself," we do not use the expression transitively, so to speak, as Aristotle claimed[110] it was meant by Plato, but absolutely, as when we say that God exists "by Himself," or that the sun shines "by itself," or that fire heats "by itself."[111] For it is not that one part of the soul moves, and another part is moved by it, but that the whole soul moves by itself, that is, of its own nature; that is, the soul can move from one subject to another in thought, and at various stages it performs the functions of nutrition, growth, and procreation.[112] This kind of temporal progression is appropriate to the soul by its own nature, because that which is superior to the soul[113] does not achieve its understanding of different things at different times as the soul does, but understands everything all at once, in one point of eternity. Therefore Plato was right[114] to locate in the soul the first motion and the first interval of time; from the soul both motion and time pass into bodies.

But since before motion there must be rest, for rest is more perfect than motion, there must be found above the changeable thinking of the soul some motionless intelligence which is intelligence in its entirety, and intelligence always completely actualized.[115] For the soul does not understand with its whole self or continuously, but only with a certain part of itself and at certain times, and it does not possess a sure power of understanding but only an ambiguous one. Therefore, in order that what is more perfect may take precedence over that which is less perfect, above the intellect of the soul, which is changeable, partial, intermittent, and doubtful, must be placed the Intellect of the Angel, which is motionless, complete, continuous, and absolutely certain; so that just as the soul, which is moved by itself, precedes the body, which is moved by something else, so the intellect, which is motionless in itself, precedes the soul, which is moved by itself. And just as the body is capable of self-motion only by virtue of the soul, and therefore not all bodies, but only those which have souls seem to move of their own accord, so the soul is always capable of understanding only by virtue of the intellect. For if intellect were present in the soul of its own nature, intellect would be found in all souls, even of beasts, like the power of self-moving. Therefore intellect does not belong to the soul of itself and from the beginning. Therefore a being which possesses intellect of itself and from the beginning must be superior to the soul. The Angel is this kind of being; it is superior to souls.

But above the Angelic Mind there must necessarily be that beginning of things and the highest Good, which Plato, in the *Parmenides*,[116] calls the One itself. Certainly above every multiplicity of a composite thing must be the one itself, simple by nature. For number is derived from one, and all compositeness is derived from simples. The Angelic[117] Mind, although it is motionless, is nevertheless not in itself, single, pure, and simple. For it understands itself. Here there seem to be these three things which are different from each other in some way: what understands, what is understood, and understanding. For its[118] reason is one thing insofar as it understands, another insofar as it is understood, and another insofar as it is understanding. Moreover, it has a potency of cognition which, before the act of cognition, is in itself completely unformed, and is given form in the act of cognition. Which potency, in the process of understanding, desires the light of truth and receives it, which it seems to have lacked before it understood. Moreover, it contains in itself the multiplicity of all the Ideas.

You see, then, how great and how varied are the multiplicity and compositeness in the Angel.[119] And so we are compelled to place the pure and simple One above it. But above the One, that is, God Himself, we cannot place anything because the true One is devoid of all multiplicity, of all compositeness. Which,[120] if it had anything above it, would necessarily derive from that. Therefore in deriving from that, it would in itself degenerate from that, as every effect does from its cause. And for this reason it would no longer be One and simple, but composed of at least two things: namely of what it has received from its cause, and of its own previous defectiveness. So the One itself, as Plato says and Dionysius the Areopagite confirms,[121] is above all things, and it is thought by both that the One itself is an excellent name for God.

The pre-eminence of which is also shown us in the principle that the highest cause must have the broadest effect and in the pre-eminence of its influence must extend itself to all things. The influence of the One does spread itself throughout the universe. For not only is the Angelic Mind one, and every soul and every body is one, but also formless Matter itself, or the absence of form,[122] is called *one* in a certain sense. For we speak of *one* silence, *one* darkness, and *one* death. But the influences of the Mind and the Soul[123] do not extend to it.[124] For the Mind confers organized shape and order. The Soul confers life and motion; but the formless first Matter of the world, the absence of form, is devoid of both shape and life. So the One itself is higher than the Mind and the Soul, since its influence is wider than theirs. For the same reason the Mind seems to be higher than the Soul, because life, the gift of the Soul, is not given to all bodies. The Mind, however, does give them all shape and order.

Chapter 16

What the relation is among God, the Angel, the Soul, and the Body[125]

Therefore, we ascend from the Body to the Soul, from this to the Angel, and from this to God. God is above eternity. The Angel is completely in eternity. Clearly its operation as well as its being remains stable. But stability is characteristic of eternity. The Soul is partly in eternity, partly in time, for its substance always remains the same, and without any change either of increase or decrease. But its operation, as we showed a little while ago, runs through intervals of time. The Body is entirely subject to time. For its substance is subject to change and all of its functions require the space of time.[126] Therefore, the One itself is above stability or motion, the Angel is in stability, the Soul is equally in stability and in motion, and the Body is only in motion. Again, the One remains above number, motion, and place; the Angel is placed in number, above motion and place; the Soul is in number and motion, but above place; the Body is subject to number, motion, and place. Although the One itself has no number, is not composed of parts, is not changed in any way from what it is, and is not enclosed in any place, the Angel certainly has a number of parts, or forms,[127] but it is free from motion and place. The Soul has multiplicity of parts and passions, and is subject to change, both in the process of thinking and in fluctuations of mood, but it is exempt from limits of place. The Body, however, is subject to all of these.

Chapter 17

What the relation is among the beauties of God,
the Angel, the Soul, and the Body

But the same relation as among these four also exists among their beauties.[128] Certainly the beauty of the Body consists in the composition of many parts; it is restricted in place, it is subject to time. The beauty of the Soul suffers changes of time, of course, and contains multiplicity of parts, but is free from limits of place. The beauty of the Angel has number alone; it is immune from the other two. But the Beauty of God suffers none of these.

The beauty of the Body you can obviously see. Do you want to see the beauty of the Soul also? Take away from corporeal beauty the weight of matter itself and the limitations of place; leave the rest. Now you have the beauty of the Soul. Do you want to see the beauty of the Angel as well? Take away, please, not only the spaces of place, but also the progression of time; keep the manifold composition; immediately you will find it. Do you want to see also the beauty of God? Take away, in addition, that manifold composition of Forms; leave utterly simple form; immediately you will have reached the beauty of God.

But what else will be left to me, after all, when those things[129] have been taken away? Do you think that beauty is anything but light? Moreover, the beauty of all bodies is that light of the sun which you see, stained with those three things: multiplicity of forms (for you see it painted with many shapes and colors), the space of place, and temporal change. Take away its base in matter, so that apart from place it retains the other two; the beauty of the Soul is exactly like this. Take away from this if you wish, temporal change; keep the rest; there remains a brilliant light, without place, without motion, but engraved with all the Reasons of all things. That is the Angel; that is the beauty of the Angel. Finally, take away that number of various Ideas; leave a single, simple, and pure light, a likeness of that light which remains within the circumference itself of the sun, and is not diffused through the air; now you comprehend in a measure the beauty of God, which excels other beauties at least as much as that light of the sun in itself, pure, single, and inviolate, surpasses the splendor of the sun dispersed through the cloudy air,[130] divided, stained, and obscured. Therefore the source of all beauty is God. Therefore the source of all love is God.

Moreover, the light of the sun in water is a kind of shadow compared to its brighter light in the air. Similarly, its brightness in the air is a shadow compared to its brilliance in fire; its brilliance in fire is a shadow compared to the light of the sun shining in the very sun itself. The same comparison exists among those four beauties of the Body, the Soul, the Angel, and God. God is certainly never so deceived as to love the shadow of His own beauty in the Angel and neglect His own true Beauty. Nor is the Angel so taken by the beauty of the Soul, which is its shadow, that it becomes preoccupied with its shadow and forsakes its own beauty. But our soul does. This is greatly to be lamented, for this is the origin of all our woe. Only our soul, I say, is so captivated by the charms of corporeal beauty that it neglects its own beauty, and forgetting itself, runs after the beauty of the body, which is a mere shadow of its own beauty.

Hence that tragic fate of Narcissus, which Orpheus records.[131] Hence the pitiable calamity of men. *Narcissus, who is obviously young,* that is, the soul of rash and inexperienced man. *Does not look at his own face,* that is, does not notice its own substance and character at all. *But admires the reflection of it in the water and tries to embrace that;* that is, the soul admires in the body, which is unstable and in flux, like water, a beauty which is the shadow of the soul itself. *He abandons his own beauty, but he never* reaches the reflection. That is, the soul, in pursuing the body, neglects itself, but finds no gratification in its use of the body. For it does not really desire the body itself; rather, seduced, like Narcissus, by corporeal beauty, which is an image of its own beauty, it desires its own beauty. And since it never notices the fact that, while it is desiring one thing, it is pursuing another, it never satisfies its desire. For this reason, *melted into tears, he is destroyed*; that is, when the soul is located outside itself, in this way, and has sunken into the body, it is racked by terrible passions and, stained by the filths of the body, it dies, as it were, since it now seems to be a body rather than a soul. It was undoubtedly in order that Socrates might avoid such a death that Diotima led him from the Body to the Soul, from this to the Angel, and from this back to God.

Chapter 18

How the soul is raised from the beauty
of the body to the beauty of God

Consider this, dear guests; imagine Diotima addressing Socrates thus.[132]

"No body is completely beautiful, O Socrates. For it is either attractive in this part and ugly in that, or attractive today, and at other times not, or is thought beautiful by one person and ugly by another.[133] Therefore the beauty of the body, contaminated by the contagion of ugliness, cannot be the pure, true, and first beauty. In addition no one ever supposes beauty itself to be ugly, just as one does not suppose wisdom to be foolish, but we do consider the arrangement of bodies sometimes beautiful and sometimes ugly. And at any one time different people have different opinions about it. Therefore the first and true beauty is not in bodies. Add the fact that many different bodies have the same family name, 'the beautiful.' Therefore there must be one common quality of beauty in many bodies, by virtue of which they are alike called 'beautiful.' But remember that just as this single quality is in another, namely matter, so it derives from another. For what cannot sustain itself can hardly derive from itself. Do you think it will derive from matter? Certainly not. For nothing ugly and imperfect can make itself beautiful and perfect. That which is one must derive from one. Therefore the single beauty of many bodies derives from some single incorporeal maker. The one maker of all things is God, who through the Angels and the Souls[134] every day renders all the Matter of the world beautiful. Therefore it must be concluded that that true Reason of beauty is to be found in God and in His ministers rather than in the Body of the world. To it you will easily ascend again, I think, O Socrates, by these steps.

"If nature had given you the eyes of a lynx, my Socrates, so that you could penetrate with your vision whatever confronted you, that outwardly handsome body of your Alcibiades would seem very ugly to you. How valuable is that which you love, my friend? It is only a surface, or rather a color, that captivates you, or rather it is only a certain reflection of lights, and an insubstantial shadow. Or a vain fantasy is deceiving you so that you love something that you are dreaming rather than something that you are seeing. But lest I seem to oppose you completely, let this Alcibiades of yours be admittedly handsome. But in what part is he handsome? Truly in all his parts except in his flat nose and his higher than normal eyebrows. These parts, however, in Phaedrus are attractive. But in him the thickness of the legs is displeasing. These things are attractive in Charmides, unless his thin neck offends you. Thus if you will observe all men individually you will praise none of them in every part. Whatever is right everywhere you will gather together; you will construct in yourself a whole figure from the observation of all, so that the absolute beauty of the human race, which is found distributed among many bodies, is collected in your soul by thinking of a single image. The beauty of any individual man, O Socrates, you will scorn if you compare it to that abstract concept of yours. You possess that concept not so much thanks to bodies as to your own soul. Therefore love that concept which your soul has created, and the soul itself, its creator, rather than that external beauty, which is defective and scattered.

"But what is it that I urge you to love in the soul? The beauty of the soul. The beauty of bodies is a light; the beauty of the soul is also a light. The light of the soul is truth, which is the only thing which your friend[135] Plato seems to ask of God in his prayers:

> Grant to me, O God, he says, *that my soul may become beautiful, and that those things which pertain to the body may not impair the beauty of the soul, and that I may think only the wise man rich.*[136]

In this prayer Plato says that the beauty of the soul consists in truth and wisdom, and that it is given to men by God. Truth, which is given to us by God single and uniform, through its various effects acquires the names of various virtues. Insofar as it deals with divine things, it is called Wisdom (which Plato asked of God above all else); insofar as it deals with natural things, it is called Knowledge; with human things, Prudence. Insofar as it makes men equal, it is called Justice; insofar as it makes them invincible, Courage; and tranquil, Temperance.[137]

"Among these, two kinds of virtues are included; I mean the moral virtues and the intellectual, which are superior to them.[138] The intellectual virtues are Wisdom, Knowledge, and Prudence; the moral virtues are Justice, Courage, and Temperance. The moral virtues are better known, because of their operations[139] and their public applications. The intellectual virtues are more mysterious, because of their hidden truth. However, anyone who is brought up on the moral virtues, since he is purer than other people, can easily ascend to the intellectual virtues. For this reason I urge you to consider first the beauty of the soul which is found in the moral virtues, so that you will understand that there is one principle in all of them, by virtue of which they are all alike called 'moral.'[140] That is, that there is a single truth of the pure life, which, through actions of Justice, Courage, and Temperance, leads us to true happiness. Therefore seek first this single truth of the moral virtues, the most beautiful light of the soul.

"But realize also that you can immediately rise above the moral virtues to the clearer truth of Wisdom, Knowledge, and Prudence,[141] if you will consider that these virtues are granted[142] to the soul brought up on the best moral virtues, and that in them is contained the highest form of moral life. Although you may think that the concepts of Wisdom, Knowledge, and Prudence all differ, remember that there is nevertheless a single light of truth in all of them, by virtue of which they are all alike called 'beautiful.' I advise you to love this light above all, as the highest beauty of the soul.

"But this single truth, embodied in many different virtues, cannot be the first truth of all, for, since it is distributed among many virtues, it is in something else. And whatever lies *in* another certainly derives *from* another. However, a single truth is not derived from a multitude of concepts. For what is one must derive from one. Therefore above the soul of man there must be some single wisdom which is not divided among various concepts, but is a single wisdom, from whose single truth the manifold truth of men derives.

"O Socrates, remember that that single light of the single wisdom is the beauty of the Angel, which you must honor above the beauty of the Soul.[143] As we have shown in the above, it[144] excels the beauty of bodies, because it is not bound by place or divided according to the parts of matter, and it is not corrupted. It also excels the beauty of the Soul, because it is completely eternal and does not move in temporal progression. But since the light of the Angel shines among the ranks of the innumerable Ideas,[145] and since above every multiplicity there must be a unity which is the origin of all number, it[146] must emanate from a single beginning of all things, which we call the One itself.

"Thus the perfectly simple light of the One itself is infinite beauty, because it is not soiled by the stains of Matter, as the beauty of the Body is, or changed by temporal progression, as the beauty of the Soul is, or dissipated in multiplicity, as the beauty of the Angel is. But any quality which is free from extraneous addition is called infinite by the natural philosophers.[147] If heat exists by itself, unimpeded by cold or moisture, and not burdened by the weight of matter, it is called infinite heat, because its force is free and is not confined by any limitations of addition. Similarly, light which is free from any body is infinite, for it shines of its own nature, without measure or limit, when it is not limited by anything else. Thus the light and beauty of God, which is utterly pure and free of all other things, may be called without the slightest question, infinite beauty. But infinite beauty also requires immense love. Therefore I beg you, O Socrates, to love other things with a certain moderation and limit, but to love God with an infinite love, and let there be no moderation in divine love."[148]

This is what Diotima said to Socrates.[149]

Chapter 19

How God is to be loved

But we, my distinguished friends, shall love God not only without moderation, as Diotima is imagined as commanding, but God alone. For the Angelic Mind is to God as the vision of our eyes is to the sun. The eye desires not only light above all else, but light alone. If we do love bodies, souls, or angels, we shall not really be loving these things, but God in them. In loving bodies we shall really be loving the shadow of God; in souls, the likeness of God; in angels, the image of God. Thus in this life we shall love God in all things so that in the next we may love all things in God. For living in this way we shall proceed to the point where we shall see both God and all things in God, and love both Him, and all things which are in Him. And anyone who surrenders himself to God with love in this life will recover himself in God in the next life. Such a man will certainly return to his own Idea, the Idea by which he was created. There any defect in him will be corrected again; he will be united with his Idea forever. For the true man and the Idea of a man are the same. For this reason as long as we are in this life, separated from God, none of us is a true man, for we are separated from our own Idea or Form. To it, divine love and piety will lead us.[150] Even though we may be dismembered and mutilated here, then,[151] joined by love to our own Idea, we shall become whole men, so that we shall seem to have first worshipped God in things, in order later to worship things in God, and to worship things in God for this reason, in order to recover ourselves in Him above all, and in loving God we shall seem to have loved ourselves.

Notes

1. That is, on the speech of Socrates, who is the sixth speaker in Plato's *Symposium*.
2. Plato *Apology* 21a. See also Diogenes Laertius *Lives of the Philosophers* 2.5.37.
3. Ficino has compiled this list of the teachers of Socrates from two sources: Aspasia and Connus are mentioned in Plato *Menexenus* 236a. Anaxagoras, Damon, and Archelaus are mentioned in Diogenes Laertius *Lives of the Philosophers* 2.5.19. Anaxagoras (c. 500–430 B.C.), the author of *Peri Phuseos*, was condemned to death for atheism but was saved by Pericles. Damon, a sophist, was one of Pericles' teachers. Archelaus was a pupil of Anaxagoras. Prodicus of Chios was a sophist and an ambassador to Athens, where he lectured on literary style. Aspasia (c. 514–430 B.C.) was the mistress of Pericles and a teacher of rhetoric. Connus was a music-teacher; he is mentioned in the *Euthydemus* 272c and 295d.
4. Plato *Symposium* 201d, 212b; see also *Phaedrus* 244b, *Lysis* 204c, and *Theages* 128b.
5. By "these feasts" Ficino means banquets such as the one which he is reporting. In modern parlance, he is saying that he does not welcome to his circle people "whose minds are in the gutter and whose only interests are alcohol and sex."
6. That is, to chastity and wisdom, as spelled out in the following two phrases.
7. Plato *Ion* 533d.
8. The four elements were thought to be arranged in layers: earth, water, air, and fire; thus Fire is the "upper" region, above the air. See chap. 3 below.
9. Plato *Symposium* 202b–203a; *Phaedrus* 245c–246a; *Philebus* 16c; *Laws* 4.

713d–5, 729c and 10.906a; *Epinomis* 984c. Although Ficino here cites his sources as works of Plato, the material on daemons in this and the following chapter actually comes largely from Chalcidius *Commentary on the Timaeus* 26–136. The other major works on daemons which Ficino knew and may have used here are: Jamblichus *De mysteriis* (Ficino, *Opera*, pp. 1876–882), Proclus *Commentary on I Alcibiades*, and Apuleius *De deo Socratis*. See Ficino's abstract of the *Commentary on I Alcibiades* in *Opera*, pp. 1908–928. There is an abstract of Proclus's *Commentary on I Alcibiades* in Proclus's own *Platonic Theology* 7.42–45.

10. The sense is that each individual body is composed not of one element only but of a mixture of all four.

11. Plato *Laws* 886a.

12. Supplied from the Italian translation; the Latin says merely, "The soul of the whole."

13. Plato *Timaeus* 36c–39b; cf. *Phaedrus* 247a, c.

14. Ficino's phrase here is *octo caeli*. As Pico explains in the *Commento* 1.2, this means the spheres of the seven planets plus the eighth sphere containing the fixed stars. This conventional allusion to the spheres Ficino seems to confuse, later in this chapter, by using the phrase *spherarum et siderum*, as if the stars were something apart from the spheres. He does not mean to separate them, however; he is simply trying to be inclusive.

15. Supplied from the Italian translation; the Latin says merely, "it must possess no less reason than earth."

16. By "The Platonists," Ficino means Plato (*Timaeus* 38e–40c) and Plotinus (*Enneads* 3.5.6).

17. For Marcel's *regione* read *regionem*.

18. The term *passible* means "subject to passion." For definitions which Ficino would have known, see *Aquinas Lexicon* 3.577, and Altenstaig (*passio et passibilitas*).

19. E.g., Proclus *Commentary on I Alcibiades* (Ficino, *Opera*, p. 1909).

20. Pseudo-Dionysius *Celestial Hierarchy* 9.2.257d–3, 261a.

21. Plato *Laws* 10.896c–899d.

22. The concept of the divine gifts has a twofold background: Proclus *Elements of Theology* 18 and 56–58, and Aquinas *ST.* 1–2. Q.68. Art.4. Ficino converts Aquinas's seven gifts of the Holy Spirit to gifts of the seven planets. The phrase "inferior gods" is Plato's term (in the *Timaeus*) for the souls of the spheres discussed in the previous chapter. The hierarchy of being described here is based on Chalcidius's *Commentary on the Timaeus* and Macrobius's *In Somnium Scipionis*.

23. Ficino means "human souls"; this paragraph interrupts the discussion of the cosmic sequence begun in the previous paragraph and resumed in the following paragraph.

24. The major source of this idea is Proclus *Elements of Theology* Prop. 209. See translation by E. R. Dodds (Oxford, 1963), p. 183 and especially his Appendix II: "The Astral Body in Neo-platonism," pp. 313–21. Some sixteenth-century discussions of the idea are reviewed in D. P. Walker, "The Astral Body in Renaissance Medicine," *JWCI* 21 (1958): 119–33. The particulars of the descent of the soul in this passage are based on Macrobius's *In Somnium Scipionis* 12.

25. Eve Adler has pointed out to me that Ficino's terminology in describing the soul's garment as *crassius* than the soul but *subtilius* than the body is exactly the ter-

minology used by Lucretius in *De rerum natura* 3.195 (*subtilibus*) and 4.1244 (*crassius*). All of Ficino's other quotations from Lucretius are concentrated in three chapters of the last section of the *Commentary* (see VII.5, 6, 11).

26. "To us" supplied on the authority of the Italian translation, but see also the first sentence of the previous paragraph.

27. The spelling out of the various classes of daemons as agents of the planets Ficino probably learned from Pletho, whose source was probably Proclus *Elements of Theology*, ed. E. R. Dodds, 2d ed. (Oxford, 1963), Prop. 40, 44.

28. These are Ficino's transliterations.

29. Plato *Phaedrus* 252c–253c.

30. That is, Ficino is giving as his example of the process of the descent only the case of souls born under Jupiter; by "the other three" Ficino presumably means those referred to in the previous paragraph: "Apollo, Mars and Juno (that is, Venus)."

31. Translation based on Italian version.

32. For Marcel's *fuit* read *fuerit*.

33. Ficino's authority for the idea that the soul creates the body is Proclus *Elements of Theology* 129.

34. That is, if the physical seed which the soul finds on earth is not well-disposed to receive the imprint of a Jovian soul, the image which the soul imprints on that seed will not be as perfect a reproduction of the soul's original pattern as that which the soul achieved in shaping its astral body.

35. That is, to its original pattern and to its first "printing" of the pattern in the astral body. Ficino's use of the term "ideas" is probably a case of deliberate ambiguity.

36. That is, born under the same astrological sign.

37. That is, at the beginning of the previous paragraph; Ficino is returning to his paradigm case of two souls born under the planet Jupiter.

38. The inversion of chronological order is Ficino's; he corrects the order in the Italian translation.

39. This idea originates in Aristotle's *De partibus animalium* 3.c.3.665.a.12, 17 and 3.c.4.666.b.14, etc. Ficino's association of the concept of spirit with the theory of love probably owes something to Avicenna's *Canon* (see *Canon* 3. Fen.1. Tr.4. cap.23). See also D. P. Walker, "Ficino's Spiritus and Music," *Annales Musicologiques* 1 (1953): 131–51. It should be pointed out that the idea was also one of the favorite esoteric doctrines of the *dolce stil nuovo* generation. Dante uses it repeatedly (in the *Vita Nuova* and elsewhere), and Cavalcanti is notorious for his use of it (e.g., Rime 8, 9, 13, 15, 16, and 23) especially in Sonnet 28, in which the word *spirit* (or a derivative) occurs in every line at least once and often twice. Ficino returns to the idea in his sections on physical love (VII), below. The humoral psychology which constitutes the basis of Ficino's discussion of physical love is the common property of a number of medical authorities surveyed by John L. Lowes in "The Loveres Maladye of Hereos," *MP* 11 (1913–14): 491–546.

40. That is, from the heart.

41. That is, soul and spirit are found in conjunction with each other in all parts of the body.

42. This sentence is written in the esoteric style. Its meaning is as follows: while looking at the images of external bodies which are reflected in the spirit, the soul creates images like them in its faculty of imagination.

43. See Robert Klein, "L'imagination comme vêtement de l'âme chez Marsile Ficin," *Revue de métaphysique et de morale* 61 (1956) : 18–39.

44. That is, in the imagination.

45. The pronoun "these" refers to the images stored in the memory. The "eye of the soul" is the intellect (*mens*), the repository of the innate ideas. In the Italian version Ficino translates the phrase *animi acies* as "the eye of the intellect."

46. Plato *Symposium* 203b–c.

47. See above, II.7. The allegorization given here of the Porus and Penia episode is based on Plotinus *Enneads* 2.5.2–10 and 5.8.13.

48. By "they" Ficino means the Platonists.

49. "This" refers to the Angelic Mind; "poverty" refers to its previous lack of light.

50. The Latin word is *rationes* (Reasons); Ficino translates it in Italian "causes." He should logically have used the term "Ideas" because he is here speaking of the Angelic Mind, and he has previously stated (V.4) that he means to use different terms for the universals, at different levels, as follows:

> Angelic Mind: Ideas
> World Soul: Reasons (i.e., Concepts)
> World Body: Forms

51. That is, in the evolution of the soul the soul's first acquisition after existence is consciousness. The phrase "vigor of life" (for existence), like the phrase "ardent benevolence" (for love), below is an example of periphrasis.

52. That is, in the World Soul.

53. That is, in the World Body.

54. That is, this affection for the body. This relative clause, like the one at the end of the next paragraph, is probably a late addition to the text.

55. That is, which were infused in us by God from the beginning.

56. The ultimate source of this distinction is Aristotle's *Nicomachean Ethics* 1.3, but the distinction occurs also in Plotinus's *Enneads* 1.3.1, and in Aquinas *ST.* 1-2. Q.69.3. Ficino discusses the distinction at greater length in the *Commentary on the Philebus* and in the *De triplici vita*. I am indebted for these suggestions to Professor Kristeller.

57. For *ebetes* read *hebetes*.

58. In the Italian translation Ficino renders *venator* as "bird-catcher" (*uccellatore*). Throughout the following discussion the Italian versions of the metaphorical references to love as a "hunting," "snaring," "being trapped," "being caught" show that it is bird-snaring which he has in mind.

59. Plato *Symposium* 203c–e. This quotation Ficino has transcribed from his Latin translation of the *Symposium*, *Opera Platonis* (Lyons, 1590), p. 328a–c, but with a number of alterations.

60. This discussion (from here to p. 123, where the Porus and Penia allegory is resumed) is continued in VII.4, 5, 7–9 below.

61. I.e., committed suicide. The Italian translation says merely "killed himself" (*sé medesimo uccise*).

62. Rhazes *Liber divisionum* chap. 11 (*De amore*). See also p. 147, n.39 above, and the article by Lowes, "Maladye of Hereos," pp. 491–546.

63. The term "thus" in this discussion ought to mean "melancholy," since that is the

only humor which has been discussed in the previous paragraph. But the term "thus" is used instead because in the ensuing discussion Ficino suddenly adds cholerics to the class of people who are especially susceptible to physical love.

64. Ficino is in error in referring to the *Nicomachean Ethics* here; the passage is actually in the *Problemata* (30.1.953a); he refers to it again below; see note 67.

65. That is, both cholerics and melancholics.

66. Ficino here uses the term *beauty* (*pulchritudo*) to mean visual attractiveness, in contradistinction to the attractiveness of sounds. Pico agrees with this view of beauty and criticizes Ficino for saying, elsewhere (see V.2), that beauty is aural as well as visual.

67. Aristotle *Problemata* 30.1.953a.

68. Sappho (c. 625–580 B.C.). Ficino may have in mind *Frag.* 46.

69. Servius says that Vergil remained chaste all of his life. See *Commentary on the Aeneid*, ed. Georgius Thilo (Leipzig, 1878), 1 : 1.

70. The last part of this sentence is a quotation from Propertius *Elegies* 2.12, as Ficino points out in a note in the Oxford manuscript (fol.34ᵛ). His reason for bringing in the Propertius quotation was apparently that he wanted to have something to say about Diotima's adjective *humble* as applied to love, and he thought that Propertius's *levissimis curis*, which he renders in Italian *vilissime cure* ("humblest worries"), might do. The rest of the paragraph has nothing to do with the adjective *humble*.

71. The force of the *also* is that there are two freedoms involved; the soul has been freed from its slavery to the body and can now also be freed from its slavery to the beloved.

72. The Italian translation shows that what Ficino has in mind here is the nervous swinging of arms or legs.

73. Ficino translates *procacitas* as "lascivious lightness."

74. Plato's phrase *en hodois*, i.e., "on roadsides," goes with "on doorsteps," indicating typical places where beggars are found asleep; Ficino takes the phrase out of context and interprets it as meaning "en route," or "on the way" to something.

75. Notice that in both of these lists Ficino introduces terms which are not present in the text quoted from Diotima in chap. 9; the quoted traits are those in italics.

76. This sentence corresponds to the sentence above beginning "*Naked*, because. . . ."

77. Plato *Protagoras* 309a. In Plato the statement is a sarcastic allusion to Socrates' homosexuality; he is said to have been hunting, not Alcibiades' "virtuous character," but his "ripeness" (*hora*).

78. Ficino here returns to the detailed explanation of the speech of Diotima, begun on p. 120 above.

79. Plato *Sophist* 231d–e.

80. Vergil *Eclogues* 2.65.

81. That is, magic. For a full discussion of Ficino's theory of magic see D. P. Walker, *Spiritual and Demonic Magic from Ficino to Campanella* (London, 1958).

82. That is, some of the ancients are said to have been closely related to daemons, either as friends. . . .

83. On Zoroaster (dates unknown), presumed author of the *Chaldaic Oracles*, see Karl Dannenfeldt, "The Pseudo-Zoroastrian Oracles in the Renaissance," *SRen* 4 (1957) : 7–30. Apollonius Tyaneus (fl. 50 A.D.) was an eclectic philosopher who was regarded in

the early Middle Ages as Anti-Christ. Porphyry (c. 232–c. 304) was a philosopher and editor of Plotinus. Porphyry's "De divinis atque daemonibus" (*De abstinentia*, Book 2) was translated by Ficino and included in his Platonic anthology (fols. 39ᵛ–41ᵛ in the Venice, 1516 edition).

84. In the Italian, Ficino supplies the missing step between this and the previous sentences by inserting a statement that the old figure is replaced by a new one.

85. The word *mens* ordinarily means specifically the faculty of the intellect, but I translate it *mind* here, since Ficino has just said that the form is deposited in the *memory* (not the intellect). Ficino himself translates *mente* here as *soul*.

86. Vergil *Aeneid* 5.743 and 8.542.

87. As the transitional phrase shows, this passage on hatred in love is an after-thought; Diotima does not say anything about hatred. The topic is treated by Aquinas in *ST*. 1–2. Q.29.2, 3; but the force of the paragraph derives from the fact that Ficino appears to be speaking personally about his feelings for Giovanni Cavalcanti.

88. Ficino italicizes these adjectives as if this were another quotation from the *Symposium*, but it is not.

89. This sentence is reported but omitted in Marcel's translation (p. 224). It is present in the Italian and in most of the Latin texts, but not in the Vatican manuscript.

90. Plato *Symposium* 207d–208b.

91. In Marcel's text *homines* should read *hominum*.

92. Plato *Symposium* 206c. This quotation is a late addition to a discussion which is based mainly on the *Meno* and the *Theatetus*, with possible attention to Aquinas *ST*. 1–2. Q.63 and 27.2.

93. Speusippus and Xenocrates were both students and disciples of Plato, but Speusippus was Plato's nephew and should therefore have looked more like him.

94. In the Italian translation Nature is capitalized here; elsewhere, as in the Latin, it is not.

95. Plato *Phaedo* 91c–92a; *Theaetetus* 157c–186e; *Meno* 75b–76c, 82b–84a.

96. Plato *Phaedrus* 253; *Meno* 85c–86a; *Phaedo* 72e.

97. That is, in his early dialogues.

98. Plato *Republic* 6.508e–509b. A variation on this idea is also stated in Plotinus *Enneads* 5.9.2.

99. For Marcel's *substinet* read *sustinet*.

100. That is, just as the sun both creates and assists the eyes.

101. *Symposium* 206c.

102. The Italian translation shows the way in which this sentence is to be understood: "The former love men rather than women and adolescents rather than boys."

103. That is, in adolescent males. The deliberate vagueness of the pronouns and the stringing together of dependent clauses in this passage are both typical devices of the esoteric style.

104. That is, the heavenly lovers.

105. That is, vulgar lovers, on the other hand, prefer women and boys.

106. In the Italian version Ficino clarifies the logic here: "But because the reproductive drive which is in the soul lacks cognition, it makes no distinction between sex and sex." For *sexum* (Marcel, p. 229) read *sexium*.

107. This sentence was added by Ficino in the Oxford manuscript (fol. 64); it is included in the Italian translation.

108. Plato *Laws* 1.636b–d, 8.836b–838c, 841d; see also *Republic* 3.403b; 6.508e–509d; and *Phaedrus* 256b. The subject of this paragraph, abortion, is irrelevant to the rest of the chapter.

109. The argument used in this chapter is based primarily on Proclus *Elements of Theology* 20 and 189. The material regarding the hypostases in this and the following chapter derives partly from Proclus *Elements of Theology* 1–96 and partly from Plotinus *Enneads* 5.1–5. By the term *Angel* Ficino means the Angelic Mind. In referring to body and soul here Ficino appears to be speaking of parts of individual human beings, but in referring to the Angel he is speaking of a part of the cosmos. I have indicated this shift by the capitalization of *Angel*.

110. Aristotle *De anima* 1.2.404b.

111. Supplied on the authority of the Italian translation.

112. The point here is brought out only in the Italian, where the cognate verbs "discorra" and "trascorra" show the contrast which Ficino has in mind. What he means to point out is that the soul moves because it is able to *shift* both from subject to subject in thought and from function to function in managing the body.

113. That is, the Angelic Mind.

114. Plato *Timaeus* 37d–38c.

115. The literal phrase is *in act*, that is, the scholastic term for *actuality* as opposed to *potentiality*. Ficino means that the Angelic Mind has no non-intellectual functions such as the soul has and is *permanently* actualized, as opposed to merely occasionally. This is explained in the following sentence.

116. Plato *Parmenides* 137c, d.

117. Supplied on the authority of the Italian translation.

118. This pronoun "its" (and "it") in this and the following three sentences refers to the Angelic Mind; this is another example of intended esotericism.

119. As the verb shows, Ficino means: how great is the multiplicity and how varied is the compositeness.

120. That is, the One.

121. Plato *Parmenides* 140c; Pseudo-Dionysius *De div. nom.* 13.184.

122. Literally "the privation of things"; my translation is based on Ficino's Italian translation. The phrase is joined to the phrase "formless matter" by *and* in two places here; but the verb in both places is singular, and we are intended to regard the "privation" phrase as an appositive. Joining appositives by *and* meaning *or* is a normal practice in Ficino.

123. Here and hereafter to the end of the chapter *Mind* refers to the Angelic Mind and *Soul* to the World Soul; Ficino is discussing the cosmos as described by Plotinus, with the One at the center and emanating first to the Angelic Mind, then to the World Soul, and then to the World Body.

124. That is, to pure Matter.

125. Throughout this chapter, the term *Angel* refers to the Angelic Mind, the term *Soul* refers to the World Soul, and the term *Body* refers to the World Body.

126. Ficino translates this phrase "temporal space."

127. This is probably a reference to the Ideas contained in the Angelic Mind.

128. This chapter is a paraphrase of Plotinus *Enneads* 5.8. As in the previous chapter, *Angel* refers to the Angelic Mind and *Soul* to the World Soul throughout.

129. That is, space, time, and multiplicity; the Italian version says "those three things."

130. For Marcel's *aera* read *aerem*.

131. Orpheus *Frag.* 315 (Abel, pp. 271–72; cited from this passage in Ficino only). The same story is told by Plotinus *Enneads* 1.6.8. See also Ovid *Metamorphoses* 3.339–510. Ficino's paragraph is a phrase-by-phrase explication of the text of Orpheus, which he italicizes, as here.

132. This chapter is mainly an amplification of Plotinus *Enneads* 1.6. The section on the moral and intellectual virtues draws on Aquinas *ST.* 1–2. Q.57–58. The whole chapter after this sentence is represented as a single speech by Diotima.

133. Cf. Plato *Symposium* 211a.

134. That is, through the Angelic Mind and the World Soul, the intermediate hypostases between God and Matter; it is these two hypostases which are referred to as God's "ministers" in the next sentence.

135. The phrase "your friend" is a late addition, found in the Oxford manuscript (fol. 69^v) and in some others.

136. Plato *Phaedrus* 279b–c.

137. In the *Symposium*, the four classical virtues are attributed to the god of love in the speech of Agathon (196c–d). Ficino states his own series in an extended zeugma which my translation partly obscures.

138. The distinction between moral and intellectual virtues is present in Aristotle's *Nicomachean Ethics* 6, but Ficino's source is probably Aquinas *ST.* 1–2. Q.57–58. For Ficino's changing view of the relative importance of the two, see Kristeller's "A Thomist Critique of Marsilio Ficino's Theory of Will and Intellect," in *Harry A. Wolfson Jubilee Volume*, English Section (Jerusalem, 1965), 2 : 463–94.

139. This is probably a technical term from Aquinas. For "operations" see *ST.* 1–2. Q.60.2. For "operatio civilis" see *Contra Gentiles* 3.63.

140. The Latin says "honesti"; the Italian translation corrects this to "belli," which is required by the analogue with the intellectual virtues in the next paragraph.

141. That is, to the truth of the intellectual virtues.

142. This doctrine of the infused virtues is from Aquinas *ST.* 1–2. Q.68.

143. As usual, the word *Soul* here means *World Soul* and *Angel* means *Angelic Mind*.

144. That is, the beauty of the Angelic Mind.

145. The Italian adds "which are in the Angelic Mind."

146. That is, the light of the Angelic Mind.

147. Aristotle *Physics* 3.5–6.

148. That is, in your love for God.

149. The Vatican manuscript places this sentence at the end of chapter 18. Both the printed editions and the Italian version place it at the beginning of chapter 19.

150. That is, piety and love of God will lead us back to our Idea.

151. Ficino deliberately mixes place and time; instead of contrasting *here* with *there* or *now* with *then*, he contrasts *here* with *then*.

Speech VII

Chapter 1

Conclusion of the aforesaid and the opinion of Guido Cavalcanti, the Philosopher

FINALLY, CRISTOFORO MARSUPPINI,[1] a man who is very thoughtful, as he was about to take the part of Alcibiades, turns to me with these words:[2]

Marsilio, I certainly congratulate very much the family of your Giovanni, which has produced, among many knights famous for both learning and deeds, Guido,[3] the philosopher, who, having deserved well of his country, and surpassing everyone of his era in the subtleties of logic, and having imitated this Socratic love[4] in conduct as well as in poetry, touched briefly upon everything you have said.[5]

For Phaedrus discussed the origin of love, emanating from the viscera of Chaos. Pausanias divided love, once born, into two kinds, namely heavenly and vulgar. Eryximachus revealed its breadth when he showed that, divided into two kinds, it is found in all things. Aristophanes then explained what the presence of this so powerful god does in everything, showing that through him men who were split are put back together. Agathon discussed how great is love's influence and power, when he argued that only by it do men become blessed. Finally, Socrates, taught by Diotima, briefly explained what love is; what its nature is;[6] whence it arose, how many parts it has, what its purpose is, and what it is worth.

All of these things Guido Cavalcanti, the philosopher, seems to have put very artfully into his verses.[7] Just as a mirror, struck in a certain way by a ray of the sun, shines back, and by that reflection of the splendor sets on fire a piece of wool placed next to it, so he thinks that the part of the soul which he calls the dark fancy and the memory (like the mirror) is struck by a certain image (like a ray) of beauty itself (taking the place of the sun), taken in through the eyes; in such a way that from that it makes another image for itself[8] (a splendor, as it were, of the first image) by which the force of desire (like the wool) is kindled and loves. He adds that this first love, kindled in the appetite of sense, is created by the form of the body seen through the eyes, but that this form itself is not impressed on the fancy in the same way in which it exists in the matter of the body, but without matter; yet in such a way that it is the image of a certain particular man placed in a definite place and time.

Then, he says, there immediately appears in the intellect another species of this image, which no longer seems to be a likeness of one particular human body, as it was in the fancy, but a common Reason or definition of the whole human race equally. And so, just as from the fancy's image, taken from the body, there arises in the appetite of sense, devoted to the body, a love inclined toward the senses, so from the intellect's universal species or Reason, which is very remote from the body, there arises in the will another love which is very foreign to commerce with the body.

The former he placed in lust, the latter in contemplation. The former he thinks revolves around the particular beauty of a single body, the latter around the universal beauty of the whole human race. He says that these two loves certainly oppose each other in man, and that the former drives him down to the bestial or voluptuous life, whereas the latter raises him up to the angelic or contemplative life. The latter he says is free from perturbation and is found in few people; the former is troubled by many passions, and seizes most people. For this reason he dismisses the latter in a few words, and is more prolix in explaining the passions of the other.

But since he explains very clearly the same things which you also have discussed above, I did not think it necessary to review them at present. But let it suffice to have learned that this philosopher included in the procreation of love a certain formlessness of Chaos, such as you have posited above, when he said that the dark fancy is illuminated, and that

from the mixture of that darkness and this light love takes its origin.
Moreover, who does not see in his words that double love, namely,
heavenly and vulgar? But he also places the first origin of that in the
beauty of divine things, the second in the beauty of bodies, for by *sun* he
means the light of God; by *ray*,[9] he means the beauty of bodies. Finally,
he says that its end corresponds to its beginning, so long as the incite-
ment of love carries some people to the beauty of the body and others to
the beauty of God.

Chapter 2

Socrates was the true lover and like Cupid

So much for love. Let us come to Alcibiades and Socrates. After the
guests had sufficiently praised the god of lovers, it remained for the
legitimate worshippers of this god to be praised. It is asserted by all that
Socrates loved the most legitimately of all. Although he served in the
camp of Cupid all of his life, openly and completely without any dissimulation, he was never accused by anyone of having loved anyone less
than virtuously. His austerity of life and frequent criticism of the vices of
others made many powerful men hostile to him (as truth often does),
especially Anytus, Meletus, and Lyco,[10] the most powerful citizens in
the state, and Thrasymachus, Polus, and Callias, the orators.[11] In addition he had Aristophanes, the comic poet, as a very biting critic. But
neither those citizens, in the accusation by which they brought Socrates
to trial, charged him with immoral loves; nor did the orators, his
enemies, hold against Socrates any such thing. Nor did Aristophanes,
the comic poet, although he brings together in his Dionysiacs[12] many
other ridiculous and absurd charges against Socrates. Now, do you
think that if he had polluted himself with a stain so filthy, or rather, if
he had not been completely above suspicion of this charge, he would
have escaped the venomous tongues of such detractors?

Did you notice, gentlemen, in the above, that when Plato pictures
love itself, he paints the whole likeness of Socrates, as if true love and
Socrates were exactly alike, and Socrates, therefore, were the true and
legitimate lover above all other? Consider now; recall to your soul that
picture of love.[13] You will see in it Socrates pictured. Put the person of
Socrates before your eyes. You will see him *thin*, *dry*, and *squalid*, that is,

a man melancholy by nature, it is said, and hairy, thin from fasting, and filthy from neglect. In addition, *naked*, that is, covered with a simple and old cloak. *Walking without shoes*; Phaedrus, in Plato,[14] describes Socrates as always accustomed to walk in that way.

Humble and low-flying. Socrates' gaze was always fixed on the ground, as Phaedo says. Moreover, he frequented humble places, for he used to be seen in the shops of Simon the tanner, or the stonecutters.[15] He used rustic and rude words, which Callicles criticizes him for in the *Gorgias*.[16] In addition, he was so gentle that even when challenged by many insults, often even beaten, in spirit he was not even ruffled, it is said.[17]

Without a home. When asked where he was from, Socrates said, "From the world. For there is my country where the Good is."[18] But not for him were Lares of his own or a soft bed, or expensive furniture.

Sleeping on doorsteps, on the road, under the sky. As applied to our Socrates, these signify his open breast and his heart lying open to all. Also that he took delight in sight and hearing, which are the doors of the soul; also that he walked confident and fearless, and also that he would sleep anywhere, if necessary, wrapped in his cloak.

Always needy. Who does not know that Socrates was the son of a stone-cutter and a midwife,[19] that even into old age he made his living with his own hands, by cutting stones, and that he never had enough to feed himself and his sons? The poverty of his mind he avowed everywhere, questioning everyone, saying that he himself knew nothing.[20]

Manly. For he was a man of constant soul and unshakable conviction, who loftily spurned even Archelaus of Macedonia and Scopus of Cranon, and Eurylochus of Larissa when he did not accept the money sent by them, nor was he himself willing to go to them.[21]

Bold and high-spirited. How great his courage was in battle Alcibiades explains at length in the *Symposium*.[22] When Socrates won the battle of Potidaea, he is said to have credited Alcibiades with the victory voluntarily.

Vehement. That is, as Zopyrus the physiognomist had rightly judged, Socrates was very excitable.[23] For often in speaking he used to wave his hands and pull at his hair, such was the vehemence of his speech.

Eloquent. When he was debating,[24] almost equal arguments on both sides presented themselves to him. Although he used unrefined words, as Alcibiades says in the *Symposium*,[25] he nevertheless moved the souls of his hearers more than Themistocles, and Pericles, and all the other orators did.

He ambushes the beautiful and the good. Alcibiades said that Socrates was always ambushing him.[26] That is, Socrates was taken prisoner by his love for those who seemed endowed with a virtuous character, and by means of his arguments he took them prisoner in turn for the study of philosophy.[27]

A crafty and keen-scented hunter. That Socrates used to hunt for the divine Beauty in the beauty of bodies has been said enough above, and Plato asserts in the *Protagoras.*[28]

A trapper. In many different ways, as the dialogues of Plato show, Socrates refuted the sophists, encouraged the young, and taught virtuous men.

Zealous of prudence. He was of such great prudence and so accurate in prophecy that anyone who did anything against his advice was lost, as is told by Plato in the *Theages.*[29]

Philosophizing all his life. In his own defense before the judges he told the judges that if they spared him from death on condition that he never afterwards philosophize, he preferred to die rather than give up philosophizing.[30]

Sorcerer, enchanter, magician, and sophist. Certainly Alcibiades said that he was soothed more by the words of Socrates than by the melody of the excellent musicians Marsyas and Olympius.[31] That a daemon was familiar to him[32] both his accusers and his friends testify. Aristophanes, the comic poet, called Socrates a Sophist also,[33] and his accusers did also. Obviously because he had an equal gift of persuading or dissuading.

Midway between wisdom and ignorance. "Although all men are ignorant," said Socrates, "I differ from the rest in this, that I am not ignorant of my ignorance, whereas the others are utterly ignorant of theirs."[34] Thus he was midway between wisdom and ignorance, since, although he did not know things themselves, at least he knew his own ignorance.

It was for these reasons that Alcibiades thought that after praising love itself,[35] they should praise Socrates, since he was the most like love and for that reason the truest lover, so that we would understand that in praising Socrates all who love in the same way have been praised. What the praises of Socrates are, you have heard here, and they lie clearly exposed in the words of Plato in the mouth of Alcibiades. How Socrates loved, anyone who remembers the teachings of Diotima can know. For Socrates loved in the way Diotima taught above.[36]

Chapter 3

On bestial love; that it is a kind of insanity

But perhaps someone may ask, "What good does this Socratic love do the human race? Why should it be celebrated with such great praises? What harm does its opposite do?" I shall tell you, beginning a few steps back.

In the *Phaedrus*,[37] our Plato defines madness as an alienation of the mind. But he teaches two kinds of alienation. One he thinks comes from human illnesses, and the other from God. The former he calls insanity, the latter, divine madness. In the sickness of insanity, a man is brought down below the species of man and in some degree is changed from a man into a beast. There are two kinds of insanity. One rises from a defect of the brain, the other from a defect of the heart. The brain often becomes too much occupied with burned bile, burned blood, or sometimes black bile. Hence men are sometimes rendered insane. Those who are troubled by burned bile, though provoked by no one, are violently enraged, scream loudly, attack those they meet, and kill themselves and others. Those who suffer from burned blood break out too much into uncontrolled laughter, make themselves conspicuous beyond common custom, promise marvels about themselves, and revel in song, and riot in dancing. Those who are oppressed by black bile lament[38] perpetually; they imagine dreams for themselves, which they fear in the present or dread in the future. And these three kinds of insanity certainly result from a defect of the brain. For when those humors are retained in the heart, they produce distress and anxiety, but not insanity; they cause insanity only when they oppress the head. Therefore these[39] are said to occur through a defect of the brain. We think that the madness by which those who are desperately in love are afflicted is, strictly speaking, caused by a disease of the heart, and that it is wrong to associate the most sacred name of love with these. But lest perhaps we seem to be too wise against the many,[40] for the sake of this discussion let us too use the name love for these.

Chapter 4

Vulgar love is a certain enchantment[41]

And now direct the attention of your ears and intellect to some things that must be said. In youth, the blood is *thin, clear, warm,* and *sweet.* For with increasing age, as the thinner parts of the blood are dissipated, the blood becomes thicker and on that account it becomes darker. Certainly that which is *thin* and rare is *clear* and transparent; but the opposite, the opposite. Why *warm* and *sweet?* Because life and the beginning of living, that is, procreation itself, consists in warmth and moisture, and semen, the first begetting of living things, is moist and *warm.* Such a nature flourishes in boyhood and youth. In later ages, it is necessarily changed, little by little, into the opposite qualities, dryness and cold. For this reason the blood in a young man is *thin, clear, warm,* and *sweet.* Because it is *thin* it seems *clear;* because it is young, it seems *warm* and moist; and because it is *warm* and moist, for this reason it seems *sweet.* For the *sweet* is in a mixture of the *warm* and the moist.

Why am I saying these things? Certainly in order that you may understand that the *spirits*[42] at this age are *thin* and *clear, warm* and *sweet.* For since these are generated from the purer blood by the heat of the heart, they are always the same in us as the humor of the blood. But, just as this vapor of the spirits is produced from the blood, so also it itself sends out rays like itself through the eyes, which are like glass windows. And also just as the heart of the world, the sun, from its circuit sends down light, and through the light sends down its own powers to lower things, so the heart of our body, through a certain perpetual motion of its own, stirring the blood nearest to it, spreads sparks of lights through all the parts certainly, but especially through the eyes. Certainly the spirit, since it is very light, flies out most to the highest parts of the body, and its light shines out more copiously through the eyes since they themselves are transparent and the most shining of all the parts.

But, that there is some light, though small, in the eyes and brain, many animals which see at night can attest. Their eyes glow in the dark. And also, if anyone has pressed the corner of his eye in some certain way with his finger and twisted it, he seems to see a certain luminous circle inside himself.[43] And it is said that the deified Augustus[44] had eyes so bright and shining that when he stared at someone very hard, he forced him to lower his eyes, as if before the glow of the sun. Tiberius[45] also is said to have had very large eyes which (this would be amazing) saw at night and in the dark, but only for a short time, and when they first opened from sleep; then they grew dim[46] again.

But the fact that a ray which is sent out by the eyes draws with it a spiritual vapor, and that this vapor draws with it blood, we observe from this, that bleary and red eyes, by the emission of their own ray, force the eyes of a beholder nearby to be afflicted with a similar disease. This shows that the ray extends as far as that person opposite, and that along with the ray emanates a vapor of corrupt blood, by the contagion of which the eye of the observer is infected.

Aristotle writes[47] that women, when the menstrual blood flows down, often soil a mirror with bloody drops by their own gaze. This happens, I think, from this: that the spirit, which is a vapor of the blood, seems to be a kind of blood so thin that it escapes the sight of the eyes, but becoming thicker on the surface of a mirror, it is clearly observed. If this falls on some less dense material, such as cloth, or wood, it is not seen, for the reason that it does not remain on the surface of that thing but sinks into it. If it falls on something dense but rough, such as stones, bricks, and the like, because of the roughness of that body it is dissipated and broken up. But a mirror, on account of its hardness, stops the spirit on the surface; on account of the evenness and smoothness of its surface, it preserves it unbroken; on account of its brightness it aids and increases the spirit's own ray; on account of its cold, it forces its very fine mist into droplets. For almost the same reason, whenever, with open jaws, we breathe[48] strongly onto glass, we sprinkle its surface with a certain very fine dew of saliva. For our breath,[49] flying out from the saliva, having been condensed on that material, falls back into saliva.

Therefore, what wonder is it if the eye, wide open and fixed upon someone, shoots the darts of its own rays into the eyes of the bystander, and along with those darts, which are the vehicles of the spirits, aims that sanguine vapor which we call spirit? Hence the poisoned dart pierces through the eyes, and since it is shot from the heart of the shooter, it seeks again the heart of the man being shot, as its proper home; it wounds the heart, but in the heart's hard back wall it is blunted and turns back into blood. This foreign blood, being somewhat foreign to the nature of the wounded man, infects his blood. The infected blood becomes sick. Hence follows a double bewitchment. The sight of a stinking[50] old man or a woman suffering her period bewitches a boy. The sight of a young man bewitches an older man. But since the humor of an older man is cold and very slow, it hardly reaches the back of the heart in the boy, and ill-fitted for passing across, moves the heart entirely too little, unless on account of infancy it is very tender. Therefore this is a light bewitchment.

But that bewitchment is very heavy by which a young man transfixes the heart of an older man. It is this, distinguished friends, which the Platonist Apuleius, complains about:

> For me, he says, you yourself are alone the whole cause and origin of my present pain, but also the cure itself and my only health. For those eyes of yours gliding down through my eyes into my inmost heart, are producing a furious fire in my marrow. Therefore have mercy on him who is dying because of you.[51]

Put before your eyes, I beg of you, Phaedrus the Myrrhinusian, and that Theban who was seized by love of him, Lysias the orator. Lysias gapes at the face of Phaedrus. Phaedrus aims into the eyes of Lysias sparks of his own eyes, and along with those sparks transmits also a spirit. The ray of Phaedrus is easily joined to the ray of Lysias, and spirit is easily joined to spirit. This vapor produced by the heart of Phaedrus immediately seeks the heart of Lysias, through the hardness of which it is condensed and turns back into the blood of Phaedrus as before, so that now the blood of Phaedrus, amazing though it seems, is in the heart of Lysias. Hence each immediately breaks out into shouting: Lysias to Phaedrus: "O, my heart, Phaedrus, dearest viscera." Phaedrus to Lysias: "O, my spirit, my blood, Lysias." Phaedrus pursues Lysias because his heart demands its humor back. Lysias pursues Phaedrus because the sanguine humor requests its proper vessel, demands its own seat. But Lysias pursues Phaedrus more ardently. For the heart can more easily do without a very small particle of its humor than the humor itself can do without its proper heart. The stream needs the spring more than the spring needs the stream. Therefore, just as iron having received the quality of the lodestone is certainly drawn toward this stone, but does not attract the lodestone, so Lysias pursues Phaedrus more than Phaedrus pursues Lysias.

Chapter 5

How easily we are ensnared by love

But, someone will say, can the weak ray, the unsubstantial spirit, the very small blood of Phaedrus contaminate the whole of Lysias so quickly, so violently, and so destructively? This will certainly not seem strange if you will consider the other diseases which arise through contagion, such as the itch, mange, leprosy, pneumonia, consumption, dysentery, pink-eye, and the plague. Indeed, the amatory infection[52] comes into being easily and becomes the most serious disease of all. Certainly that spiritual vapor and blood which is injected by a young man directly into an older has four qualities, as we have said. It is *clear, thin, warm,* and *sweet.* Because it is *clear,* it harmonizes very well with the clarity of the eyes and spirits in the older man; it entices and allures them. Whence it happens that it is eagerly swallowed up by them. Because it is *thin,* it flies into the heart very quickly. From there through the veins and arteries it easily spreads throughout the whole body. Because it is *warm,* it acts and moves vigorously, it infects the blood of the older man very powerfully, and changes it into its own nature. This Lucretius touches on thus: *"Hence first that drop of Venus' honey distilled in your heart, and then came freezing pain."*[53]

Moreover, because it is *sweet,* it comforts the viscera in some way; it feeds, and pleases them. Hence it happens that all the blood of the older man, when it has been converted into the nature of young blood, seeks the body of the youth in order to inhabit its own veins, and also in order that humor of the young blood may flow in equally young and tender veins. It also happens that this sick one is touched by pleasure and pain at the same time. By pleasure on account of the clarity and sweetness of that vapor and blood. Certainly the former attracts and the latter pleases. By pain on account of the *thinness* and *warmth* of the same. Certainly the former divides and plucks to pieces the viscera; the latter takes away from the man that which is his own and changes it into the nature of the other, through which change clearly it does not permit him to rest in himself, but always draws him toward the person by whom he has been infected. This Lucretius hinted at thus:

And the body seeks that whence the mind is wounded by love, for we all fall for the most part toward the wound, and the blood spurts out in the direction whence we are struck by the blow; and if he is nearby, the red humor seizes the enemy.[54]

In these verses Lucretius can only mean that the blood of a man wounded by a ray of the eyes flows forward into the wounder, just as the blood of a man slain with a sword flows back onto the slayer. If you ask the reason for this miracle, so to speak, I will give it:

Hector wounds Patroclus[55] and kills him. Patroclus sees Hector wounding him, and from this his thought judges that he should be avenged. Immediately his bile is kindled to vengeance. By that his blood is inflamed, and hastens immediately to the wound, partly in order to help that part of the body, partly also for vengeance. To the same place rush also the spirits; these, because they are light, fly out toward Hector and pass into him; by his heat they are preserved for a time, say seven hours. During that same period, if Hector is near the corpse's wound and looks at it intently, the wound spurts blood toward Hector, for gore can somehow flow out toward an enemy, partly because all of its heat is not yet extinguished, its inner motion not yet stilled, partly because it had been aroused against him a little while before, and finally partly because the blood seeks its own spirits, and also those spirits attract their own blood. That in some similar way the blood of a man wounded by love hastens against the wounder, Lucretius implies, and we very much agree.

Chapter 6

On a certain strange effect of vulgar love

Shall I say what follows, chaste gentlemen, or shall I rather omit it? I shall certainly say it, since the subject requires it, even if it seems out of place to say. For who can say offensive things inoffensively?[56]

The great transformation which occurs in an older man who is inclined toward the likeness of a younger causes him to want to transfer his whole body into the youth, and to draw the whole of the youth into himself, in order that either the young humor may obtain young arteries, or the younger arteries may obtain younger blood. Hence they are driven to do many sinful things together. For since the genital semen flows down from the whole body, they believe that merely by ejaculating or receiving this, they can give or receive the whole body. The Epicurean philosopher, Lucretius, the most unhappy of all lovers, perceived this very thing:

Thus, therefore, he who receives wounds from the arrows of Venus, whether it is a boy with girlish limbs who shoots him or a woman sending out love from her whole body, tends thither whence he is wounded and longs to come together; and to send out the humor drawn from his body into its body. . . . They hungrily form a body, and join salivas, and pressing lips with teeth, they breathe from each other's mouths, but in vain, since they can rub off nothing thence, nor penetrate and pass over into its body with the whole body, for they sometimes seem to wish and to be struggling to do this. They cling passionately in the couplings of Venus up to the point where their parts, violently shaken for a moment by the force of ecstasy, melt.[57]

This is what Lucretius the Epicurean says. That lovers desire to take the whole beloved into themselves Artemisia, the wife of King Mausolus of Caria, also showed, who is said to have loved her husband beyond the belief of human affection and to have ground up his body, when he died, into a powder, and to have drunk it, dissolved in water.[58]

Chapter 7

Vulgar love is a perturbation of the blood

That this passion is in the blood there is evidence in the fact that this kind of heat has no periodic break. Any fever which is continuous is located by natural philosophers in the blood; one which gives six-hours of rest, in the phlegm; one which gives one day, in the bile, and one which gives two, in the humor of black bile. Therefore, we are right in placing this fever in the blood; in blood, that is, which is melancholic,[59] as you have heard in the speech of Socrates. Fixation of thought always accompanies this kind of blood.

Chapter 8

How the lover becomes like the beloved

For this reason none of you should be surprised if you have heard that some lover has taken on in his own body a certain similarity of likeness to his beloved. Often pregnant women think vehemently about wine which they avidly desire. The vehement thought moves the internal spirits and paints on them an image of the thing being thought about. The spirits similarly move the blood, and express an image of the wine in the very soft matter of the foetus. But a lover desires his pleasures more feverishly than pregnant women theirs, and thinks about them more vehemently and more constantly. What wonder if the features are so firmly implanted and embedded in the breast by mere thought that they are imprinted on the spirit, and by the spirit are immediately imprinted on the blood?[60] Especially since the very soft blood of Phaedrus has already been generated in the veins of Lysias, so that the face of Phaedrus can very easily be reflected in its own blood. But since all parts of the body, as they dry out every day, so they revive every day, having taken moisture from food, it follows that from day to day the body of each man which has gradually dried out is little by little restored. But the parts are restored by the blood flowing from the channels of the veins. Therefore will you be surprised if blood imprinted with a certain likeness has impressed that likeness on the parts of the body, so that eventually Lysias will seem to have become like Phaedrus in some colors, or features, or feelings, or gestures?

Chapter 9

By whom especially we are ensnared

Perhaps someone will ask, by whom especially, and in what way, lovers are ensnared, and how they are freed. Women, of course, catch men easily, and even more easily women who display a certain masculine character. Men catch men still more easily, since they are more like men than women are, and they have blood and spirit which is clearer, warmer, and thinner, which is the basis of erotic entrapment. But among males those attract men or women most quickly who are predominately sanguine but partly choleric, and who have large eyes, blue and shining; and especially if they live chastely, and have not, through coitus, exhausting the clear sap of the humors, disfigured their serene faces. For these qualities are required in order for the arrows themselves which wound the heart to be sent out properly, as we have explained above.[61]

In addition they are quickly ensnared at whose birth Venus was in Leo, or Luna looked vehemently on Venus, and those who are endowed with the same complexion. Phlegmatics, in whom phlegm dominates, are never caught. Melancholics, in whom black bile dominates, are rarely caught, but once caught are never afterward freed. When a sanguine captures a sanguine, it is a light yoke, an agreeable bond, for a like complexion creates mutual love. Moreover, the amiability of this humor offers faith and hope to the lover. When a choleric captures a choleric, the bondage is more intolerable. Certainly their likeness of complexion affords some interchange of good will between them, but that fiery humor of bile disturbs them with frequent irascibility. When a sanguine captures a choleric, or vice versa, on account of the combination of a pleasant humor and a painful one together, a certain alternation of irascibility and affability, pleasure and pain results. When a sanguine harnesses a melancholic, the knot is permanent, but not unpleasant. Certainly the sweetness of the sanguine tempers the bitterness of the melancholy. But when a choleric traps a melancholic, the disease is the most destructive of all. The very painful humor of the younger glides throughout the viscera of the older. The soft flame eats his marrow. The unfortunate lover is consumed. Choler provokes to wrath and killings. Melancholy provokes to sulking and perpetual complaining; for these the issue of love is often the same as it was for Phyllis, Dido, and Lucretius.[62] But a phlegmatic or melancholy young man, on account of the thickness of his blood and spirits, catches no one.

Chapter 10

How lovers are bewitched

How lovers are bewitched we seem to have explained sufficiently above,[63] if only we may add that mortals are bewitched the most when, by very frequent gazing, directing their sight eye to eye, they join lights with lights and drink a long love together, poor wretches. As Musaeus says,[64] the whole cause and origin of this illness is certainly the eye. For this reason anyone who is powerful in the shining of his eyes,[65] even if he is less attractive in his other parts, drives people mad who look at him very often, for the reason we have given. He who is conversely disposed[66] excites only a certain moderate good will rather than ardor. The harmony of the other parts besides the eyes seems not to have the power to cause this disease but only a tendency to occasion it. Certainly such an arrangement[67] encourages one looking at it from a distance to come nearer. Then when he is looking close at hand, it detains him for a long time in mere contemplation of it. But it is only the sight[68] which wounds him as he lingers. But as for that moderate love which participates in divinity, and which is the main subject in this banquet, not only the eye but the harmony and pleasantness of all the parts concur in causing it.

Chapter 11

The way of escaping from love[69]

Thus far we have discussed how and by whom we may be ensnared. It remains that we teach in a few words how we are freed. The freeing is twofold, one certainly of nature, and the other of diligence.[70] The natural is that which is brought about by certain intervals of time. Which applies not only to this but all diseases. For an itch in the skin remains only so long as the residue of decaying blood remains in the veins, or the saltiness of the phlegm is strong in the parts. When the blood has been purged and the phlegm deadened, the itch ceases and the foul stains of the skin are cleared up. However, a deliberate[71] care in evacuation contributes most. A precipitous evacuation or ointment is judged very dangerous. Also the disquiet of lovers necessarily lasts as long as that infection of the blood, injected into the viscera through bewitchment, lasts; it presses the heart with heavy care, feeds the wound through the veins, and burns the members with unseen flames. For its passage is made from the heart into the veins, and from the veins into the members. When this infection is finally purged away, the disquiet of the erotics (or rather erratics)[72] ceases. This purging requires a long space of time in all, but longest in melancholics, especially if they were snared under the influence of Saturn. And also very bitter[73] if they were subjugated when Saturn was retrograde or in conjunction with Mars, or in opposition to the Sun. Also they are ill the longest at whose birth Venus was in the house of Saturn, or was looking vehemently on Saturn and the Moon.

To be added to this natural purgation is the industry of the most careful art. We must watch out in the first place lest we try to pull up or cut off things not yet mature, and lest we tear apart with the greatest danger things which we can more safely unstitch. A breaking off of habitual relations must be achieved. One must be especially careful lest the lights of the eyes be joined with the lights.[74] If there is any defect in the soul or body of the beloved, it is to be diligently revolved by the soul.[75] The soul is to be kept busy with many, varied, and demanding matters. The blood is to be drawn often. A clear wine is to be used, sometimes even with intoxication, in order that when the old blood has been evacuated, new blood may approach and new spirit. It is important to use exercise, often to the point of perspiration, by which the pores of the body may be opened, for expurgation to be achieved. In addition, all those things which physicians employ for protection of the heart and nourishment of the brain are very useful. Lucretius also prescribes frequent coitus:

> But it is fitting to avoid images and remove from himself the foods of love, and turn his mind elsewhere, and cast the accumulated humor into various bodies and not retain it, once it has been infected by love for a certain person.[76]

Chapter 12

How harmful vulgar love is

But lest we go mad talking further about madness, let us conclude briefly thus. That anxious care by which vulgar lovers are vexed day and night is a certain species of madness. As long as the love lasts, they are afflicted first by the burning of the bile, then by the burning of the black bile, and they rush into frenzies and fire, and as if blind do not know where they are being precipitated. How destructive this adulterous love is, to beloveds as well as to lovers, Lysias the Theban and Socrates in Plato's *Phaedrus* show.[77] Thus by this madness man sinks back to the nature of beast.

Chapter 13

How useful divine love is, and its four kinds

But by the divine madness he is raised above the nature of man and passes into a god.[78] The divine madness, however, is an illumination of the rational soul through which, after the soul has fallen from higher things to lower, God draws it back from lower to higher. The fall of the soul from the One itself, the beginning of all things, to bodies is brought about through four grades; through Intellect, Reason, Opinion, and

Nature. For since in the whole order of things there are six grades,[79] of which the One itself holds the highest and the body, the lowest; but the middle ones are the four which we have just mentioned; it is necessary for whatever falls down from the first to the last to fall through the middle four. The One itself, the limit and measure of all things, is devoid of confusion and multiplicity. The Angelic Mind is certainly a multiplicity (of Ideas), but stable and eternal. The Reason of the Soul is a multiplicity (of notions and arguments), mobile but ordered. Opinion, however, is a disordered and mobile multiplicity (of images), but unified in substance and in points,[80] since the Soul itself, in which Opinion resides, is a single substance, occupying no place. Nature, that is, the power of nourishing from the Soul, and the animal complexion likewise,[81] except that it is distributed through the points of the Body. The Body, however, is an indeterminate multiplicity (of parts and accidents), subject to motion, and divided in substance, in points, and in moments.[82]

All of these[83] our soul looks back upon. Through these it descends; through these it also ascends. For as it is produced from the One itself, which is the beginning of all things, it has received a certain unity[84] which unifies its whole essence, its powers and its actions, from which and to which the other things which are in the soul go, just as the radii go from the center and to the center of a circle. It unites not only the parts of the soul to each other, and to the whole Soul, but also the whole Soul to the One itself, the cause of all things. As it[85] shines with a ray of the divine Mind, it contemplates the Ideas of all things, through its intellect by a motionless act. As it pays attention to itself, it thinks about the universal Reasons of things, and by reasoning proceeds from beginnings to conclusions. As it pays attention to bodies, it considers by Opinion the particular forms and images of movable things received through the senses. As it relates to Matter, it uses Nature as an instrument by which it unifies, moves, and forms Matter. Whence generations, increases, and their opposites originate. You see therefore that from the One, which is above eternity, it falls into multiplicity, from eternity into time, from time into place and matter. It falls, I say, when it departs from that purity in which it is born, embracing the body too long.

Chapter 14

By what grades the divine madnesses raise the soul

Therefore, just as it descends through four grades, it is necessary that it ascend through four. But the divine madness is that which raises to higher things, as is established in its definition. Therefore there are four species of divine madness. The first certainly is poetic madness, the second, mysterial, the third, prophecy, the fourth, amatory feeling. But poetry is from the Muses; mystery from Dionysus; prophecy from Apollo; love from Venus.

Obviously the soul cannot return to the One unless it itself becomes one. But it has become many because it has fallen into the body, is distributed into various operations, and pays attention to the infinite multiplicity of corporeal things. As a result its higher parts are almost asleep; the lower parts dominate the others. The former are affected by torpor, the latter, by perturbation. The whole soul is filled with discord and disharmony. Therefore first there is need for the poetic madness, which, through musical sounds, arouses those parts of the soul which are asleep, through harmonious sweetness calms those which are perturbed, and finally, through the consonance of diverse things, drives away dissonant discord and tempers the various parts of the soul.

Nor is this enough. For multiplicity still remains in the soul. There is added, therefore, the mystery pertaining to Dionysus, which by expiations and sacrifices, and every divine worship, directs the attention of all the other parts to the intellect, by which God is worshipped. In this way since all the parts of the soul are reduced to intellect alone, the soul has already been made a certain single whole out of many.

But there is still need for a third madness which leads the intellect back to unity itself, the head of the soul.[86] This Apollo brings about through prophecy. For when the soul rises above intellect into unity, it foresees future things.

Finally, when the soul has been made one, one, I say, which is in the nature and being of the soul, it remains that it immediately recall itself to that One which is above being, that is God. This that celestial Venus completes, through love, that is the desire for the divine beauty and thirst for the Good.

And so the first madness tempers the unharmonious and dissonant things. The second makes the tempered things into a single whole from parts. The third makes it a single whole above parts. The fourth leads it to the One which is above being and above the whole.

In the *Phaedrus*[87] Plato calls the intellect, devoted to divine things, the charioteer in the soul of man; the unity of the soul, the head of the charioteer; reason and opinion, running through natural things, the good horse; confused fancy and the appetite of the senses, the evil horse. The nature of the whole soul is the chariot because its motion is circular; beginning in itself it finally returns to itself, when it considers its own nature. Here its attention, having started out from the soul, returns to the same. He attributes to the soul wings, on which it is carried to the sublime; of these we think that one is that investigation by which the intellect assiduously strives toward truth; the other is the desire for the Good by which our will is always influenced. These parts of the soul[88] lose their order when they are confused by the perturbing body.

And so the first madness distinguishes the *good horse*,[89] that is, reason and opinion, from the *evil horse*, that is, from confused fancy and the appetite of the senses. The second madness subjects the evil horse to the good, and the good to the charioteer, that is, the intellect. The third directs the charioteer to *his own head*, that is, to his unity, the apex of the intellect. The last turns the head of the charioteer toward the head of all things. Here the charioteer is *blessed*, and *stopping his horses*, that is, accommodating all parts of the soul subject to himself *at the stable*, that is, at the divine beauty, *he puts before them ambrosia and, more than that, nectar to drink*, that is, the vision of beauty, and from that vision happiness. These are the works of the four madnesses. Plato discusses them generally in the *Phaedrus*;[90] but the poetic madness specifically in the *Ion* and the amatory madness in the *Symposium*.[91] That Orpheus was seized by all of these madnesses, his books can testify. That Sappho, Anacreon, and Socrates were seized especially by the amatory madness we have already heard.[92]

Chapter 15

Of all these madnesses love is the most excellent

The most powerful and most excellent of all is the amatory; *most powerful* I say, on account of the fact that all the others necessarily need it. For we achieve neither poetry nor mysteries, nor prophecy without vast zeal, burning piety, and sedulous worship of divinity. But what else do we call zeal, piety, and worship except love? Therefore all exist through the power of love. It is also the most excellent since the others are related to this as to an end. Moreover, this joins us most closely to God.

Certainly an equal number of adulterous emotions seem falsely to imitate these four madnesses. Certainly that vulgar music which pleases only the ears imitates the poetic. The vain superstition of many men, the mysterial. The false conjecture of human prudence, the prophetic. The impulse of lust, the amatory. For true love is nothing other than a certain effort of flying up to divine beauty, aroused by the sight of corporeal beauty. But adulterous love is a falling down from sight to touch.

Chapter 16

How useful the true lover is

You ask what good Socratic Love does?[93] First, certainly, it benefits Socrates himself for recovering the wings by which to fly back to his homeland; next, it benefits his state greatly, for living virtuously and happily. Certainly, not stones but men make a state. But men from a tender age, like plants from their younger years, must be cared for and directed toward the best fruit. The care of boys, parents and teachers look after. Young men do not transgress the rules of their parents and teachers until they are corrupted by the wicked companionship of the crowd. They would certainly follow the superior standard of life which they learned at home if they were not diverted from it by the association and intercourse of wicked men, especially of those who flatter them. What therefore will Socrates do? Will he permit youth, which is the seed of the future state, to be corrupted by the contagion of the shameful? But where is his love of country? Therefore Socrates will come to the aid of the country and will free its sons, his own brothers, from destruction. Perhaps he will write laws by which he will segregate lascivious men from the company of youths. But we cannot all be Lycurguses and Solons.[94] To few is given the authority to make laws; very few obey the laws already made. What then? Will he bring on force, and drive older men away from youth by his own hand? But only Hercules is said to have fought with monsters; for others this kind of violence is very dangerous. Perhaps he will warn, rebuke, or scold the wicked men? But a perturbed soul scorns the words of a warner, and what is worse, rages against the warner. On this account, when Socrates tried this he was struck with a fist by one and a stone by another. There remains a single way of safety for the young, the companionship of Socrates. Therefore, devoted to this through love, that wisest of the Greeks mingles everywhere, and he walks[95] with a great crowd of youths accompanying him.

Thus the true lover, like a shepherd, protects his flock of lambs from the abyss[96] and plague of false lovers, or wolves. But since equals associate most easily with equals, he makes himself equal to the younger men in purity of life, simplicity of words, games, jokes, and jests. From an old man he makes himself a boy at first in order eventually to render boys old men by domestic and agreeable familiarity. Since youth is inclined to pleasure, it is held by pleasure alone; it flees from strict teachers. Hence our protector of youth, for the good of his country, neglecting the administration of his own affairs,[97] undertakes the care of the young, and first captures them by the attractiveness of his pleasant company. When they are thus snared, he warns them, then a little more severely, and finally he chastises them with stricter censure. In this way he saved Phaedo, a very young man,[98] who was a prostitute in a public brothel, from this calamity and made him into a philosopher. He persuaded Plato, who was dedicated to poetry, to give his tragedies to the fire and undertake more valuable studies. He led Xenophon from vulgar luxury to the sobriety of the wise. He changed Aeschines and Aristippus from paupers into rich men, Phaedrus from an orator into a philosopher, and Alcibiades from an ignorant man into a most learned one. Charmides he made earnest and modest, and Theages a just and brave citizen in the state. Euthydemus and Meno he brought over from the quibbles of the Sophists to true wisdom. Thus it happened that the companionship of Socrates was not so enjoyable as useful, and Socrates was loved much more ardently by young men than he loved them, as Alcibiades says.[99]

Chapter 17

How thanks are to be given to the Holy Spirit which
has illuminated and kindled us for this disputation

Now, therefore, distinguished guests, we seem to have found out successfully what love is, what a true lover is, and what is the usefulness of the lover, first from your disputation and then from mine. But consider that the cause and teacher in this very successful finding out was without a doubt the very same love which has been found out. For having been kindled by love, so to speak, of finding love, we have sought and found love, so that thanks must be given to him equally for the seeking and the finding. O the wonderful magnificence of this god! O the incomparable beneficence of love! For other gods finally reveal themselves with difficulty, for a short time, after you have sought them for a long time. Love runs to meet us even before we start looking. Therefore men acknowledge that they owe much more to him than to the others.

There are some who often dare to curse the divine Power as the punisher of our crimes. Some also hate the divine Wisdom[100] as the exposer of all of our shames. But the divine Love, the giver of all goods, we are not able not to love. Let us worship this love, which is so propitious to us, with such a mind that we may revere his Wisdom and admire his Power, so that under the leadership of love we may keep the whole of God, so to speak, propitious, and loving the whole with the burning of love, we may also enjoy the whole God with eternal love.

Notes

1. See Introduction, Section IV, p. 27, n.1.

2. As in earlier speeches, since the whole speech is a quotation, there is no need for quotation marks.

3. Guido Cavalcanti (c. 1250–1300).

4. This, not "Platonic love," is the term which Ficino uses for idealized love in the *Commentary*. See also VII.16, below. Ficino apparently did invent the term "Platonic love," but not until about 1476–77, in a letter to Alamanno Donati. See *Opera*, p. 716.

5. This slip (for "we have said") shows the fragility of the banquet fiction in the *De amore*. Marsuppini here refers to everything that Ficino has said, whereas, according to the fiction, Ficino has not said anything at all.

6. Literally, *quid* vs. *qualis*.

7. Guido Cavalcanti, "Donna me prega," in *Rime*, ed. Guido Favati (Milan, 1957), pp. 214–40. Cavalcanti says none of the things about the sun and its rays which Ficino attributes to him in this paragraph. Ficino's material actually comes from a commentary on Cavalcanti's canzone by Egidio Colonna. See *Il Canzoniere Vaticano-Barberino Latino 3953*, ed. Gino Lega (Bologna, 1905), pp. 93–94.

8. That is, in such a way that from the visual image the soul makes another image for itself.

9. These terms are italicized as if being quoted from Cavalcanti's canzone, "Donna me prega," but they do not occur in that poem any more than any of the rest of this chapter does.

10. Socrates mentions these three as accusers at his trial. See Plato *Apology* 23e.

After Socrates' death, Anytus was exiled, Meletus stoned to death, and Lyco banished.

11.   Thrasymachus of Chalcedon, a sophist, was a contemporary of Lysias; he is one of the speakers in Plato's *Republic*, Book 1. Polus of Agrigento was a sophist and a student of Gorgias; he is refuted in the dialogue entitled *Gorgias*. Callias was a wealthy Athenian at whose house the *Protagoras* takes place, but Professor Kristeller points out that Ficino probably means here Callicles, another speaker in the *Gorgias*, mentioned below.

12.   That is, his comedies, *The Clouds* 423; *The Frogs* 1491. According to Diogenes Laertius (2.5.36), Socrates is reported to have said that he did not at all object to being satirized by "comic poets."

13.   That is, the description given in VI.9 (pp. 120–30), based on the *Symposium* 203c–e.

14.   Plato *Phaedrus* 229a; see also Kristeller, *Suppl.*, 2 : 100.

15.   Plato *Apology* 22d.

16.   Plato *Gorgias* 494d.

17.   Diogenes Laertius 2.5.21.

18.   Cicero *Tusculan Disputations* 5.37.108.

19.   Diogenes Laertius 2.5.18.

20.   Plato *Apology* 31b, c.

21.   Diogenes Laertius 2.5.25. Archelaus was the King of Macedonia; he sent Scopus and Eurylochus as an embassy to Socrates to try to induce him to visit the Macedonian court, but Socrates would have nothing to do with them.

22.   Plato *Symposium* 220d–221c. Ficino's account does not correspond with Plato's. What Plato says is that at Potidaea Socrates saved Alcibiades' life, and as a result Alcibiades tried to get the generals to give Socrates credit for the victory in the battle.

23.   Cicero *Tusculan Disputations* 4.37.80.

24.   For Marcel's *differeret* read *dissereret*.

25.   Plato *Symposium* 215e.

26.   Plato *Symposium* 213c.

27.   Plato *Symposium* 222b.

28.   Plato *Protagoras* 309a. See also *Symposium* 210b–212c.

29.   Plato *Theages* 128d–129a.

30.   Plato *Apology* 29d.

31.   Plato *Symposium* 215b, c.

32.   Plato *Apology* 31d–40b; *Phaedrus* 242b, c. Xenophon also comments on how notorious Socrates' "deity" was and how seriously his "sign" was taken (*Memorabilia* 1.1.2–4).

33.   Aristophanes *The Clouds* 112 ff.

34.   Plato *Apology* 21d.

35.   That is, in the first six speeches of the dialogue.

36.   This sentence is based on the printed editions and several manuscripts. The passage reads *Ita enim amavit Socrates, ut supra Diotima docuit*. It is given in a note by Marcel (p. 245). See Kristeller, *Suppl.*, 1 : 87.

37.   Plato *Phaedrus* 265a.

38.   For *merent* read *maerent*.

39. That is, the three kinds of insanity. Here and in the rest of the paragraph Ficino uses this pronoun euphemistically for "genuine mental illness."

40. That is, too self-confident about differing from the opinion of the majority. In the Italian translation Ficino gives a different idea: lest we seem to be using the term in too technical a sense.

41. The Italian translates *fascinatio* as *male d'occhio*, "the evil eye."

42. See p. 121 above.

43. In the Italian translation, Ficino amplifies his description to make clear that it is the inner corner, near the tear duct, which is to be pressed with the twisting finger and that the luminous circle will appear within the eye.

44. Suetonius *Lives of the Caesars*: Augustus, chap. 79.

45. Suetonius *Lives of the Caesars*: Tiberius, chap. 68. In this sentence for *esset* the printed editions read *est*. The Italian translation gives a different account of Tiberius's powers.

46. For Marcel's *ebescebant* read *hebescebant*. Marcel's translation "turned red" is based on a reading of *erubescebant*.

47. Aristotle *De insomniis* 2.459.b.30.

48. For Marcel's *hanelamus* read *anhelamus*.

49. For *alitus* read *halitus*.

50. For *fetidi* read *foetidi*.

51. Apuleius *Metamorphoses* 10.3.

52. In describing love as a disease Ficino usually draws on medical works, but this particular passage probably reflects his reading of Dino del Garbo's *Commentary* on the canzone of Guido Cavalcanti, discussed in Chapter 1 of Speech VII above. The relevant passage in del Garbo, who was himself a physician, is on p. 130 of Bird's translation of "The Commentary of Dino del Garbo on Cavalcanti's 'Canzone d'amore,'" in *Medieval Studies* 2 (1940) : 150–203 and 3 (1941) : 117–60.

53. Lucretius *De rerum natura* 4.1059–060.

54. Lucretius *De rerum natura* 4.1047–051.

55. Cf. Plato *Symposium* 179e.

56. In the Italian translation Ficino attributes the whole of the following paragraph to Lucretius, but he omits the quotation altogether.

57. Lucretius *De rerum natura* 4.1052–056, 1108–114.

58. Aulus Gellius *Attic Nights* 10.18.

59. The identification of love as a disease associated with the melancholy humor may be seen in Avicenna's *Canon* 3. Fen.1. Tr.4. cap.23, among other sources which Ficino may have used.

60. The Italian translation makes clear that the features are those of the beloved, but the breast, thought, spirit, and blood are those of the lover.

61. That is, in VII.4.

62. That is, suicide. On Phyllis see Ovid *Remedia amoris* 591–608 and *Heroides* 2. On Dido see Vergil *Aeneid* 1 and 4 and Ovid *Heroides* 7. On Lucretius, see above, p. 121.

63. Cf. VII.4 above.

64. Museus *Hero and Leander* 94 ff.

65. That is, has beautiful eyes.

66. That is, who is very attractive in his other parts but does not have beautiful eyes.

67. Of parts; that is, physical beauty.

68. That is, it is only when the two look into each other's eyes that love occurs. The Italian translation provides this explanation.

69. The Italian title specifies vulgar love.

70. Ficino's suggestions for curing the disease of love are borrowed from a number of medical authorities but primarily from Rhazes *Liber derisionum* chap. 11 (*De amore*). For others see the Lowes article cited, p. 147, n.39 above. As the Italian translation and the following paragraph show, *diligence* here means *art* (i.e., medical skill) as opposed to *nature* as a mode of remedy. Ficino makes a similar distinction in *Opera*, p. 761, in speaking of philosophy.

71. For Marcel's *natura* read *matura*.

72. My translation is an effort to preserve Ficino's play on words: *amantium immo vero amentium*. In the Italian translation he eliminates the pun altogether.

73. That is, the purgation is very uncomfortable.

74. That is, the lovers must stop looking into each other's eyes.

75. That is, one should keep reminding oneself of any undesirable aspects of the beloved.

76. Lucretius *De rerum natura* 4.1062–066.

77. Plato *Phaedrus* 231a–234e, 238d–241d.

78. The material of this and the following chapter appears again in Ficino's commentary on the *Ion* (*Opera*, pp. 1281–284).

79. This redescription of the hierarchy of being as having six levels and the specification of the various faculties as Intellect, Reason, Opinion, and Nature (i.e., the vegetative functions) suggest that this chapter and the chapter following may be based on Proclus *Commentary on I Alcibiades* (especially section 71–72, 140–41, in the O'Neill translation). Cf. Ficino's abstract of this work (*Opera*, pp. 1908–928). Professor Kristeller points out, however, that similar ideas are also present in Plotinus. See P. O. Kristeller, *The Philosophy of Ficino* (New York, 1943), pp. 74–91, 166–69, and 232–33. See p. 28, n.8 above.

80. By "points" in this passage Ficino means simply "space."

81. That is, Nature, which is the World Soul's faculty for creating living things and includes the souls of all individual animals, is also disordered, changeable, and multiple, like Opinion.

82. That is, in time.

83. That is, these levels of the hierarchy of being.

84. See p. 59, n.18 above.

85. That is, the human soul. Strictly speaking, the subject should still be "unity" of the human soul.

86. See p. 59, n.18 above.

87. Plato *Phaedrus* 246b. See Michael Allen, *Marsilio Ficino and the Phaedran Charioteer* (Berkeley, 1981).

88. That is, intellect and will.

89. Ficino introduces italics here for the various parts of the allegory of the charioteer, from the *Phaedrus*. This suggests that this passage may originally have been written for a commentary on that dialogue, but the *Phaedrus* itself is not quoted verbatim at the

beginning of the discussion, and the terms are therefore not previously italicized.

90. Plato *Phaedrus* 244b–245c, 247d–249e, 265b.

91. Plato *Ion* 533d–536d; *Symposium* 205d–207c, 210–212a.

92. The passage referred to is in VI.9 (p. 122 above), where Socrates and Sappho are said to have been melancholics. Anacreon is not mentioned there.

93. See p. 174, n.4.

94. Both of these figures were famous law-givers: Lycurgus, of Sparta, and Solon (c. 638–558), of Athens. Solon's achievements as a begetter of laws are mentioned in the *Symposium* 209d.

95. For Marcel's *incendit* read *incedit*.

96. Marcel, following the Italian translation, renders *voragine* "voracity."

97. Plato *Apology* 31b.

98. The following examples of Socrates' influence on various young men are taken from the biography by Diogenes Laertius in *Lives of the Philosophers* and from Xenophon's biography in *Memorabilia*. Xenophon, the author of the *Anabasis*, was a pupil of Socrates as well as his biographer. Aeschines was an Athenian philosopher, also a pupil of Socrates. Aristippus, though a student of Socrates, later became a hedonist philosopher. Charmides was Plato's maternal uncle but is represented, in the dialogue bearing his name, as a pupil of Socrates. Theages, the son of Demodocus, appears in a dialogue named after him. Euthydemus, a sophist, was born at Chios. Plato's dialogue is named after him, not after Euthydemus the disciple of Socrates, mentioned in Xenophon's *Memorabilia* (1.2.29) and Plato's *Symposium* (222). Meno was a leader in the expedition of Cyrus in 401 B.C.; Plato's dialogue is named after him.

99. Possibly a reference to Plato *Symposium* 222b.

100. That is, the *Wisdom* of God, paralleling the *Power* of God mentioned (also indirectly) in the previous sentence. The Pauline distinction becomes clearer in the second sentence below.

Appendix

Renaissance Letters Concerning the *De Amore*

1. Letter from Ficino to Giovanni Cavalcanti, prefaced to the holograph copy of the *De amore* (Marcel, *Life*, p. 341)

Marsilio Ficino to Giovanni Cavalcanti, best of friends: Eu prattein!

A long time ago, dear Giovanni, I learned from Orpheus that love existed, and that it held the keys to the whole world; then from Plato I learned the definition of love and its nature. But what power and influence this god has, had lain hidden from me until I was thirty-four years old, when a certain divine hero, glancing at me with heavenly eyes, showed me, by a certain wonderful nod, how great the power of love is. Being in that way fully informed, as it seems to me, about amatory things, I have composed a book *On Love*. This book, written in my own hand, I have decided to dedicate exclusively to you, so that I may return to you what belongs to you. Farewell.

2. Letter from Ficino to Bishop Giovanni Antonio Campano
   (Kristeller, *Suppl.*, 1 : 89)

Marsilio Ficino to Bishop Campano: Eu prattein!

My servant Gerard will hand you, with this letter, a commentary which I wrote a little while ago on Plato's dialogue on love. In this commentary I have included almost all of Plato's own words, except for the "I said"s and the "he said"s, and a few inconsequential questions which the context of the dialogue requires. I hope you will send this little offering of ours on to the Cardinal of Siena, by Gerard, and that you will embellish it with a few words and commendations of your own. Some other time, if God permits, I shall send you a better gift.

Such as it is, because it is about love, I thought I should dedicate it to Francesco Piccolomini, who is the most loving and most beloved of men. I hear that Bishop Campano also practices Socratic love and worships the Platonic Muses. Not only do others praise many divine things about you and your Cardinal, but also Baccio Ugolini often sings your praises in the Academy, so that you are now called by all of us a pillar of the Academy. Farewell.

3. Dedication of the Italian translation
   (Kristeller, *Suppl.*, 1 : 89-91)

Marsilio Ficino to Bernard del Nero and Antonio Manetti:

As a general rule, a thing which a man does frequently and often, after long experience he does well, and the longer he is accustomed to it, the better he does it. But in the case of love, this rule, because of our stupidity, and much to our sorrow, does not hold.

We all love continuously in some way, but almost all of us love wrongly, and so the more we love, the worse it becomes. And if one in a hundred thousand loves rightly, because his is not the common practice, no one follows his example.

We fall into this great error, unfortunately for us, because we boldly start out upon this difficult journey of love before we know its destination or how to travel the perilous path of the journey. The farther we go, the farther we stray, to our great undoing; and losing our way in the dark forest of love is more serious than on other journeys because we travel there in larger numbers and more often.

In order to lead us back to the straight path which we had missed, the supreme love of Divine Providence inspired a chaste woman in ancient Greece called Diotima the priestess, who, under divine inspiration, finding the philosopher Socrates devoted above all else to love, explained to him what this ardent passion is and how by means of it we can fall into the greatest evil, or soar to the highest Good.

Socrates, in turn, revealed these holy mysteries to our Plato, and Plato, the most pious of all philosophers, immediately wrote a book about them for the salvation of the Greeks. For the salvation of the Latins, I translated Plato's book from Greek into Latin, and, encouraged by our Magnificent Lorenzo de' Medici, commented upon the more difficult ideas in the book; and in order that this health-giving manna, sent to Diotima from heaven, might be easily available to more people, I have translated from Latin into Tuscan both the Platonic mysteries and my own commentary.

This volume I dedicate especially to you, Bernardo del Nero and Antonio Manetti, my dear friends, because I am certain that the love which your Marsilio Ficino sends you, you will receive with love, and that you will explain that love to anyone who might presume to read this book carelessly or with malice, a thing which no one will ever be able to do, because the diligence of love is not to be understood through negligence, and love itself is not grasped through hatred.

May the Holy Spirit, that Divine Love which inspired Diotima, enlighten our intellects and kindle our wills so that we may love Him in all His beautiful works, and then love His works in Him, and at last infinitely enjoy His infinite Beauty.

4. Preface to the first Italian edition, by Cosimo Bartoli
   (Kristeller, *Suppl.*, 1 : 91–92)

To His Most Illustrious and Noble Lordship,
Signor Cosimo de' Medici, Duke of Florence,
Most Respectful Greetings:

Your Illustrious Excellency, the goodness and beneficence of our Marsilio Ficino were great and wonderful. He was a worthy pupil, certainly, of the great Cosimo de' Medici, in whose illustrious memory your Excellency has been named. Ficino, not content with having given Plato to readers of Latin, commented upon and explained by many learned writings of his own, desired to help those who could read nothing but Italian no less than he had formerly desired to gratify the honored and useful advice of your Lorenzo the Magnificent, and he deigned to translate into our native tongue the *Commentary on Plato's Symposium*, which he had written in Latin, dedicating this Italian translation to Bernardo del Nero and Antonio Manetti, his dear friends, as is indicated in his own dedicatory epistle.

Though his intention was truly generous and holy, it has not yet hit the mark at which he himself aimed, since this treasure of his has lain hidden, as it were, up to our time, or has been really appreciated by few. For this reason, both because of the beneficent intention of Marsilio and because of the benefits which could result if only the *Commentary* could be read and understood now with the faith and conviction with which he himself wrote and translated it, and because I had access to a manuscript copied from the original itself, I wished to share it with all who understand our language, but under the noble name of your Excellency, to whom I must not only render this, because it belongs to him by hereditary right, but also everything that I now am or ever could be.

Therefore accept this, your Excellency, with generous spirit, and know that it is printed with as much care as possible. And do not wonder that you do not find the text of Plato before the commentary, because I preferred to follow the example of Marsilio, and risk the charge of having been too lazy to translate it, than give to the unlearned, who usually consider only the surface of things, occasion to kindle in their minds, because of his figurative and profound mode of expression, those emotions which are discussed there perhaps more completely than is appropriate in a language of the common people, such as Italian. This is really the reason why Marsilio translated it and commented on it for readers of Latin but did not wish to translate into Italian anything more than the commentary, because the original was a thing truly Christian, and not to be desecrated.

Therefore, read it, your Excellency, and continue, as you have done so beneficently heretofore, to encourage students of this language, to honor and enrich it with every ancient fine art and wholesome science, and remember me as the most faithful servant of your Excellency.

Most Devotedly,
Cosimo Bartoli

Bibliography

Note: This bibliography is a selected list of primary and secondary materials which are important to a study of Ficino's *De amore* and its influence in western culture. Since most students of it come not from the history of philosophy but from a study of its influence on the various arts, I have arranged the bibliography according to the principal areas of that influence.

I. Editions and Translations

II. General Secondary Works

III. Italy

IV. France

V. Spain

VI. Britain

VII. Other Countries

VIII. Visual Arts and Music

Table of Abbreviations

ABR	*American Benedictine Review*
AHDLM	*Archives d'histoire doctrinale et littéraire du Moyen Age*
Altenstaig	Joannes Altenstaig, *Vocabularius theologiae*
Aquinas Lexicon	Roy J. Deferrari, ed. *Lexicon of St. Thomas Aquinas*
AUMLA	*Journal of Australasian Univ. Lang. & Lit. Assoc.*
BAAL	*Boletín de la Academia Argentina de Letras*
BHR	*Bibliotheque d'humanisme et renaissance*
BHS	*Bulletin of Hispanic Studies*
BSUF	*Ball State University Forum*
CDI	*Comprehensive Dissertation Index, 1861–1972*
CL	*Comparative Literature*
CLS	*Comparative Literature Studies*
CSR	*Christian Scholar's Review*
DAI	*Dissertation Abstracts International*
DVLG	*Deutsche Vierteljahrsschrift für Literaturwissenschaft und Geistesgeschichte*
EIC	*Essays in Criticism*
ELH	*English Literary History*
ELN	*English Language Notes*
ELR	*English Literary Renaissance*
EM	*English Miscellany*
FSI	*La filosofia delle scuole italiane*
GCFI	*Giornale critico della filosofia italiana*
GSLI	*Giornale storico della letteratura italiana*
HLQ	*Huntington Library Quarterly*
HR	*Hispanic Review*
IMU	*Italia medioevale et umanistica*
JEGP	*Journal of English and Germanic Philology*
JHI	*Journal of the History of Ideas*
JHPh	*Journal of the History of Philosophy*
JMRS	*Journal of Medieval and Renaissance Studies*
JWCI	*Journal of the Warburg and Courtauld Institutes*
MLN	*Modern Language Notes*
MLQ	*Modern Language Quarterly*
MLR	*Modern Language Review*
MP	*Modern Philology*
MRS	*Medieval and Renaissance Studies*
N&Q	*Notes and Queries*
PBSA	*Papers of the Bibliographical Society of America*
PMLA	*Publications of the Modern Language Association of America*
PQ	*Philological Quarterly*
RBPH	*Revue Belge de philologie et d'histoire*
RES	*Review of English Studies*
RFNS	*Rivista di filosofia neo-scolastica*
RH	*Revue Hispanique*
RLC	*Revue de la littérature comparée*
RN	*Renaissance News*
RPL	*Revue philosophique de Louvain*

RQ	*Renaissance Quarterly*
RSH	*Revue des sciences humaines*
SAQ	*South Atlantic Quarterly*
SCN	*Seventeenth-Century News*
SEL	*Studies in English Literature*
SFr	*Studi francesi*
SMC	*Studies in Medieval Culture*
SP	*Studies in Philology*
SPCT	*Studi e problemi di critica testuale*
SQ	*Shakespeare Quarterly*
SRen	*Studies in the Renaissance*
UTQ	*University of Toronto Quarterly*
ZFK	*Zeitschrift für Kirchengeschichte*
ZKT	*Zietschrift für katholische Theologie*

I. Editions and Translations

1. Editions with other works

> *Opera Platonis*: Florence, 1484; and at least 26 later editions.
> *Opera Ficini*: Basle, 1576; reprinted 1959 and 1962.

2. Separate editions

Italian		Florence, 1544
Italian	ed. Guiseppe Rensi	Lanciano, 1914
Latin	ed. Sears Jayne	Columbia, 1944
Italian	ed. James Wadsworth	Harvard Diss., 1950
	(from Laurenziana MS 76, 73)	
Latin	ed. Raymond Marcel	Paris, 1956
Italian	ed. G. Ottaviano (reprints Rensi)	Milan, 1973

3. Translations

Italian	Hercole Barbarasa	Rome, 1544
French	Jean de La Haye	Poitiers, 1545, 1546
French	Guy Le Levre de la Boderie	Paris, 1578, 1588
German	Karl P. Hasse	Leipzig, 1914
Roumanian	Sorin Ionescu	Budapest, 1942
English	Sears Jayne	Columbia, 1944
French	Raymond Marcel	Paris, 1956
Spanish	Adolfo Ruíz Díaz	Mendoza, 1968

4. In addition, there are partial English translations as follows:

> V.3–6: by J. J. S. Peake, in Erwin Panofsky, *Idea*, pp. 128–41. Columbia, S.C., 1968.
> VI.11–19: by Gordon Neal, in *Renaissance Views of Man*, edited by Stevie Davies, pp. 31–61. Manchester, 1979.
> VII.14: by Michael Allen, in *Marsilio Ficino and the Phaedran Charioteer*, pp. 220–23. Berkeley, 1981.

II. General Secondary Works

Allen, Don Cameron. *Mysteriously Meant.* Baltimore, 1970.

Allen, Michael J. B. "Cosmogony and Love: the Role of Phaedrus in Ficino's *Symposium* Commentary." *JMRS* 10 (1980) : 131–53.

———. "Ficino's Lecture on the Good?" *RQ* 30 (1977) : 160–71.

———. "Ficino's Theory of the Five Substances and the Neoplatonists' *Parmenides.*" *JMRS* 12 (1982) : 19–44.

———. *Marsilio Ficino and the Phaedran Charioteer.* Berkeley, 1981.

———. "Marsilio Ficino on Plato's Pythagorean Eye." *MLN* 97 (1982) : 171–82.

———. *Marsilio Ficino: The "Philebus" Commentary.* Berkeley, 1975.

———. "The Absent Angel in Ficino's Philosophy." *JHI* 36 (1975) : 219–40.

———. "The Sibyl in Ficino's Oaktree." *MLN* 95 (1980) : 205–10.

———. "Two Commentaries on the 'Phaedrus': Ficino's Indebtedness to Hermias." *JWCI* 43 (1980) : 110–29.

Allen, Michael J. B. and White, Roger A. "Ficino's Hermias Translation and a New Apologue." *Scriptorium* 35 (1981) : 39–47.

Allers, Rudolf. "Microcosmus from Anaximander to Paracelsus." *Traditio* 2 (1944) : 319–408.

Altenstaig, Joannes. *Vocabularius theologiae.* Hagenau, 1517.

Alverny, Marie Thérèse d'. "Quelques aspects du symbolisme de la 'Sapientia' chez les humanistes." In *Umanesimo e esoterismo,* edited by Enrico Castelli, pp. 321–33. Padua, 1960.

Anichini, Giuseppe. "Umanesimo e salvezza in Marsilio Ficino." *RFNS* 33 (1941) : 205–21.

Avicenna. *Treatise on Love.* Translated by Emil Fackenheim. In *Medieval Studies* 7 (1945) : 208–28.

Avisani, P., Billanovitch, G., and Pozzi, G., eds. *Miscellanea Marciana di Studi Bessarionei.* Padua, 1976.

Balbino, Giuliano. *L'idea religiosa di Marsilio Ficino e il concetto di una dottrina esoterica.* Cerignola, 1904. Not seen.

Barfucci, Enrico. *Lorenzo de'Medici e la società artistica del suo tempo.* 2d ed. Florence, 1964.

Baron, Hans. "Willensfreiheit und Astrologie bei Marsilio Ficino und Pico della Mirandola." In *Kultur-und Universalgeschichte. Festschrift Walter Goetz,* pp. 145–70. Leipzig, 1927.

Beierwaltes, Werner, ed. *Platonismus in der Philosophie des Mittelalters.* Darmstadt, 1969.

Boas, George. "Philosophies of Science in Florentine Platonism." In *Art, Science, and History in the Renaissance,* edited by Charles S. Singleton, pp. 239–54. Baltimore, 1963.

Börje, Knös. "Gémiste Pléthon et son souvenir." *Bulletin de l'Association Guillaume Budé* 10 (1950) : 97–184.

Brown, Clarence A. *The Platonic doctrine of inspiration . . . in Renaissance literary criticism.* Dissertation, Wisconsin, 1941. *CDI.*

Brussels, University of. *L'univers à la renaissance; microcosme et macrocosme.* Colloque international, 1968. Brussels, 1970.

Bruyne, Edgar de. *Etudes d'esthétique médiévale.* 3 vols. Bruges, 1946.

Burke, John G. "Hermeticism as a Renaissance World View." In *The Darker Vision of the Renaissance*, edited by Robert S. Kinsman, pp. 95–118. Berkeley, 1974.

Canavero, Alessandra T. "Agostino e Tommaso nel Commento di Marsilio Ficino all' *Epistola ai Romani*." *RFNS* 65 (1973) : 815–24.

_____. "L'amicizia nell' epistolario di Marsilio Ficino." *RFNS* 67 (1975) : 422–31.

_____. "Il *De triplici vita* di Marsilio Ficino . . . una strana vicenda ermeneutica." *RFNS* 69 (1977) : 697–717.

_____. "S. Agostino nella *Teologia Platonica* di Marsilio Ficino." *RFNS* 70 (1978) : 626–46.

Cantimori, Delio. "Anabattismo e Neoplatonismo nel XVI secolo in Italia." *Rendiconti della R. Academia Nazionale dei Lincei*. Classe di scienze morali, storiche e filologiche, series 6, 12 (1937) : 521–61.

Carbonara, Cleto. *Il secolo XV. Storia della filosofia italiana*, ch. 2, 6. Milan, 1943.

_____. "La tradizione ontologica e l'importanza storica del platonismo." *GCFI* 24 (1943) : 242–72.

_____. "Umanesimo teologico e umanesimo della prassi." *Logos* 2 (1971) : 336–62. Not seen.

Cassirer, Ernst. "Ficino's Place in Intellectual History." *JHI* 6 (1945) : 483–501.

_____. *The Individual and the Cosmos in Renaissance Philosophy*. New York, 1963.

Castelli, Enrico, ed. *Umanesimo e esoterismo*. Convegno internazionale di studi umanistici. Padua, 1960.

Collins, Ardis B. "Love and Natural Desire in Ficino's *Platonic Theology*." *JHPh* 9 (1971) : 435–42.

_____. *The Secular is Sacred*. Hague, 1974.

Comito, Terry. *The Idea of the Garden in the Renaissance*, pp. 51–88. New Brunswick, 1977.

Corradi, Mario. "Alle origini della letteratura neoplatonica del *Convito*: Marsilio Ficino e il *De Amore*." *RFNS* 69 (1977) : 406–22.

Corsano, Antonio. *Il pensiero religioso italiano*, pp. 15–31. Bari, 1937.

Coulter, James. *The Literary Microcosm*. Leiden, 1976.

Crahay, Franz. "Perspectives sur les philosophies de la renaissance." *RPL* 72 (1974) : 655–77.

Cristiani, Emilio. "Una inedita invettiva giovanile di Marsilio Ficino." *Rinascimento* 6 (1966) : 209–22.

Danielou, Jean. *Platonisme et théologie mystique*. Paris, 1944.

Dannenfeldt, Karl H. "The Pseudo-Zoroastrian Oracles in the Renaissance." *SRen* 4 (1957) : 7–30.

Deferrari, Roy J. et al., eds. *A Lexicon of St. Thomas Aquinas*. 5 vols. Washington, D.C., 1948–49.

Della Torre, Arnaldo. *Storia dell' Accademia Platonica di Firenze*. Florence, 1902.

Delumeau, Jean. "Platon et Aristote à la Renaissance." *Revue d'histoire moderne et contemporaine* 24 (1977) : 415–19.

De Mattei, Rodolfo. "Difese italiane di Platone nel cinque e nel seicento." *Scritti in memoria di W. Cesarini Sforza*, pp. 263–88. Milan, 1968.

De Ruggiero, Guido. *Rinascimento, riforma e contrariforma*. Bari, 1947.

Devereux, James. "The Object of Love in Ficino's Philosophy." *JHI* 30 (1969) : 161–70.

_____. "The Textual History of Ficino's *De amore*." *RQ* 28 (1975) : 173–82.

Dress, Walter. *Die Mystik des Marsilio Ficino*. Berlin, 1929.

Fabro, Cornelio. "Influenze tomistiche nella filosofia del Ficino." *Studia Patavina* 3 (1959) : 396–413.

_____. *La nozione metafisica di partecipazione secondo S. Tomasso d'Aquino*. 3d ed. Turin, 1963.

Ferri, Luigi. "Di Marsilio Ficino e delle cause della rinascenza del platonismo nel quattrocento." *FSI* 28 (1883) : 180–201.

_____. "L'Accademia Platonica di Firenze e le sue vicende." *Nuova Antologia*, series 3, 34 (1891) : 226–44.

_____. "Platonismo di Ficino: Dottrina dell' amore." *FSI* 29 (1884) : 269–94.

_____. "Storia della filosofia: il platonismo di Marsilio Ficino." *FSI* 29 (1884) : 237–60.

Festugières, Jean. "Dante et Marsile Ficin." Comité Français Catholique pour la célébration du Sixième Centenaire de la mort de Dante Alighieri. *Bulletin du Jubilé*, no. 5 (1922) : 535–43.

Ficino, Marsilio. *De triplici vita*. Translated by Charles Boer. Dallas, 1981.

_____. *In convivium Platonis*. Edited by Raymond Marcel. Paris, 1956.

_____. *Lessico greco-latino*. Edited by Rosario Pintaudi. (Laur. Ashb. 1439). Rome, 1977.

_____. *Letters*. Vol. I. Translated by members of the Language Department, School of Economic Science, London, 1975. Vol. 2. London, 1978. Vol. 3. London, 1981.

_____. *Opera*. 2 vols. Reprint of Basle, 1576 ed. Turin, 1962.

_____. *Supplementum Ficinianum*. Edited by P. O. Kristeller. 2 vols. Florence, 1937.

_____. *Theologia Platonica*. Edited by Raymond Marcel. 3 vols. (Vol. 3 contains some of *Epistolae*). Paris, 1964–70.

Gabotto, Ferdinando. "L'Epicureismo di Marsilio Ficino." *Rivista di filosofia scientifica* 10 (1891) : 428–42.

Galli, Ettore. *La morale nelle lettere di Marsilio Ficino*. Pavia, 1897.

Gandillac, Maurice de. "Astres, anges et génies chez Marsile Ficin." In *Umanesimo e esoterismo*, edited by Enrico Castelli, pp. 85–109. Padua, 1960.

_____. "Le platonisme au xiie et au xiiie siècle." *Association Guillaume Budé. Congrès de Tours et Poitiers*, pp. 266–85. Paris, 1954.

Garin, Eugenio. "Aristotelismo e platonismo del rinascimento." *La Rinascita* 2 (1939) : 641–71.

_____. "Ficino." In *Storia della filosofia italiana*, pp. 373–436. 2d ed. Turin, 1966.

_____. "Images and Symbols in Marsilio Ficino." In *Portraits from the Quattrocento*, translated by Victor A. and Elizabeth Velen, pp. 142–60. New York, 1972.

_____. *Italian Humanism: Philosophy and Civic Life in the Renaissance*. New York, 1965. Italian ed. Bari, 1952.

_____. *La cultura filosofica del rinascimento italiano*. Florence, 1961.

_____. *La filosofia*. Vol. 1, pp. 286–352; Vol. 2, pp. 66–94. Milan, 1947.

_____. "La teologia ficiniana." In *Umanesimo e Machiavellismo*, edited by Enrico Castelli, pp. 21–33. Padua, 1949.

_____. "Magia ed astrologia nella cultura del rinascimento." *Belfagor* 5 (1951) : 657–67.

_____. _Medioevo e rinascimento: Studi e ricerche._ Bari, 1954.

_____. "Per la storia della cultura filosofica del Rinascimento." _Rivista critica di storia della filosofia_ 12 (1957) : 3-21.

_____. "Problemi di religione e filosofia nella cultura fiorentina del Quattrocento." _BHR_ 14 (1952) : 70-82.

_____. "Recenti interpretazioni di Marsilio Ficino." _GCFI_ 21 (1940) : 299-318.

_____. "Ricerche sulle traduzioni di Platone nella prima metà del sec. XV." _Medioevo e rinascimento: Studi in onore di Bruno Nardi._ Vol. 1, pp. 339-74. Florence, 1955.

_____. _Studi sul platonismo medievale._ Florence, 1958.

Gentile, Giovanni. _Il pensiero italiano del rinascimento._ Florence, 1940.

Gentile, Sebastiano. "Per la storia del testo del'Commentarium in Convivium'di Marsilio Ficino." _Rinascimento_ 21 (1981) : 3-27.

George of Trebizond. _Comparationes philosophorum Aristotelis et Platonis._ Venice, 1523. Reprinted Frankfort, 1965.

Gilbert, C. D. "Blind Cupid." _JWCI_ 33 (1970) : 304-05.

Gilson, Etienne. "Marsile Ficin et le _Contra Gentiles._" _AHDLM_ 24 (1957) : 101-13.

Goffis, Cesare F. "Il sincretismo Lucreziano-Platonico negli _Hymni Naturales_ del Marullo." _Belfagor_ 24 (1969) : 386-417.

Gould, Thomas. _Platonic Love._ London, 1963.

Hadot, Pierre. "L'amour magicien' aux origines de la notion de 'magia naturalis': Platon, Plotin, Marsile Ficin." _Revue philosophique de la France et de l'étranger_ 172 (1982) : 283-92.

Hak, H. J. _Marsilio Ficino._ Amsterdam, 1934.

Harvey, E. Ruth. _The Inward Wits._ London, 1975.

Hazo, Robert A. _The Idea of Love._ New York, 1967.

Heitzman, Marian. "Etudes sur l'Académie Platonicienne de Florence." _Bulletin International de l'Académie Polonaise de Sciences et des Lettres._ Classe de Philologie, d'Histoire et de Philosophie. (1932) : 18-22; (1933) : 35-39.

_____. "L'agostinismo avicennizzante e il punto di partenza della filosofia di Marsilio Ficino." _GCFI_ 16 (1935) : 295-322, 460-80; 17 (1936) : 1-11.

_____. "La libertà e il fato nella filosofia de Marsilio Ficino." _RFNS_ 28 (1936) : 350-71; 29 (1937) : 59-82.

Heninger, S. K. _Touches of Sweet Harmony: Pythagorean Cosmology and Renaissance Poetics._ San Marino, 1974.

Henry, Paul. "Les manuscrits grecs de travail de Marsile Ficin, le traducteur des _Enneades_ de Plotin." In _Association Guillaume Budé. Congres de Tours et Poitiers,_ pp. 323-28. Paris, 1954.

Hillman, James. "Plotino, Ficino, and Vico as Precursors of Archetypal Psychology." In _Loose Ends,_ pp. 146-69. Irving, Texas, 1978. Italian translation in _Rivista di Psicologia Analitica_ 4 (1973) : 322-40.

_____. _Re-Visioning Psychology,_ pp. 197-202. New York, 1975.

Hirst, Désirée. _Hidden Riches._ London, 1964.

Horský, Zdeněk. "La cosmologie de Marsile Ficin." Translated by Jaromir Kopecký. _Acta Historica_ 2 (1966) : 57-68.

_____. "Le Rôle du Platonisme dans l'origine de la cosmologie moderne." *Organon* (Poland) 4 (1967) : 47–54.

Hough, Samuel J. "An Early Record of Marsilio Ficino." *RQ* 30 (1977) : 301–04.

Huit, Charles. *Le Platonisme pendant la Renaissance*. Monograph published piecemeal in *Annales de Philosophie Chrétienne*, series 2, 32 (1895)–40 (1899). Collected copy at Columbia University.

Huszti, Guiseppe. "La prima redazione del *Convito* di Marsilio Ficino." *GCFI* 8 (1927) : 68–71.

Ivanka, Endre Von. "Apex mentis, Wanderung und Wandlung eines stoischen Termines." *ZKT* 72 (1950) : 129–76.

Ivanoff, N. "Remarques sur M. Ficin." *Revue d'Esthétique* 1 (1948) : 381–92.

Joukovsky, Françoise. "Plotin dans les éditions et les commentaires de Porphyre, Jamblique et Proclus de la Renaissance." *BHR* 42 (1980) : 387–400.

_____. "Plotin et la Renaissance." In *Etudes seiziémistes* (Festschrift for V.-L. Saulnier), edited by Robert Aulotte, pp. 19–32. Geneva, 1980.

Keller, A. "Two Byzantine Scholars and their Reception in Italy." *JWCI* 20 (1957) : 363–70.

Kieszkowski, Bohdan. *Studi sul Platonismo del Rinascimento*. Firenze, 1936.

Klein, Robert. "L'Enfer de Ficin." In *Umanesimo e esoterismo*, edited by Enrico Castelli, pp. 47–84. Padua, 1960.

_____. "L'imagination comme vêtement de l'âme chez Marsile Ficin et Giordano Bruno." *Revue de métaphysique et de morale* 51 (1956) : 18–39.

Klibansky, Raymond. *The Continuity of the Platonic Tradition during the Middle Ages*. London, 1939.

_____. "Ein Proklos-Fund und seine Bedeutung." *Sitzungsberichte der Heidelberger Akademie der Wissenschaften* (*Phil.–Hist. Klasse*) 19 (1929) : 3–41.

_____. "Plato's *Parmenides* in the Middle Ages and the Renaissance." *Medieval and Renaissance Studies* 1 (1943) : 281–335.

Kristeller, Paul O. "An Unpublished Description of Naples by Francesco Bandini." In *Studies in Renaissance Thought and Letters*, pp. 395–410. Rome, 1956.

_____. *The Classics and Renaissance Thought*. Cambridge, Mass., 1955.

_____. "L'état présent des études sur Marsile Ficin." In *Platon et Aristote à la Renaissance*, pp. 59–77. Colloque international de Tours. Paris, 1976.

_____. "The European Diffusion of Italian Humanism." *Italica* 39 (1962) : 1–20.

_____. "The European Significance of Florentine Platonism." In *Medieval and Renaissance Studies* 3, edited by John M. Headley, pp. 206–29. Chapel Hill, N.C., 1968.

_____. "Ficino and Renaissance Platonism." *Personalist* 36 (1955) : 238–49.

_____. "The First Printed Edition of Plato's Works and the Date of its Publication (1484)." In *Science and History: Studies in Honor of Edward Rosen*, pp. 25–35. Wroclaw, 1978.

_____. "Florentine Platonism and its Relations with Humanism and Scholasticism." *Church History* 8 (1939) : 201–11.

_____. "Humanist Learning in the Italian Renaissance." *Centennial Review* 4 (1960) : 243–66.

_____. "The Impact of Early Italian Humanism on Thought and Learning." In *Developments in the Early Renaissance*, edited by Bernard S. Levy, pp. 120–57. Albany, 1972.

_____. "Marsilio Ficino as a Beginning Student of Plato." *Scriptorium* 20 (1966) : 41–54.

_____. "Marsilio Ficino as a Man of Letters and the Glosses Attributed to him in the Caetani Codex of Dante." *RQ* 36 (1983) : 1–47. Italian original in *Quaderni della Fondazione Camillo Caetani* 3 (1981).

_____. "Movimenti filosofici del Rinascimento." *GCFI* 29 (1950) : 275–88.

_____. *The Philosophy of Marsilio Ficino.* Translated by Virginia Conant. New York, 1943. Also available in German (Frankfort, 1972) and Italian. I have used the Italian translation, by the author, *Il Pensiero filosofico di Marsilio Ficino.* Florence, 1953.

_____. "The Platonic Academy of Florence." *RN* 14 (1961) : 147–58.

_____. "Platonismo bizantino e fiorentino e la controversia su Platone e Aristotle." *Venezia e l'Oriente,* pp. 103–16. Florence, 1966.

_____. *Renaissance Concepts of Man, and Other Essays.* New York, 1972.

_____. "Renaissance Platonism." In *Facets of the Renaissance,* edited by W. H. Werkmeister, pp. 103–23. 2d ed. Los Angeles, 1963.

_____. *Renaissance Thought.* 2 vols. New York, 1961 and 1965.

_____. *Renaissance Thought and its Sources.* Edited by Michael Mooney. New York, 1979.

_____. "Some Original Letters and Autograph Manuscripts of Marsilio Ficino." In *Studi di bibliografia e di storia in onore di Tammaro De Marinis.* Vol. 3, pp. 5–33. Verona, 1964.

_____. *Studies in Renaissance Thought and Letters.* Rome, 1956.

_____. *Supplementum Ficinianum.* 2 vols. Florence, 1937.

_____. "La teoria dell' appetito naturale in Marsilio Ficino." *GCFI,* series 2, 5 (1937) : 234–56.

_____. "A Thomist Critique of Marsilio Ficino's Theory of Will and Intellect." *Harry A Wolfson Jubilee Volume* (English Section), 2 : 463–94. Jerusalem, 1965.

_____. *La tradizione classica nel pensiero del Rinascimento.* Florence, 1965.

_____. *La tradizione aristotelica nel rinascimento.* Padua, 1962.

_____. "Un nuovo trattatello inedito di Marsilio Ficino." *Rinascimento* 1 (1950) : 25–42.

_____. "Volontà e amore divino in Marsilio Ficino." *GCFI,* series 2, 6 (1938) : 185–214.

Kuczyńska, Alicja. *Filozofia i teoria peikna Marsilia Ficina.* Warsaw, 1970.

LeFevre d'Etaples, Jacques. *Prefatory Epistles.* Edited by Eugene F. Rice. New York, 1977.

Lloyd, A. K. "Primum in genere: The Philosophical Background." *Diotima* 4 (1976) : 32–36.

Lowes, John I. "The Loveres Maladye of Hereos." *MP* 11 (1913–14) : 491–546.

Maimonides, Moses. *The Guide for the Perplexed.* Translated by M. Friedlander. 2d ed. New York, 1956.

Marcel, Raymond. "L' apologétique de Marsile Ficin." In *Pensée Humaniste et tradition Chrétienne,* edited by Henri Bédarida, pp. 159–68. Paris, 1950.

_____. "La Fureur poétique et l'humanisme florentin." *Mélanges Georges Jamati,* pp. 177–93. Paris, 1956.

_____. *Marsile Ficin.* Paris, 1958.

Margolin, Jean-Claude. "Platon et Aristote à la Renaissance." *BHR* 36 (1974) : 157–73.

Masai, François. *Plethon et le Platonisme de Mistra.* Paris, 1956.

_____. "Le platonisme italien et le probleme des influences byzantines." In *Association Guillaume Budé. Congrès de Tours et Poitiers,* pp. 320–21. Paris, 1954.

_____. "Pléthon, l'Averroisme et le probleme réligieux." In *Le Néoplatonisme*, pp. 437–46. Colloques internationaux du Centre National de la Recherche Scientifique. Paris, 1971.

_____. "Platonisme et christianisme au XVe siècle." *Revue de l' Université de Bruxelles* 10 (1958) : 392–412.

_____. "Renaissance platonicienne et controverses trinitaires, à Byzance au XVe siecle" In *Platon et Aristote à la Renaissance*, pp. 25–43. Colloque international de Tours (1973). Paris, 1976.

_____. "La Restauration du Paganisme par Georges Gemiste Pléthon." *Il Mondo Antico nel Rinascimento*, pp. 57–62. Convegno internazionale di studi sul Rinascimento. Florence, 1958.

Maurer, A. A. *Medieval Philosophy*, pp. 328–37 (on Ficino). New York, 1962.

Maylender, Michel. *Storia delle accademie d'Italia*. 5 vols. Bologna, 1926–30.

Mohler, Ludwig. *Kardinal Bessarion als Theologe, Humanist und Staatsmann*. 3 vols. Paderborn, 1923–42.

Mönch, Walter. "Platon und Marsilio Ficino." In *Das Gastmahl*, pp. 11–87. Hamburg, 1947.

Monfasani, John. *George of Trebizond*. Leiden, 1976.

Nardi, Bruno. *Dante e la cultura medievale*. 2d ed. Bari, 1949.

Nedoncelle, M. "Nature et valeur permanente de l'amour platonique." *Studi internazionali di filosofia* 8 (1976) : 27–38.

Nelson, John Charles. "Platonism in the Renaissance." In *Dictionary of the History of Ideas*, edited by Philip Weiner. Vol. 3, pp. 508–15. New York, 1973.

Nobili, Flaminio. *Il Trattato dell'amore humano*. Edited by Pier D. Pasolini. Rome, 1895.

Norford, Don P. "Microcosm and Macrocosm in Seventeenth-Century Literature." *JHI* 38 (1977) : 409–28.

Nygren, Anders. *Agape and Eros*, pp. 668–80. London, 1953.

Oberman, Heiko. "A Nominalistic Glossary." In *The Harvest of Medieval Theology*, pp. 459–76. Cambridge, Mass., 1963.

_____. "Some Notes on the Theology of Nominalism, with Attention to its Relations to the Renaissance." *Harvard Theological Review* 53 (1960) : 47–76.

_____. *Itinerarium Italicum*. Leiden, 1975.

Partee, Charles. "The Revitalization of 'The Christian Philosophy' in Renaissance Humanism." *CSR* 3 (1974) : 360–69.

Pfeiffer, Rudolf. *A History of Classical Scholarship 1300–1850*. Oxford, 1976.

Plotinus. *Enneads*. Edited by Emile Bréhier. Paris, 1924–28.

_____. *Enneads*. Translated by Stephen MacKenna and B. S. Page. 3d ed. London, 1962.

Poppi, Antonino. "Il problema della filosofia morale nella scuola Padovana del Rinascimento." In *Platon et Aristote à la Renaissance*, pp. 105–46. Colloque international de Tours (1973). Paris, 1976.

Pouillon, Henri. "La beauté, propriété transcendentale, chez les scolastiques (1220–1270)." *AHDLM* 15 (1946) : 263–329.

Proclus. *Alcibiades I*. Translated by William O'Neill. Hague, 1965.

_____. *Commentary on the First Alcibiades of Plato.* Edited by L. G. Westerink. Amsterdam, 1954.

_____. *The Elements of Theology.* Edited by E. R. Dodds. 2d ed. Oxford, 1963.

_____. *Théologie Platonicienne.* Edited by H. D. Saffrey and L. G. Westerink. 6 vols., in progress. Paris, 1968–.

Pugliese, Olga Zorzi. "Quattrocento Views on Love and Existence." *Canadian Journal of Italian Studies* 1 (1977) : 97–107.

Purnell, F. "Hermes and Sibyl: A Note on Ficino's *Pimander.*" *RQ* 30 (1977) : 305–10.

Pusino, Ivan. "Ficinos und Picos religiös-philosophische Anschauungen." *ZFK* 44 (1925) : 504–43.

Reypens, R. P. "Ame." *Dictionnaire de Spiritualité.* Vol. 1, pp. 434–67. Paris, 1933.

Rist, J. M. *Studies in Eros and Psyche.* Toronto, 1964.

Robb, Nesca. *Neoplatonism of the Italian Renaissance.* London, 1935.

Robin, Leon. *La Théorie Platonicienne de l' amour.* Paris, 1933.

Rocholl, R. "Der Platonismus der Renaissancezeit." *ZFK* 13 (1892) : 47–104.

Rosa, Romano. "S. Tomasso e Marsilio Ficino." *Sapienza* 25 (1972) : 335–45.

Rousselot, Pierre. *Pour l' histoire du problème de l' amour au moyen âge.* Beiträge zur Geschichte der Philosophie des Mittelalters. Vol. 6. Munster, 1908.

Russo, Luigi. "La poetica di Platone e il Rinascimento." *Belfagor* 16 (1961) : 401–15.

Saffrey, H. D. "Notes Platoniciennes de Marsile Ficin dans un manuscrit de Proclus." *BHR* 21 (1959) : 161–84.

Saitta, Giuseppe. "La rivendicazione di Epicuro nell 'umanesimo.'" *Filosofia italiana e umanesimo,* pp. 53–82. Venice, 1928.

_____. *Marsilio Ficino e la filosofia dell' umanesimo,* esp. pp. 193–238. 3d ed. Bologna, 1954.

Saurat, Denis. *Literature and the Occult Tradition.* New York, 1930.

Schelhorn, J. "De vita, moribus et scriptis Marsilii Ficini commentatio." In *Amoenitates literariae.* Leipzig, 1730.

Schiavone, Michele. *Problemi filosofici in Marsilio Ficino.* Milan, 1957.

Schmitt, Charles B. *Cicero Scepticus.* Hague, 1972.

_____. "L'introduction de la philosophie platonicienne dans l'enseignment des universités à la Renaissance. In *Platon et Aristote à la Renaissance,* pp. 93–104. Colloque international de Tours (1973). Paris, 1976.

_____. "Perennial Philosophy: From Agostino Steuco to Leibniz." *JHI* 27 (1966) : 505–32.

_____. "Prisca theologia e philosophia perennis: due temi del rinascimento italiano e la loro fortuna." *Il pensiero italiano del rinascimento e il tempo nostro,* pp. 211–36. Convegno internazionale del centro di studi umanistici. Florence, 1970.

Scholz, Heinrich. *Eros und Caritas: die platonische Liebe und die Liebe im Sinne des Christentums.* Halle, 1929.

Schwartz, Jerome. "Aspects of Androgyny in the Renaissance." In *Human Sexuality in the Middle Ages and Renaissance,* edited by Douglas Radcliffe-Umstead, pp. 121–31. Pittsburgh, 1978.

Scott, William O. "Perotti, Ficino, and Furor Poeticus." *Res Publica Litterarum* 4 (1981) : 273–84.

Sheppard, Anne. "The Influence of Hermias on Marsilio Ficino's Doctrine of Inspiration." *JWCI* 43 (1980) : 97–109.

Shorey, Paul. *Platonism Ancient and Modern*. Berkeley, 1938.

Shumaker, Wayne. *The Occult Sciences in the Renaissance*. Berkeley, 1972.

Sicherl, Martin. "Neuentdeckte Handschriften von Marsilio Ficino und Johannes Reuchlin." *Scriptorium* 16 (1962) : 50–61.

Siedlmayer, Michael. "Religiös–ethische Probleme des italienisches Humanismus." *Germanisch-Romanische Monatsschrift*. N.F., 8 (1958) : 105–26.

Simonin, H. D. "Autour de la solution Thomiste du problème de l'amour." *AHDLM* 6 (1931) : 174–272.

Smalley, Beryl. "Gregory IX and the Two Faces of the Soul." *MRS* 2 (1950) : 179–82.

Soellner, Rolf. "Shakespeare, Aristotle, Plato, and the Soul." In *Deutsche Shakespeare Gesellschaft Jahrbuch 1968*, pp. 56–71. Heidelberg, 1968.

Soldati, Benedetto. *La poesia astrologica nel quattrocento*. Florence, 1906.

Solinas, G. "Sull' estetica di M. Ficino." *Annali della Facoltà di lettere di Cagliari* 16 (1949) : 367–80. Not seen.

Stein, Heinrich von. *Sieben Bücher zur Geschichte des Platonismus*. Göttingen, 1875.

Stewart, H. L. "The Platonic Academy of Florence." *Hibbert Journal* 43 (1945) : 226–36.

Tanturli, Giuliano. "I Benci copisti." *Studi di filologia italiana* 36 (1978) : 197–313.

Tateo, Francesco. "Il Platonismo e la crisi dell' umanesimo." In *Il Quattrocento*, by Achille Tartaro and Francesco Tateo. La Letteratura italiana: storia e testi, edited by Carlo Muscetta, vol. 3.1, pp. 375–421. Bari, 1971.

Taylor, John W. *Gemisthus Pletho's Criticism of Plato and Aristotle*. Menasha, 1921.

Thorndike, Lynn. "Marsilio Ficino und Pico della Mirandola und die Astrologie." ZFK 46 (1927) : 584–85.

Tigerstedt, Eugene N. *The Decline and Fall of the Neoplatonic Interpretation of Plato*. Helsinki, 1974.

_____. "Furor poeticus: Poetic Inspiration in Greek Literature before Democritus and Plato." *JHI* 31 (1970) : 163–70.

_____. *Plato's Idea of Poetical Inspiration*. Helsinki, 1969.

_____. "The Poet as Creator: Origins of a Metaphor." *CLS* 5 (1968) : 455–88.

Tsouyopoulos, N. "Der Einfluss des Neoplatonismus auf die Wissenschaft der Renaissance." *Sudhoffs Archiv* 60 (1976) : 33–44.

Valency, Maurice. *In Praise of Love*. New York, 1958.

Vieri, Francesco de'. *Lezzioni d'amore*. Edited by John Colaneri. Munich, 1973.

Vinge, Louise. *The Five Senses: Studies in a Literary Tradition*. Lund, 1975.

Vossler, Karl. *Die philosophischen Grundlagen zum süssen neuen Stil des Guido Guinicelli, Guido Cavalcanti und Dante*. Heidelberg, 1904.

Walker, D. P. "The Astral Body in Renaissance Medicine." *JWCI* 21 (1958) : 119–33.

_____. "Orpheus the Theologian and the Renaissance Platonists." *JWCI* 16 (1953) : 100–20. Reprinted, revised in *The Ancient Theology*, pp. 22–41. Ithaca, 1972.

Wallis, R. T. *Neoplatonism*. London, 1972.

Walzel, Oskar. "Von Plotin, Proklos und Ficinus." *DVLG* 19 (1941) : 407–29.

Weinstein, Donald. *Savonarola and Florence.* Princeton, 1970.

Westerink, L. G. "Ficino's Marginal Notes on Olympiodorus in Riccardiana Greek MS 37." *Traditio* 24 (1968) : 351–78.

Zambelli, Paola. "Platone, Ficino e la magia." In *Studia Humanitatis, Ernesto Grassi zum 70. Geburtstag*, edited by Eginhard Hora and Eckhard Kessler, pp. 121–42. Munich, 1973.

Zanier, Giancarlo. *La medicina astrologica e la sua teoria: Marsilio Ficino e i suoi critici contemporanei.* Rome, 1977. Not seen.

III. Italy

Bérence, Fred. "Pietro Bembo et les *Dialogues d'Amour.*" *Cahiers du Sud* 305 (1951) : 101–18.

Buck, August. *Der Einfluss des Platonismus auf die volkesprachliche Literatur im florentiner Quattrocento.* Krefeld, 1966.

_____. *Der Platonismus in den Dichtungen Lorenzo de' Medicis.* Berlin, 1936.

Chastel, André. "Melancholia in the Sonnets of Lorenzo de' Medici." *JWCI* 8 (1945) : 61–67.

Colonna, Egidio. *L'espositione sopra la canzone d'amore di Guido Cavalcanti.* Siena, 1602.

Cordova, G. Capra. *Il platonismo nei trattati d'amore del cinquecento . . .* Cerignola, 1902. Not seen.

Crane, T. F. *Italian Social Customs of the Sixteenth Century and their Influence on the Literatures of Europe.* New Haven, 1920.

Del Vita, Alessandro. "Trattati d'amore." *Vasari* 17 (1959) : 143–60.

Dethier, Hubert. "Michelangelo Buonarroti en de Florentintynse Academie." *Dialoghi* 7 (1966) : 1–9. Not seen.

De Venditis, L. "Il platonismo agostiniano del Petrarca." *Medioevo romanzo* 5 (1978) : 320–46.

Equicola, Mario. *Libro di natura d'amore.* Venice, 1531.

Ercole, Pietro, ed. *Guido Cavalcanti e sue rime.* Livorno, 1885.

Farinelli, Arturo. *Michelangelo e Dante.* Turin, 1918.

Fletcher, Jefferson B. *The Religion of Beauty in Woman.* New York, 1911.

Floriani, Pietro. *Bembo e Castiglione.* Rome, 1976.

Frachetta, Girolamo. *La spositione . . . sopra la canzone di Guido Cavalcanti.* Venice, 1586.

Friedrich, Hugo. *Epochen der italienischen Lyrik.* Frankfort, 1964

Garin, Eugenio. "Marsilio Ficino, Girolamo Benivieni e Giovanni Pico." *GCFI* 23 (1942) : 93–99.

Griswold, Jerry. "Aquinas, Dante, and Ficino on Love, An Explication of the Paradiso: XXVI.25–39." *SMC* 8–9 (1976) : 151–61.

Hettner, Hermann. *Das Wiederaufleben des Platonismus in italienische Studien.* Braunschweig, 1897. Not seen.

Ingegno, Alfonso. "Il primo Bruno e l'influenza di Marsilio Ficino." *Rivista critica di storia della filosofia* 23 (1968) : 149–70.

Kristeller, Paul O. "Francesco da Diacceto and Florentine Platonism in the Sixteenth Century." *Miscellanea Giovanni Mercati* 4 (1946) : 260–304. Reprinted in Kristeller, *Studies*, pp. 267–336.

_____. "Lorenzo de' Medici Platonico." *Studies in Renaissance Thought and Letters*, pp. 213–19. Rome, 1956

Lega, Gino. *Il Canzoniere Vaticano-Barberino Latino 3953*. Bologna, 1905

Lorenzetti, Paolo. *La bellezza e l' amore nei trattati del cinquecento*. Pisa, 1922.

Luzi, Mario. "Un'illusione platonica." In *Un'illusione platonica e altri saggi*, pp. 19–38 (on Castiglione). Florence, 1941. Reprinted 1972, pp. 19–33

Maiorino, Giancarlo. "The Breaking of the Circle: Giordano Bruno and the Poetics of Immeasurabale Abundance." *JHI* 38 (1977) : 317–27

Mann, Thomas. "La concezione dell' amore nella poesia di Michelangelo." *Letterature Moderne* 1 (1950) : 427–34.

Marcel, Raymond. "Le Platonisme de Pétrarque à Léon l' Hébreu." *Association Guillaume Budé. Congrès de Tours et Poitiers*, pp. 293–319. Paris, 1954.

Melczer, William. "Neoplatonism and Petrarchism: Familiar or Estranged Bedfellows in the High Renaissance." *Neohelicon* 3 (1975) : 9–27.

Merrill, Robert V. "Platonism in Petrarch's Canzoniere." *MP* 27 (1929) : 161–74.

Meylan, Edouard F. "L' évolution de la notion d' amour platonique." *Humanisme et Renaissance* 5 (1938) : 418–42.

Michel, Paul Henri. "Renaissance Cosmologies." *Diogenes* 18 (1957) : 93–107.

_____. *The Cosmology of Giordano Bruno*. Translated by R. E. W. Maddison. Ithaca, 1973.

Nelson, John Charles. "The Poetry of Michelangelo." In *Developments in the Early Renaissance*, edited by Bernard S. Levy, pp. 15–35. Albany, 1972.

_____. *Renaissance Theory of Love: The Context of Giordano Bruno's Eroici Furori*. New York, 1958.

[Orpheus] *Orphica*. Edited by Eugene Abel. Leipzig, 1885.

Pappalardo, F. "Per una rilettura della canzone d'amore del Cavalcanti." *SPCT* 13 (1976) : 47–76.

Patterson, Annabel M. "Tasso and Neoplatonism: The Growth of his Epic Theory." *SRen* 18 (1971) : 105–33.

Pozzi, Mario. "Mario Equicola e la cultura cortigiana." *Lettere italiane* 32 (1980) : 149–71.

Radetti, Giorgio. "Demoni e sogni nella critica di Callimaco Esperiente al Ficino." In *Umanesimo e esoterismo*, edited by Enrico Castelli, pp. 111–21. Padua, 1960.

Robb, Nesca. *Neoplatonism of the Italian Renaissance*. London, 1935.

Rocchi, Ivonne. "Per una nuova cronologia e valutazione del *Libro de natura de amore* di Mario Equicola." *GSLI* 93 (1976) : 566–85.

Rosi, Michele. *Saggio sui trattati d'amore nel 500*. Recanati, 1889.

_____. *Scienza d'amore*. Milan, 1904.

Saitta, Guiseppe. *Le teoria dell' amore e l' educazione nel rinascimento*. Bologna, 1947.

Santayana, George. "Platonic Love in Some Italian Poets." *Interpretations of Poetry and Religion*, pp. 118–46. New York, 1900.

Savino, Lorenzo. *Di alcuni trattati e trattatisti d' amore italiani*. Naples, 1912.

Scarano, Nicola. "Il Platonismo nelle poesie di Lorenzo de' Medici." *Nuova antologia*, series 3, 46 (1893) : 605–28; 47 (1893) : 49–66.

Thomas, Gabriel. "Michel-Ange, poète: étude sur l'expression de l'amour platonique dans la poésie italienne du Moyen Age et de la Renaissance." *Mémoires de l'Académie de Stanislas*, series 5, 8 (1890) : 291–454.

Thompson, David. "Pico della Mirandola's Praise of Lorenzo (and Critique of Dante and Petrarch)." *Neophilologus* 54 (1970) : 123–27.

Toffanin, Guiseppe. *Il Cortegiano nella trattatistica del rinascimento*. Naples, 1961.

Tonelli, Luigi. *L'amore nella poesia e nel pensiero del rinascimento*. Florence, 1933.

Trinkaus, Charles. *In Our Image and Likeness*, esp. vol. 2. Chicago, 1970.

Vallese, Giulio. "La filosofia dell' amore nel rinascimento: dal Ficino al Bembo," and "da Leone Ebreo ai Minori." *Le Parole e Idee* 6 (1964) : 15–30 and 207–18. Reprinted in *Grande Antologia Filosofica* 11. Milan, 1965; and in *Studi di umanesimo*, pp. 43–89. Naples, 1971.

Vieri, Francesco de' (Il Verino Secondo). *Compendio della dottrina di Platone*, ch. 2. Florence, 1577.

_____. *Lezzioni d'amore*. Edited by John Colaneri. Munich, 1973.

Wadsworth, James B. "Landino's *Disputationes Camaldulenses*, Ficino's *De Felicitate*, and *L' Altercazione* of Lorenzo de' Medici." *MP* 50 (1952) : 23–31.

_____. "Lorenzo de' Medici and Marsilio Ficino: An Experiment in Platonic Friendship." *Romanic Review* 4–6 (1955) : 90–100.

Walker, D. P. *Spiritual and Demonic Magic from Ficino to Campanella*. London, 1958.

_____. "Esoteric Symbolism." In *Poetry and Poetics from Ancient Greece to the Renaissance*, edited by G. M. Kirkwood, pp. 218–32. Ithaca, 1975.

Yates, Frances A. *Giordano Bruno and the Hermetic Tradition*. Chicago, 1964.

Zonta, G. *Trattati d' Amore*. Bari, 1912.

IV. France

Adam, Antoine. "La théorie mystique de l'amour dans *l'Astrée* et ses sources italiennes." *Revue d'histoire de la philosophie et d'histoire générale de la civilisation* 15 (1936) : 193–206.

Antonioli, Roland. "Aspects du monde occulte chez Ronsard." In *Lumieres de la Pléiade*, pp. 195–230. Stage international d'études humanistes. Tours, 1965. Paris, 1966.

_____. "Un medecin lecteur du *Timée*, S. Champier." In *Colloque sur l'humanisme lyonnais au XVIe siècle* (1972), pp. 53–62. Grenoble, 1974.

Baillou, Jean. "L' influence de la pensée philosophique de la Renaissance italienne sur la pensée francaise." *Revue des études italiennes* 1 (1936) : 116–55.

Bazan, Paul. *L'influence neo-platonicienne sur la poésie courtoise*. Paris, 1973.

Becker, A. *Un humaniste au xvie siècle: Louis Le Roy de Coutances*. Paris, 1896.

Brann, Noel L. "Melancholy and the Divine Frenzies in the French Pléiade." *JMRS* 9 (1979) : 81–100.

Brody, Jules. "Platonisme et classicisme." *Saggi e ricerche di letteratura francese* 2 (1961) : 7–30. Milan, 1961.

Burgess, Robert M. *Platonism in Desportes*. Chapel Hill, N.C., 1954.

Castor, Grahame. *Pléiade Poetics: A Study in Sixteenth-Century Thought and Terminology*. New York, 1964.

Cavazza, Silvano. "Platonismo e riforma religiosa: la theologia vivificans di Jacques Lefèvre d'Etaples." *Rinascimento* 22 (1982) : 99–149.

Clements, Robert J. *Critical Theory and Practice of the Pléiade.* Cambridge, Mass., 1942.

_____. "Ronsard and Ficino on the Four Furies." *Romanic Review* 45 (1954) : 161–69.

Coleman, Dorothy. *Maurice Scève, Poet of Love.* Cambridge, 1975.

Copenhaver, Brian P. *Symphorien Champier and the Reception of the Occultist Tradition in Renaissance France.* Hague, 1979.

Dagens, Jean. "Hermétisme et cabale en France, de Lefèvre d'Etaples à Bossuet." *RLC* 35 (1961) : 5–16.

Dexter, G. "L'imagination poétique." *BHR* 27 (1975) : 49–62. [On Platonism in B. Aneau].

Dresden, Sam. "The Profile of the Reception of the Italian Renaissance in France." In *Itinerarium Italicum,* edited by Heiko Oberman, pp. 119–89. Leiden, 1975.

Fenoaltea, D. "The Final Dizains of Scène's *Délie* and the *Dialogo d'Amore* of Sperone Speroni." *SF* 20 (1976) : 201–25.

Festugière, Jean. *La philosophie de l'amour de Marsile Ficin.* 2d ed. Paris, 1941.

Françon, Marcel. "Pétrarquisme et Néo-platonisme chez Peletier du Mans." *Italica* 36 (1959) : 28–35.

Gadoffre, Gilbert. "Ronsard et la Pensée Ficinienne." *Archives de philosophie* 26 (1963) : 45–58.

Gauna, S. M. "De genio Pantagruelis: An Examination of Rabelaisian Demonology." *BHR* 33 (1971) : 557–70.

Gundersheimer, Werner I. *The Life and Works of Louis Le Roy.* Geneva, 1966.

Hall, Kathleen H. *Pontus de Tyard and his "Discours philosophiques."* Oxford, 1963.

Hawkins, Richmond L. "The *Querelle des amies*: the Platonism of Charles Fontaine." In *Maistre Charles Fontaine, Parisien,* pp. 70–119. Cambridge, Mass., 1916.

Hébréo, Léon. *Dialogues d'amour.* Translated by Pontus de Tyard. Edited by Theodore Anthony Perry. Chapel Hill, N.C., 1974.

Hornik, Henry. "Guy le Fevre de la Boderie's *La Galliade* and Renaissance Syncretism." *MLN* 76 (1961) : 735–42.

_____. "More on Ronsard's Philosophy, the *Hymnes* and Neoplatonism." *BHR* 27 (1965) : 435–43.

_____. "More on the Hermetica and French Renaissance Literature." *SFr.* 52 (1974) : 1–12.

Huit, Charles. "La platonisme en France au XVIIe siècle." *Annales de philosophie chrétienne.* *CDI* (1906) : 473–505 and *CDI* 2 (1906) : 134–60, 516–35. Not seen.

Johnson, Leonard W. "Literary Neoplatonism in Five French Treatises of the Early Seventeenth Century." *Romanic Review* 60 (1969) : 233–50.

Keating, L. C. *Studies in the Literary Salon in France 1550–1615.* Cambridge, Mass., 1941.

Kerr, W. A. R. "Antoine Héroet's Parfaite Amye." *PMLA* 20 (1905) : 567–83.

_____. "Le Cercle d'Amour." *PMLA* 19 (1904) : 33–63.

_____. *Platonic love theories in the Renaissance with Special Regard to France.* Dissertation, Harvard, 1904. *CDI.*

_____. "The Pléiade and Platonism." *MP* 5 (1908) : 407–21.

Kushner, Eva. "Le personnage d' Orphée chez Ronsard." In *Lumières de la Pléiade*, pp. 271–302. Stage international d'études humanistes. Tours, 1965. Paris, 1966.

_____. "Le *Solitaire premier* de Pontus de Tyard." *RBPH* 50 (1972) : 760–67.

Lajarte, Philippe de. "*L'Heptaméron* et le Ficinisme." *RSH* 147 (1972) : 339–71.

Lebègue, Raymond. "Le Platonisme en France au XVIe siècle." *Association Guillaume Budé. Congrès de Tours et Poitiers*, pp. 331–51. Paris, 1954.

Leclerc, Hélène. "Du mythe platonicien aux fêtes de la Renaissance." *Revue de la Société d'histoire du théatre* 11 (1959) : 105–71.

Lefranc, Abel. "La platonisme et la littérature en France à l'époque de la Renaissance." *Revue de l'histoire littéraire de la France* 3 (1896) : 1–44. Reprinted in *Grands écrivains français de la Renaissance*, pp. 63–137. Paris, 1914.

_____. "Marguerite de Navarre et le platonisme de la Renaissance." *Bibliotheque de l'Ecole de chartes* 58 (1897) : 3–81. Reprinted in *Grands écrivains français de la Renaissance*, pp. 139–249. Paris, 1914.

Levi, Anthony H. T. *French Moralists*, esp. pp. 165–76 and 202–13. Oxford, 1964.

_____. "The Neoplatonist calculus: the exploitation of Neo-platonist themes in French Renaissance Literature." In *Humanism in France*, pp. 229–48. New York, 1970.

Ley, Klaus. *Neuplatonische Poetik und nationale Wirklichkeit*. (on DuBellay). Heidelberg, 1975.

Lorenzetti, Paolo. *Riflessi del pensiero italiano nell' "Heptameron" di Margherita di Navarre*. Voghera, 1916.

McFarlane, I. D., ed. *The Délie of Maurice Scève*. Cambridge, 1966.

Margolin, Jean-Claude. "Le Roy traducteur de Platon et la Pléiade." In *Lumières de la Pléiade*, pp. 49–62. Stage international d'études humanistes. Tours, 1965. Paris, 1966.

Marichal, Robert. "L'attitude de Rabelais devant le Neoplatonisme et l' italianisme." In *François Rebelais: Ouvrage publié pour le quatrième centenaire de sa mort 1533–1953*. Vol. 7, pp. 181–209. Geneva, 1953.

Masters, George M. "The Hermetic and Platonic Traditions in Rabelais." *SFr*. 10 (1966) : 15–29.

_____. *Rabelaisian Dialectic and the Platonic–Hermetic Tradition*. Albany, 1969.

Mathieu-Castellani, Gisele. *Les thèmes amoureuses dans la poésie française 1570–1600*. Paris, 1975.

Merrill, Robert V. "Eros and Anteros." *Speculum* 19 (1944) : 265–84.

_____, and Clements, Robert J. *Platonism in French Renaissance Poetry*. New York, 1957.

_____. "Platonism in Pontus de Tyard's *Erreurs Amoureuses, 1549*." *MP* 35 (1937) : 144–48.

_____. "The Pléiade and the Androgyne." *CL* 1 (1949) : 97–112.

Mesnard, Pierre. "Le Platonisme de Jean Bodin." *Association Guillaume Budé. Congrès de Tours et Poitiers*, pp. 352–61. Paris, 1954.

Mönch, Walter. *Die italienische Platonrenaissance und ihre Bedeutung für Frankreichs Literatur und Geistesgeschichte, 1450–1500*. Berlin, 1936.

_____. "Le sonnet et le platonisme." In *Association Guillaume Budé. Congrès de Tours et Poitiers*, pp. 376–80. Paris, 1954.

_____. "Marsiglio Ficino und die Nachwirkung Platons in der französischen Literatur und Geistesgeschichte." *Kant Studien* 40 (1935) : 165–79.

Nothnagle, John T. "Poet or Hierophant: A New View of the Poetic Furor." *Esprit Créateur* 4 (1966) : 203–07.

Nurse, Peter H. "Christian Platonism in the Poetry of Bonaventure des Periers." *BHR* 19 (1957) : 234–44.

Pantin, I. "Un débat sur les influences astrales (1507); Champier et Ficin." *BHR* 39 (1977) : 545–47.

Perry, Theodore Anthony. *Erotic Spirituality.* University, Ala., 1980.

Pézard, André. "Nymphes platoniciennes au Paradis Terrestre." *Association Guillaume Budé. Congrès de Tours et Poitiers*, pp. 321–23. Paris, 1954.

Picot, Emile. *Les Françaises italianisants au XVIe siècle.* 2 vols. Paris, 1906–07.

Pierrefeu, Nita de. "Marguerite de Navarre la platonicienne." *Cahiers d'Etudes Cathares* 24 (1973) : 15–27.

Pouilloux, Jean-Yves. "Problèmes de traduction: L. Le Roy et le Xe livre de la *République*." *BHR* 31 (1969) : 47–66.

Renaudet, A. *Préréforme et humanisme à Paris.* 2d ed. Paris, 1953.

Rice, Eugene, Jr. "The Humanist Idea of Christian Antiquity: Le fevre d'Etaples and his Circle." *SRen* 9 (1962) : 126–60.

Roger, J. "La situation d'Aristote dans l'oeuvre de Symphorien Champier. In *Colloque sur l'humanisme lyonnais au XVIe siècle* (1972), pp. 41–51. Grenoble, 1974.

Saulnier, V. L. "Marguerite de Navarre: art médiéval et pensée nouvelle." *Revue Universitaire* 63 (1954) : 154–62.

Schmidt, Albert-Marie. *La Poésie Scientifique en France au seizième siècle.* Paris, 1970.

_____. "Poètes lyonnais du XVIe siècle." In *Études sur le XVIe siècle*, pp. 173–94. Paris, 1967.

_____. "Traducteurs français de Platon (1536–1550)." In *Études sur le XVIe siècle*, pp. 18–44. Paris, 1967.

Secret, François. *L'Esoterisme de Guy le Fevre de la Boderie.* Geneva, 1969.

Sigal, Stephanny C. *Le platonisme et le sensualisme dans l'oeuvre de Louise Labé.* Dissertation, Tulane, 1975. *DAI* 36 : 5341A.

Sozzi, Lionello. "La 'dignitas hominis' dans la littérature française de la Renaissance." In *Humanism in France*, edited by A. H. T. Levi, pp. 176–98. New York, 1970.

_____. "La 'dignitas hominis' chez les auteurs lyonnais du XVIe siècle." In *Colloque sur l'humanisme lyonnais au XVIe siècle* (1972), pp. 295–338. Grenoble, 1974.

Spitzer, Leo. "The Poetic Treatment of a Platonic Christian Theme." *CL* 6 (1954) : 193–217.

Staub, Hans. "Scève, poète hermétique." *Cahiers de l'association internationale des études françaises* 15 (1963) : 25–39.

Stegmann, André. "L'inspiration platonicienne dans les *Hymnes* de Ronsard." *RSH* 31 (1966) : 193–210.

Stone, Donald. *The Platonic Ladder: the Function of Love in Ronsard's Poetic Creation.* Dissertation, Yale, 1963. *CDI.*

Taylor, Mary E. *The Influence of Platonism on Certain French Authors of the 16th Century.* M. Litt. thesis, Cambridge, 1930. Not seen.

Tiemann, Barbara. *Fabel und Emblem* (on Corrozet). Munich, 1974.

Tilley, Arthur. *The Dawn of the French Renaissance.* Cambridge, 1918.

Varga, A. K. "Poésie et cosmologie au XVIe siècle." In *Lumières de la Pléiade*, pp. 135–55 (on Héroet). Stage international d'études humanistes. Tours, 1965.

Varty, Kenneth. "Louise Labé and Marsilio Ficino." *MLN* 71 (1956) : 508–10.

Vasoli, Cesare. "Temi e fonti della tradizione ermetica in uno scritto di Symphorien Champier." In *Umanismo e esoterismo*, edited by Enrico Castelli, pp. 235–89. Padua, 1960.

Wadsworth, James B. "Filippo Beroaldo the Elder and the Early Renaissance in Lyons." *Medievalia et Humanistica* 11 (1957) : 78–89.

_____. *Lyons 1473–1503: The Beginnings of Cosmopolitanism.* Cambridge, Mass., 1962.

_____. *Le livre de vraye Amour.* Edited by Symphorien Champier. The Hague, 1962.

Walker, D. P. "The Prisca Theologia in France." *JWCI* 17 (1954) : 204–59. Reprinted, revised, in *The Ancient Theology*, pp. 63–131. Ithaca, 1972.

Weber, Henri. *La création poétique au XVIe siècle en France.* 2 vols. Paris, 1956.

_____. "Platonisme et sensualité dans la poésie amoureuse de la Pléiade." In *Lumières de la Pléiade*, pp. 157–94. Stage international d'études humanistes. Tours, 1965. Paris, 1966.

_____. "La Poésie amoureuse de la Pléiade." In *Übersetzung und Nachahmung im europaischen Petrarkismus*, compiled by Luzius Keller, pp. 42–88. Stuttgart, 1974.

_____. "Thèmes d'amour platonicien dans le *Printemps* d'Agrippa d'Aubigné." *Association Guillaume Budé. Congrès de Tours et Poitiers*, pp. 361–64. Paris, 1954.

_____. "Y-a-t-il une poésie hermétique au xvie siècle en France?" *Cahiers de l'association internationale des études françaises* 15 (1963) : 41–58.

Williams, Thomas A. "The Question of Platonism in the *Erreurs Amoureuses* of Pontus de Tyard." *High Point College Studies* 3 (1963) : 7–12.

Wilson, Dudley. "Ronsard's Orphism in the *Hymnes*." In *Histoire et littérature: Les Ecrivains et la politique*, pp. 237–63. Centre d'étude et de recherche d'histoire des idées. Paris, 1977.

Yates, Frances A. *The French Academies of the Sixteenth Century.* London, 1947.

V. Spain

Arciniegas, Germán. "El Inca Garcilaso y Léon Hebreo." *Cuadernos*, no. 45 (Nov.–Dec. 1960) : 5–11.

_____. "El Inca Garcilaso y Léon Hebreo, o cuatro diálogos de amor." *Miscelanea de Estudos a Joaquim de Carvalho*, no. 4 (1960) : 359–67.

Arocena, Luis A. *El Inca Garcilaso y el humanismo renacentista.* Buenos Aires, 1949.

Arrando, María del Pilar. *Auzias March y Garcilaso de la Vega: poetas doloridos de amor.* Mexico, 1948.

Avalle-Arce, Juan Battista. *La novela pastoril española.* Madrid, 1959.

Baez, Morenzo. *Diana.* Edited by Jorge de Montemayor. Introd. Madrid, 1955.

Bataillon, Marcel. *Érasme et l'Espagne.* Paris, 1937.

Bell, Aubrey. *Luis de Léon: A Study of the Spanish Renaissance.* Oxford, 1925.

Cobos, Jean. "Léon l'Hébreu et ses *Dialogues de l'Amour.*" In *Penseurs hétérodoxes du monde hispanique*, edited by Pierre Maxime Schuhl, pp. 11–79. Toulouse, 1974.

Damiens, Suzanne. *Amour et intellect chez Léon Hébreu.* Toulouse, 1971.

Darst, David H. "Renaissance Platonism and the Spanish Pastoral Novel." *Hispania* 52 (1969) : 384–92.

Dionisotti, Carlo. "Appunti su Leone Ebreo." *IMU* 2 (1959) : 409–28.

Estelrich, J. "Coup d' oeil sur le platonisme en Espagne." *Association Guillaume Budé. Congrès de Tours et Poitiers*, pp. 382–83. Paris, 1954.

Estrada, Francisco Lopez. "La influencia italiana en la *Galatea de Cervantes.*" *CL* 4 (1952) : 161–69.

Fontanesi, Guiseppina. *Il problema dell' amore nell' opera di Leone Ebreo.* Venice, 1934.

Giannini, A. "La *Carcel de Amore* y el *Cortegiano* de Castiglione." *RH* 46 (1919) : 547–68.

Gonzalez de la Calle, Pedro Urbano. *Sebastian Fox Morcillo.* Madrid, 1903.

Green, Otis H. *Spain and the Western Tradition.* 4 vols. Madison, 1963.

_____ and Leonard, Irving A. "On the Mexican Book Trade in 1600." *HR* 9 (1941) : 1–40. Reprinted in Irving Leonard, *Books of the Brave*, pp. 241–57. Cambridge, Mass., 1949.

_____. "Boscan and *Il Cortegiano.*" *Boletin del Instituto Caro y Cuervo* (Bogota) 4 (1948) : 90–101.

_____. *Courtly Love in Quevedo.* Boulder, 1952.

_____. "Courtly Love in the Spanish Cancioneros." *PMLA* 64 (1949) : 293–300.

_____. "Fingen los poetas: Notes on the Spanish Attitude toward Pagan Mythology." In *Estudios dedicados a Menendez Pidal.* Vol. 1, pp. 275–88. Madrid, 1950.

Guy, Alain. *El pensamiento filosofico de Fray Luis de Léon.* Madrid, 1960.

Hathaway, Robert L. *Love in the Early Spanish Theater.* Madrid, 1976.

Holloway, James E. "Lope's Neoplatonism: *La Dama Boba.*" *BHS* 49 (1972) : 236–55.

Ivanoff, N. "La beauté dans la philosophie de Marsile Ficin et de Léon Hébreu." *Humanisme et Renaissance* 3 (1936) : 12–21.

Janakiram, Alur. "Leone Ebreo and Shakespeare." *English Studies* 61 (1980) : 224–35.

Jones, Royston O. "Bembo, Gil Polo, Garcilaso: Three Accounts of Love." *RLC* 40 (1966) : 526–40.

_____. "El 'Tomas Moro' de Fernando de Herrera." *Boletin de la Real Academia de España* 30 (1950) : 423–38.

_____. "Góngora and Neoplatonism Again." *BHS* 43 (1966) : 117–20.

_____. "Neoplatonism and the *Soledades.*" *BHS* 40 (1963) : 1–16.

_____. "The Idea of Love in Garcilaso's Second Eclogue." *MLR* 46 (1951) : 388–95.

Keniston, Hayward E. *Garcilaso de la Vega.* New York, 1922.

Krebs, Ernesto. "El *Cortesano* de Castiglione en España." *BAAL* 8 (1940) : 93–146, 423–35; 9 (1941) : 135–42, 517–43; 10 (1942) : 53–118, 689–748.

Leo Hebreo. *Dialogos de amor.* Translated by Garcilaso Inca de la Vega. Edited by Eduardo J. Martinez. Madrid, 1941.

McAllister, Robin. *The Reader as Pilgrim and Poet in Góngora's "Soledades."* Dissertation, Princeton, 1975. *DAI* 36 : 4546A.

Maio, Eugene Anthony. *The Imagery of Eros: A Study of the Influence of Neoplatonism on the Mystical Writings of St. John of the Cross.* Dissertation, UCLA, 1967. *DAI* 28 : 684A.

Marasso, Arturo. *Góngora: Hermetismo poetico y alguimia.* Buenos Aires, 1965.

Marcelino, Gutiérrez. *Fray Luis de Léon y la filosofía del Renacimiento.* Madrid, 1929.

Margolin, Jean-Claude. "Vives, lecteur et critique de Platon et d'Aristote." In *Classical Influences on European Culture, A.D. 1500-1700,* edited by R. R. Bolgar, pp. 245-58. Cambridge, 1976.

Melczer, William. "Platonisme et Aristotelisme dans la pensée de Léon l'Hébreu." In *Platon et Aristote à la Renaissance,* pp. 293-306. Colloque international de Tours (1973). Paris, 1976.

Menéndez y Pelayo, M. *Historia de las Ideas Estéticas en Espana.* Vol. 2, pp. 7-76. Santander, 1947.

Mönch, Walter. "Le Sonnet et le platonisme." *Association Guillaume Budé. Congrès de Tours et Poitiers,* pp. 376-80. Paris, 1954.

Morreale, Margherita. *Castiglione y Boscan.* 2 vols. Madrid, 1959.

Orcibal, J. "Une formule de l' amour extatique de Platon à Saint Jean de la Croix et au cardinal de Berulle." In *Mélanges offerts à E. Gilson,* pp. 447-63. Paris, 1959.

Perry, Anthony. "Dialogue and Doctrine in Leone Ebreo's *Dialoghi d'amore.*" *PMLA* 88 (1973) : 1173-179.

Pflaum, Heinz. *Die Idee der Liebe: Leone Ebreo.* Tubingen, 1926.

_____. "Leone Ebreo." *Heidelberger Abhandlungen zur Philosophie,* no. 7 (1926) : 42-158.

Reyes, Alfonso. "La prueba platonica." *Cuentos y ensavos.* Mexico City, 1944. Not seen.

Ricard, Robert. "Notes et matériaux pour l'étude du 'socratisme chretien' chez sainte Thérèse et les spirituels espagnols." *Bulletin Hispanique* 49 (1947) : 5-37.

Rivers, Elias L. "The Sources of Garcilaso's Sonnet VIII." *Romance Notes* 2 (1961) : 96-100 (on Castiglione).

Solé-Lerís, A. "The Theory of Love in the two *Dianas:* A Contrast." *BHS* 36 (1959) : 65-79.

Somville, Pierre. "Platonisme chez Fray Luis de Léon et chez Pascal." *Revue des langues vivantes* 36 (1970) : 27-34.

Sturm, H. G. "From Plato's Cave to Sigismund's Prison: The Four Levels of Reality and Experience." *MLN* 89 (1974) : 280-89 (influence of Plato on Calderon's *La Vida es Sueño*).

Trueblood, Alan S. "Plato's *Symposium* and Ficino's Commentary in Lope de Vega's *Dorotea.*" *MLN* 73 (1958) : 506-14.

_____. *Experience and Artistic Expression in Lope de Vega,* pp. 196-97. Cambridge, Mass., 1974.

Vinci, Joseph. "The Neoplatonic Influence of Marsilio Ficino on Fray Pedro Malón de Chaide." *HR* 29 (1961) : 275-95.

Walker, Roger M. "Towards an Interpretation of the *Libro de buen amor.*" *BHS* 43 (1966) : 1-10.

VI. Britain

Ackerman, Caroline. "John Lyly and Platonism in Caroline Poetry." *Lock Haven Bulletin* 1 (1961) : 19–23.

Arthos, John. "Milton, Ficino, and the Charmides." *SRen* 6 (1959) : 261–74.

Atkins, J. W. H. *English Literary Criticism: The Renascence.* London, 1947.

Austin, Eugene M. *The Ethics of the Cambridge Platonists.* Philadelphia, 1935.

Battenhouse, Roy W. "Chapman and the Nature of Man." *ELH* 12 (1948) : 87–107.

———. "Chapman's *The Shadow of Night*: an Interpretation." *SP* 38 (1941) : 584–608.

———. "The Doctrine of Man in Calvin and in Renaissance Platonism." *JHI* 9 (1948) : 447–71.

Beachcroft, T. O. "Traherne and the Cambridge Platonists." *Dublin Review* 186 (1930) : 278–90.

Becker, Carole R. "Clothing the Soul: A Study of . . . George Chapman." Dissertation, Minnesota, 1975. *DAI* 36 : 5310A.

Bennett, Josephine W. "Spenser's *Fowre Hymnes*: Addenda." *SP* 32 (1935) : 131–57.

———. "Spenser's Garden of Adonis." *PMLA* 47 (1932) : 46–80.

———. "Spenser's Venus and the Goddess of Nature in the *Cantos of Mutabilitie*." *SP* 30 (1933) : 159–92.

———. "The Theme of Spenser's *Fowre Hymnes*." *SP* 28 (1931) : 18–57.

Berleth, Richard J. "'Heavens favorable and free': Belphoebe's Nativity in the *FQ*." *ELH* 40 (1973) : 479–500.

Bhattacharya, Mohinimohana. *Platonic Ideas in Spenser.* Calcutta, 1935.

Bieman, Eliz. "Neoplatonism, the Ghost in Spenser's Fictions." In *Spenser: Classical, Medieval, Renaissance, and Modern*, edited by David A. Richardson, pp. 306–17. Cleveland, 1977.

Bjorvand, Einar. "Spenser's Defense of Poetry and Some Structural Aspects of the *Fowre Hymnes*." In *Fair Forms*, edited by Maren-Sofie Rostvig, pp. 13–53, 203–06. Totowa, 1975.

Blumenberg, Hans. "Neoplatonismen and Pseudo-platonismen in der Kosmologie und Mechanik der Früher Neuzeit." In *Le neoplatonisme*, pp. 447–74. Colloques internationaux du Centre National de la Recherche Scientifique. Paris, 1970.

Bottrall, Margaret. "Chapman's Defense of Difficulty in Poetry." *Criterion* 16 (1937) : 638–54.

Bowden, Karen. *Love's Mightie Mysteries.* Dissertation, Berkeley, 1978. *DAI* 40 : 835A (on Spenser, Ficino, Hebreo, and Orphica, i.a.).

Boyette, Purvis E. "Milton's Eve and the Neoplatonic Graces." *RQ* 20 (1967) : 341–44.

———. "Something More About the Erotic Motive in *Paradise Lost*." *Tulane Studies in English* 15 (1957) : 19–30.

Brown, James Neil. "Spenser and Ficino." *N&Q* 24 (1977) : 517.

———. "Elizabethan Pastoralism and Renaissance Platonism." *AUMLA* 44 (1975): 247 –67. Not seen.

Bush, Douglas. *Mythology and the Renaissance Tradition.* Minneapolis, 1932.

Cain, Thomas H. "Spenser and the Renaissance Orpheus." *UTQ* 41 (1971) : 24–47.

Caldiero, Frank M. "The Source of Hamlet's 'What a piece of work Is a Man.'" N&Q 196 (1951) : 421–24.

Camé, Jean-François. "Marvell's Platonism in 'The Garden.'" Cahiers Elisabéthains 17 (1980) : 71–76.

Casady, Edwin. "The Neo-Platonic Ladder in Spenser's Amoretti." In Renaissance Studies in Honor of Hardin Craig, edited by Baldwin Maxwell et al., pp. 92–103. Stanford, 1941. Reprinted from PQ 20 (1941) : 284–95.

Cassirer, Ernst. The Platonic Renaissance in England. London, 1953.

Cinquemani, A. M. "Henry Reynolds' Mythomystes and the Continuity of Ancient Modes of Allegoresis in Seventeenth Century England." PMLA 85 (1970) : 1041–049.

Cirillo, A. R. "Spenser's Epithalamion: The Harmonious Universe of Love." SEL 8 (1968) : 19–34.

Clanton, Jann. "Love Descending: A Study of Spenser's Fowre Hymnes and Milton's "Nativity Ode." DAI 39 (1978) : 3593A.

Cody, Richard. The Landscape of the Mind. Oxford, 1969.

Colby, Frances L. "Thomas Traherne and Henry More." MLN 62 (1947) : 490–92.

Collins, Joseph B. Christian Mysticism in the English Renaissance. Baltimore, 1940.

Comito, Terry. "A Dialectic of Images in Spenser's Fowre Hymnes." SP 74 (1977) : 301–21.

Cope, Jackson I. The Theater and the Dream. Baltimore, 1973.

Coudert, Allison. "A Cambridge Platonist's Kabbalist Nightmare." JHI 36 (1975) : 633–52.

Council, Norman. "O Dea Certe: The Allegory of The Fortress of Perfect Beauty." HLQ 39 (1976) : 329–42.

Cox, Gerard H. "Traherne's Centuries: A Platonic Devotion of 'Divine Philosophy.'" MP 69 (1971) : 10–24.

Craig, D. H. "A Hybrid Growth: Sidney's Theory of Poetry in An Apology for Poetry." ELR 10 (1980) : 183–201.

Da Crema, Joseph J. The Neoplatonic Element in John Lyly. Dissertation, Temple, 1968. DAI 29 : 1204A.

Dahl, Rolf. "Platonismen og den engelske renessanse (1497–1535)." Kirke og Kultur (Oslo) 79 (1974) : 169–82.

Dannenberg, Friedrich. Das Erbe Platons in England bis zur Bildung Lylys. Berlin, 1932.

Day, Malcolm M. "Traherne and the Doctrine of Pre-Existence." SP 65 (1968) : 81–97.

Dees, Jerome S. "Spenser's Anti-Platonism." In Spenser: Classical, Medieval, Renaissance, and Modern, edited by David A. Richardson, pp. 271–305. Cleveland, 1977.

De Neef, A. L. "Spenserian Meditation: the 'Hymne of Heavenlie Beautie.'" ABR 25 (1974) : 317–34.

Doebler, Bettie Anne. "Donne's Incarnate Venus." SAQ 71 (1972) : 504–12.

Doggett, Frank A. "Donne's Platonism." Sewanee Review 42 (1934) : 274–92.

Dowlin, Cornell M. "Sidney's Two Definitions of Poetry." MLQ 3 (1942) : 573–81.

Dreher, Diane. "Traherne's Second 'Century': A Source in Ficino." N&Q 26 (1979) : 434–36.

Durkan, John. "The Beginnings of Humanism in Scotland." *Innes Review* 4 (1953) : 1–20.

Durr, Robert A. *On the Mystical Poetry of Henry Vaughan.* Cambridge, Mass., 1962.

Dust, Philip. "Another Source for Spenser's *Faerie Queene*." *EM* 23 (1972) : 15–19.

Einstein, Lewis. *The Italian Renaissance in England.* New York, 1902.

Ellrodt, Robert. *Neoplatonism in the Poetry of Spenser.* Geneva, 1960. Reprinted New York, 1975.

———. *Les poétes métaphysiques anglais.* Paris, 1960.

Elton, William R. *Shakespeare's World,* pp. 153–75. New York, 1979.

Evans, Frank B. "Platonic Scholarship in 18th Cent. England." *MP* 41 (1943) : 103–10.

Evans, Maurice. "Platonic Allegory in *The Faerie Queene*." *RES* n.s., 12 (1961) : 132–43.

Ferruolo, Arnolfo. "Sir Philip Sidney e Giordano Bruno." *Convivium* 17 (1948) : 686–99.

Fletcher, Jefferson B. "A Study in Renaissance Mysticism: Spenser's *Fowre Hymnes.*" *PMLA* 26 (1911) : 452–75.

———. "Benivieni's Ode of Love and Spenser's 'Fowre Hymnes.'" *MP* 8 (1911) : 545–60. Reprinted in *The Religion of Beauty in Woman,* pp. 116–46. New York, 1911.

Foreman, Jack. "An Unacknowledged Use of the *Cratylus* by Thomas Elyot." *N&Q* 22 (1975) : 532–34.

Fowler, Alastair. "Emanations of Glory: Neoplatonic Order in Spenser's *Faerie Queene*." In *Theater for Spenserians,* edited by Judith M. Kennedy, pp. 53–82. Toronto, 1973.

———. *Spenser and the Numbers of Time.* London, 1964.

Fuzier, Jean. "Le *Banquet* de Shakespeare: Les Sonnets et le platonisme authentique." *Etudes Anglaises* 34 (1981) : 1–15.

Galyon, Linda. "Some Questions and Neo-Platonic Answers." In *Spenser and the Middle Ages,* edited by David A. Richardson, pp. 196–210. Cleveland, 1976.

———. "Sapience in Spenser's *Hymne of Heavenlie Beautie*." *Fourteenth Century English Mystics Newsletter* 3 (1977) : 9–12.

Gannon, C. C. "Lyly's *Endimion*: from Myth to Allegory." *ELR* 6 (1976) : 220–43.

Geller, Lila. "The Acidalian Vision: Spenser's Graces in Book VI of *The Faerie Queene*." *RES* 23 (1972) : 267–77.

———. "Venus and the Three Graces: A Neoplatonic Paradigm for Book III of *The Faerie Queene*." *JEGP* 75 (1976) : 56–74.

Gleason, John B. "Sun-Worship in More's *Utopia*." In *Le Soleil à la Renaissance,* pp. 435–45. Brussels, Université Libre, Institut pour l'Etude de la Renaissance et de l'Humanisme. Brussels, 1965.

Gordon, D. J. "The Imagery of Ben Jonson's *The Masque of Blacknesse and the Masque of Beautie*." *JWCI* 6 (1943) : 122–41. Reprinted, revised in *England the Mediterranean Tradition,* pp. 102–21. Oxford, 1945. Also in *The Renaissance Imagination,* edited by Stephen Orgel, pp. 134–56. Berkeley, 1975.

Guffey, George R., ed. *Traherne and the Seventeenth Century English Platonists 1900–1966.* [A bibliography.]. London, 1969.

Guilfoyle, Cherrell. "The 'Paragraph Poems' in *Silex Scintillans*." *Etudes Anglaises* 33 (1980) : 296–307.

Gupta, O. S. "Depiction of Love as a Cosmic Force in *Colin Clout's Come Home Againe*." *Rajasthan University Studies in English* 9 (1976) : 17–23. Not seen.

Gutsell, James B. *Irony in the Fallen World of George Chapman*. Dissertation, Conn., 1969. *DAI* 29 : 2674A.

Hamilton, Gertrude K. *Three Worlds of Light in Marsilio Ficino, Thomas Vaughan and Henry Vaughan*. Dissertation, Rochester, 1974. *DAI* 35 : 2222A.

Hankins, John. *Source and Meaning in Spenser's Allegory*. Oxford, 1971.

Harrison, John S. *Platonism in English Poetry*. New York, 1903.

Heninger, S. K. "Sidney and Serranus' *Plato*." *ELR* 13 (1983) : 146–61.

Hirst, Désirée. *Hidden Riches*. London, 1964.

Hughes, Merritt Y. "The Lineage of 'The Extasie.'" *MLR* 27 (1932) : 1–5.

———. "Milton and the Symbol of Light." *SEL* 4 (1964) : 14–18.

Hutin, Serge. *Henry More*. Hildesheim, 1966.

Hutton, Sarah. "Thomas Jackson, Oxford Platonist and William Twisse, Aristotelian." *JHI* 39 (1978) : 635–52.

Hyma, Albert. "The Continental Origins of English Humanism." *HLQ* 4 (1940) : 1–25.

Jacquot, Jean. "Le platonisme de Ralph Cudworth." In *Association Guillaume Budé. Congrès de Tours et Poitiers*, pp. 380–82. Paris, 1954.

———. "L'élément platonicien dans *L'histoire du monde* de Sir Walter Ralegh." In *Mélanges d'histoire littéraire de la renaissance offerts à Henri Chamard*, pp. 347–53. Paris, 1951.

Jayne, Sears. "Ficino and the Platonism of the English Renaissance." *CL* 4 (1952) : 214–38.

———. "The Subject of Milton's Ludlow *Mask*." In *A Mask at Ludlow: Essays on Milton's Comus*, edited by John Diekhoff, pp. 165–87. Cleveland, 1968.

Jenkins, Harold. *Edward Benlowes*. London, 1952.

Jones, Judith P. "The *Philebus* and the Philosophy of Pleasure in Thomas More's *Utopia*." *Moreana* 32 (1971) : 61–70.

Kermode, Frank. "The Banquet of Sense." *Bulletin of the John Rylands Library* 44 (1961) : 68–99. Reprinted in his *Shakespeare, Spenser, and Donne*, pp. 84–115. London, 1971.

Koskimies, Rafael. "The Question of Platonism in Shakespeare's Sonnets." *Neuphilologische Mitteilungen* 71 (1970) : 260–70.

Krouse, F. Michael. "Plato and Sidney's Defence of Poesie." *CL* 6 (1954) : 138–47.

Lakin, Barbara. "The Magus and the Poet." *Sixteenth Century Journal* 10 (1979) : 1–14 (on Bruno and Chapman).

Lee, R. W. "Castiglione's Influence on Spenser's Early *Hymnes*," *PQ* 7 (1928) : 65–77.

Legocka, Eva. "Man and the Hierarchy of Christian Platonism as Presented in Selected Poems of Edmund Spenser." *Studia Anglica Posnaniensia* 7 (1976) : 149–57. Not seen.

Lepick, Julie Ann. *That Faire Hermaphrodite*. Dissertation, SUNY (Buffalo), 1976. *DAI* 37 : 3644A.

Levinson, Ronald B. "Milton and Plato." *MLN* 46 (1931) : 85–91.

Lewis, C. S. "Neoplatonism in the Poetry of Spenser." *Etudes Anglaises* 14 (1961) : 107–16.

———. *Spenser's Images of Life*. Cambridge, 1967.

Lichtenstein, Aharon. *Henry More: The Rational Theology of a Cambridge Platonist*. Cambridge, Mass., 1962.

Lockwood, William. *The Thought and Lyrics of Sir Walter Ralegh.* Dissertation, Penn., 1970. *DAI* 30 : 5414A.

McAdoo, H. R. *The Spirit of Anglicanism,* pp. 81–155 (on Cambridge Platonists). London, 1965.

Mackinnon, Flora L. *The Philosophy of John Norris of Bemerton.* Baltimore, 1910.

McNulty, Robert. "Bruno at Oxford." *RN* 13 (1960) : 300–05.

Mahoney, John L. "Platonism as Unifying Element in Spenser's *Fowre Hymnes.*" *Bulletin de la faculté des lettres de Strasbourg* 42 (1963) : 211–19.

Major, John. *Sir Thomas Elyot and Renaissance Humanism.* Lincoln, 1964.

Marcel, Raymond. "Les découvertes d'Erasme en Angleterre." *BHR* 14 (1952) : 117–23.

Marc' Hadour, Germain. "Thomas More entre Aristote et Platon." In *Platon et Aristote à la Renaissance,* pp. 483–91. Colloque international de Tours. Paris, 1976.

Marks, Carol. See Sicherman, Carol.

Martz, Louis. *The Paradise Within.* New Haven, 1964.

Maskell, David. "Robert Gaguin and Thomas More, Translators of Pico della Mirandola." *BHR* 37 (1975) : 63–68.

Massa, Daniel. "Giordano Bruno's Ideas in Seventeenth Century England." *JHI* 38 (1977) : 227–42.

Mayr, Roswitha. *The Concept of Love in Sidney and Spenser.* Salzburg, 1978.

Micheletti, Mario. "L'ateismo come alienazione nel pensiero di Benjamin Whichcote e John Smith." *RFNS* 67 (1975) : 432–41.

Michener, Richard. "The Great Chain of Being: Three Approaches." *BSUF* 1 (1970) : 60–71.

Miles, Leland. *John Colet and the Platonic Tradition.* La Salle, Ill., 1961.

Moloney, Michael F. "Plato and Plotinus in Milton's Cosmogony." *PQ* 40 (1961) : 34–43.

Moreau, Joseph. "Introduction à la lecture des *Hymnes* de Spenser." *Revue de théologie et de philosophie,* series 3, 14 (1964) : 65–83.

Morillo, M. "Donne's 'The Relique' as Satire." *Tulane Studies in English* 21 (1974) : 47–55.

Myers, James P. "This curious Frame: Chapman's *Ovid's Banquet of Sense.*'" *SP* 65 (1968) : 192–206.

Nathanson, Leonard. *The Strategy of Truth.* Chicago, 1967.

Nestrick, William V. "Spenser and the Renaissance Mythology of Love." *Literary Monographs* 6 (1975) : 35–70.

Nohrnberg, James. *The Analogy of 'The Faerie Queene.'* Princeton, 1976.

Orgel, Stephen. *The Jonsonian Masque.* Cambridge, Mass., 1965.

Osgood, Charles G. "Spenser's Sapience." *SP* 14 (1917) : 167–77.

Partee, Morriss. "Anti-Platonism in Sidney's *Defense.*" *EM* 22 (1971) : 7–29.

_____. *Plato and the Elizabethan Defense of Poetry.* Dissertation, Texas, 1966. *DAI* 27 : 459A.

_____. "Sir Philip Sidney and the Renaissance Knowledge of Plato." *English Studies* (Neth.) 51 (1970) : 411–24.

_____. "Sir Thomas Elyot on Plato's Aesthetics." *Viator* 1 (1973) : 327–35.

Passmore, John A. *Ralph Cudworth: An Interpretation.* Cambridge, 1951.

Pearson, Lu Emily. *Elizabethan Love Conventions*. Berkeley, 1933.

Pellegrini, Angelo M. "Giordano Bruno at Oxford." *HLQ* 5 (1941) : 301–16.

Perry, Theodore Anthony. *Erotic Spirituality*. University, Ala., 1980.

Peterson, Richard S. "Virtue Reconciled to Pleasure: Jonson's 'A Celebration of Charis.'" *Studies in the Literary Imagination* 6 (1973) : 219–68.

Pickett, Penny. "Sidney's Use of *Phaedrus* in *The Lady of May*." *SEL* 16 (1976) : 33–50.

Pinto, Vivian de Sola. *Peter Sterry: Platonist and Puritan, 1613–1672*. Cambridge, 1934.

Praz, Mario. "Stanley, Sherburne, and Ayres as Translators and Imitators of Italian, Spanish, and French Poets." *MLR* 20 (1925) : 280–94 and 419–31.

Quitslund, Jon A. "Spenser's Image of Sapience." *SRen* 16 (1969) : 181–213.

_____. "Spenser's Amoretti VIII and Platonic Commentaries on Petrarch." *JWCI* 36 (1973) : 256–76.

Reyher, Paul. *Les Masques anglais*. Paris, 1909.

Reynolds, Henry. *Mythomystes*. Edited by Arthur F. Kinney. London, 1972.

Richmond, Hugh M. *Puritans and Libertines*. Berkeley, 1981.

Rivers, Isabel. *Classical and Christian Ideas in English Renaissance Poetry*, ch. 3. London, 1979.

Roberts, James D. *From Puritanism to Platonism in Seventeenth Century England*. Hague, 1968.

Rostvig, Maren-Sofie. "Ars aeterna: Renaissance Poetics and Theories of Creation." *Mosaic* 3 (1970) : 40–61. Reprinted in *Silent Poetry*, edited by Alastair Fowler, pp. 32–72. London, 1970.

_____. "The Hidden Sense: Milton and the Neoplatonic Method of Numerical Composition." In *The Hidden Sense and Other Essays*, pp. 1–112. Oslo, 1963.

_____. "Images of Perfection." In *Seventeenth-Century Imagery*, edited by Earl Miner, pp. 1–24. Berkeley, 1971.

Ryan, John K. "John Smith (1616–1652): Platonist and Mystic." *The New Scholasticism* 20 (1946) : 1–25.

Samuel, Irene. "The Influence of Plato on Sir Philip Sidney's *Defense of Poesie*." *MLQ* 1 (1940) : 383–91.

_____. *Plato and Milton*. Ithaca, 1947.

Satterthwaite, Alfred W. *Spenser, Ronsard, and DuBellay*. Princeton, 1960.

Saurat, Denis. *Milton, Man and Thinker*. New York, 1935.

Savage, J. B. "*Comus* and its Traditions." *ELR* 5 (1975) : 58–80.

Saveson, J. E. "The Library of John Smith, The Cambridge Platonist." *N&Q* 203 (1958) : 215–16.

_____. *Some Aspects of the Thought and Style of John Smith, the Cambridge Platonist*. Dissertation, Cambridge, 1955.

Schoell, Frank L. *Etudes sur l'humanisme continental en Angleterre à la fin de la renaissance*. Paris, 1926.

Schrinner, Walter. *Castiglione und die englische Renaissance*. Berlin, 1939.

Schroeder, Kurt. *Platonismus in der Englischen Renaissance*. Berlin, 1920.

Seebohm, Frederic. *The Oxford Reformers*. London, 1938.

Sells, A. Lytton. *The Italian Influence in English Poetry*. Bloomington, 1955.

Sensabaugh, George. "John Ford and Platonic Love at Court." *PMLA* 36 (1939) : 206–26.

_____. "Love Ethics in Platonic Court Drama." *HLQ* 1 (1938) : 277–304.

_____. "Platonic Love and the Puritan Rebellion." *SP* 37 (1940) : 457–81.

_____. "Platonic Love in Shirley's *The Lady of Pleasure.*" In *A Tribute to George Coffin Taylor*, pp. 168–77. Chapel Hill, N.C., 1952.

Sicherman, Carol M. "Traherne's Ficino Notebook." *PBSA* 63 (1969) : 73–81.

_____. "Thomas Traherne and Cambridge Platonism." *PMLA* 81 (1966) : 521–34.

_____. "Thomas Traherne and Hermes Trismegistus." *RN* 19 (1966) : 118–31.

_____. "Thomas Traherne's Commonplace Book." *PBSA* 58 (1964) : 458–65.

Siegel, Paul N. "The Petrarchan Sonneteers and Neo-Platonic Love." *SP* 42 (1945) : 164–82.

Sims, Dwight J. "The Syncretic Myth of Venus in Spenser's Legend of Chastity." *SP* 71 (1974) : 427–50.

Smith, Charles G. "The Ethical Allegory of the Two Florimels." *SP* 31 (1934) : 140–51.

Smith, Susan. *Diana and the Renaissance Allegory of Love.* Dissertation, Princeton, 1979. *DAI* 40 : 1486A.

Snare, Gerald. "Spenser's Fourth Grace." *JWCI* 34 (1971) : 350–55.

Southall, Raymond. "Love Poetry in the Sixteenth Century." *EIC* 22 (1972) : 362–80. See discussion in *EIC* 23 (1973) : 435–40 and 24 (1974) : 216–18.

Staudenbauer, Craig A. "Galileo, Ficino, and Henry More's *Psychathanasia.*" *JHI* 29 (1968) : 168–78.

_____. *The Metaphysical Thought of Henry More.* Dissertation, Johns Hopkins Univ., 1961. *CDI.*

_____. "Platonism, Theosophy, and Immaterialism: Recent Views of the Cambridge Platonists." *JHI* 35 (1974) : 157–69.

Steadman, John M. "'Like Two Spirits': Shakespeare and Ficino." *SQ* 10 (1959) : 244–46.

_____. "Herbert's Platonic Lapidary: A Note on 'The Foil.'" *SCN* 30 (1972) : 59–62.

Steintrager, James. "Plato and More's *Utopia.*" *Social Research* 36 (1969) : 357–72.

Swardson, H. R. *Poetry and Light.* Columbia, 1962.

Taylor, A. B. "Sir John Davies and George Chapman: A Note on the Current Approach to 'Ovid's Banquet of Sence.'" *ELN* 12 (1975) : 261–65.

Trapp, Joseph B. "John Colet, his Manuscripts, and the Pseudo-Dionysius." In *Classical Influences on European Culture A.D. 1500–1700*, edited by R. R. Bolgar, pp. 205–21. Cambridge, 1976.

Tucker, Virginia. "Directing Threds Through the Labyrinth. The Moral Use of Platonic Conventions and Patterns of Imagery in Sidney's *Astrophil and Stella.*" *DAI* 34 (1973) : 2583A.

Vinge, Louise. "Chapman's 'Ovid's Banquet of Sence.'" *JWCI* 38 (1975) : 234–57.

Waddington, Raymond B. "Chapman's *Andromeda Liberata*: Mythology and Meaning." *PMLA* 81 (1966) : 34–44.

_____. "The Iconography of Silence in Chapman's Hercules." *JWCI* 33 (1970) : 248–63.

_____. *The Mind's Empire: Myth and Form in George Chapman's Narrative Poems.* Baltimore, 1974.

Walker, D. P. *The Decline of Hell*, pp. 104–78. Chicago, 1964.

Wallace, Roderick S. "Chapman's Debt to Ficino." *N&Q* 17 (1970) : 402–03.

Warnlof, Jessica. *The Influence of Giordano Bruno on the Writings of Sir Philip Sidney.* *DAI* 34 (1974) : 4222A.

Watkin, E. I. *Poets and Mystics*, pp. 238–56 (on John Smith), pp. 272–300 (on H. Vaughan). London, 1953.

Welsford, Enid. *Spenser: The Fowre Hymnes and Epithalamion.* Oxford, 1967.

Williams, Gordon. "Spiritual Love and Sexual Death in Edward Herbert's Poetry." *Language and Literature* 2 (1974) : 16–31. Not seen.

Winstanley, Lilian, ed. *The Fowre Hymnes.* Cambridge, 1930.

Wittreich, Joseph A. "Milton's 'Destined Urn': The Art of *Lycidas*." *PMLA* 84 (1969) : 60–70.

VII. Other Countries

Ancyal, Andrea. "Tradizione neoplatonica e umanesimo Ungharese." In *L'opera e il pensiero di Giovanni Pico della Mirandola*, edited by A. Rotondò. Vol. 2, pp. 389–97. Convegno internazionale. Florence, 1965.

Cytowska, Maria. "Erasme de Rotterdame et Marsile Ficin, son maître." *Eos* 63 (1975) : 165–79.

Dambre, O. "Ficiniaanse achtergronden bij Justus de Harduwijns *Roose-mund* (1613)." *Studia Germanica Gandensia* 5 (1963) : 45–76.

Farra, Maria L. dal. "H. Helder leitor de Camoés." *Rev. canon.* 1 (1978) : 67–90 (on Hebreo). Not seen.

Gandillac, M. de. "Le platonisme en Allemagne aux XIVe et XVe siècles." In *Association Guillaume Budé. Congrès de Tours et Poitiers*, pp. 372–75. Paris, 1954.

―――. "Platonisme et Aristotelisme chez Nicolas de Cues." In *Platon et Aristote à la Renaissance*, pp. 7–23. Colloque international de Tours. Paris, 1976.

Glaser, E. "Frei Heitor Pinto's *Imagem da Vida Crista*." *Portuguesische Forschungen der Gorresgesellschaft* 3 (1962) : 47–90.

Huszti, Giuseppe. "Tendenze Platonizzanti alla corte di Mattia Corvino." *GCFI* 2 (1930) : 1–37, 135–62, 220–36, 272–87.

Lindroth, Sten. *Paracelsismen i Sverige.* Uppsala, 1943.

Llinares, Armand. "Platon et Aristote dans les dialogues de Heitor Pinto." In *Platon et Aristote à la Renaissance*, pp. 439–52. Colloque international de Tours (1973). Paris, 1976.

Mansfield, B. E. "Erasmus and the Mediating School." *Journal of Religious History* 4 (1967) : 302–16.

Manzoni, Claudio. "La cosmologia della *Cristianismo restituto* di Michel Serveto e l'influenza del neoplatonismo di Ficino." *La Cultura* 9 (1971) : 314–41.

―――. "L'hermetismo nella *Christianismi restitutio* di Michele Serveto." *La Cultura* 9 (1971) : 15–41.

Pina Martins, Jośe de. "Pico della Mirandola e o humanismo italiano nas origens do humanismo portugûes." *Estudos Italianos em Portugal*, no. 23 (1964) : 107–46.

_____. "Platon et le Platonisme dans la culture portugaise du XVIe siecle." In *Platon et Aristote à la Renaissance*, pp. 421–37. Colloque international de Tours (1973). Paris, 1976.

Pugliese, Olga. "Quattrocento Views on Love and Existence." *Canadian Journal of Italian Studies* 1 (1977) : 97–107.

Pusino, Ivan. "Der Einfluss Picos auf Erasmus." *ZFK* 46 (1927) : 75–96.

Saraiva, A. J. *Historia da Cultura em Portugal*. Lisbon, 1955.

Spitz, Lewis. "Occultism and Despair of Reason in Renaissance Thought." *JHI* 27 (1966) : 464–69.

_____. "Pythagoras and Cabala for Christ." *Archiv für Reformationsgeschichte* 47 (1966) : 1–20.

_____. *The Religious Renaissance of the German Humanists*. Cambridge, Mass., 1963.

_____. "The *Theologia Platonica* in the Religious Thought of the German Humanists." In *Middle Ages, Reformation, Volkskundes: Festschrift for John G. Kunstmann*, pp. 118–33. Chapel Hill, N.C., 1959.

VIII.   Music and the Visual Arts

Arnoux, Georges. *Musique platonicienne: âme du monde*. Paris, 1960.

Blunt, Anthony. *Artistic Theory in Italy 1450–1600*. Oxford, 1940.

Chastel, André. *Art et humanisme a Florence au temps de Laurent le Magnifique*. Paris, 1959.

_____. *Marsile Ficin et l' art*. Geneva, 1954. Reprint, 1975.

_____. "Marsilio Ficino et l' art." *Archivio di filosofia* 1 (1952) : 137–53.

_____. "Le platonisme et les arts à la Renaissance." In *Association Guillaume Budé. Congrès de Tours et Poitiers*, pp. 384–411. Paris, 1954.

_____. "Problèmes de l' art et de l' humanisme en Italie: revue de publications récentes." *BHR* 10 (1948) : 195–202.

De Tolnay, Charles. *The Art and Thought of Michelangelo*. New York, 1964.

Fellerer, Karl Gustav. "Agrippa von Nettesheim und die Musik." *Archiv für Musikwissenschaft* 16 (1959) : 77–86.

Ferruolo, Arnolfo. "Botticelli's Mythologies, Ficino's *De Amore*, Poliziano's *Stanze per la Giostra*: Their Circle of Love." *Art Bulletin* 37 (1954) : 17–25.

Finney, Gretchen. *Musical Backgrounds for English Literature 1580–1650*. New Brunswick, 1962.

Gilbert, Creighton E. *Antique Frameworks for Renaissance Art Theory*. New York, 1946.

Gombrich, E. H. "Botticelli's Mythologies: A Study in the Neoplatonic Symbolism of His Circle." *JWCI* 8 (1945) : 7–60.

_____. "*Icones Symbolicae*: The Visual Image in Neoplatonic Thought." *JWCI* 11 (1948) : 163–92.

Heninger, S. K. "Sidney and Boethian Music." *SEL* 23 (1983) : 37–46.

Hersey, George L. "Marsilio Ficino's Cosmic Temple." In *Collaboration in Italian Renaissance Art*, edited by Wendy S. Sheard and John T. Paoletti, pp. 91–97. New Haven, 1978.

Kemp, Martin. "'Ogni dipintore dipinge se': a Neoplatonic Echo in Leonardo's Art Theory?" In *Cultural Aspects of the Italian Renaissance*, edited by Cecil Clough, pp. 311–23. Manchester, 1976.

Kinkeldey, Otto. "Franchino Gafori and Marsilio Ficino." *Harvard Library Bulletin* 1 (1947) : 379–82.

Klibansky, Raymond et al. *Saturn and Melancholy*. London, 1964.

Kristeller, Paul O. "Music and Learning in the Early Italian Renaissance." *Journal of Renaissance and Baroque Music* 1 (1947) : 255–74. Reprinted in Paul O. Kristeller, *Studies in Renaissance Thought and Letters*, pp. 451–70. Rome, 1956.

Lebègue, Raymond. "Ronsard et la Musique." In *Musiques et Poésie au XVIe Siècle*, pp. 106–19. Colloques internationaux du Centre National de la Recherche Scientifique, no. 5. Paris, 1954.

Leclerc, Hélène. "Du mythe platonicien aux fêtes de la Renaissance." *Revue d'Histoire du Théatre* 11 (1959) : 105–71.

Panofsky, Erwin. "Die Entwicklung der Proportionslehre als Abbild der Stilentwicklung." *Monatshefte für Kunstwissenschaft* 14 (1921) : 188–209.

———. *Idea*. Columbia, S.C., 1968.

———. *Studies in Iconology: Humanistic Themes in the Art of the Renaissance*. New York, 1962.

Parronchi, Alessandro. "Il Programma della volta." *La Nazione* (on Ficino and the Sistine ceiling). Florence, January 5, 1971.

Saulnier, Verdun I. "Maurice Scève et la Musique." In *Musique et Poésie au XVIe Siècle*, pp. 89–103. Colloques internationaux du Centre National de la Recherche Scientifique, no. 5. Paris, 1954.

Terverant, Guy de. "Eros and Anteros or Reciprocal love in Ancient and Renaissance art." *JWCI* 28 (1965) : 205–08.

Tiemann, Barbara. *Fabel und Emblem* (on emblems). Munich, 1974.

Wadsworth, James B. "Marsilio Ficino's Fable of Phoebus and Lucilia and Botticelli's *Primavera*." *Aquila* 3 (1976) : 190–200.

Walker, D. P. "Ficino's Spiritus and Music." *Annales Musicologiques* 1 (1953) : 133–50.

———. "Le Chant Orphique de Marsile Ficin." In *Musiques et Poésie au XVIe siècle*, pp. 17–33. Colloques internationaux du Centre National de la Recherche Scientifique, no. 5. Paris, 1954.

Welliver, Warman. *Botticelli's Court of Venus, Poliziano's Stanze, and Lorenzo*. Indianapolis, 1960. Not seen.

Wind, Edgar. *Pagan Mysteries in the Renaissance*. New York, 1968.

Zupnick, I. L. "Imitation or Essence: the Dilemma of Renaissance Art." In *Platon et Aristote à la Renaissance*, pp. 469–79. Colloque international de Tours. Paris, 1976.